This study shows Lowell as a modern epic poet, political in the largest sense. In his career from *Life Studies* onward, I was self-examina conscious ba understandin statesmen a argues that I  ward a psychological vision of political behavior akin to the later Freud's. Through this vision, Lowell's so-called confessional or self-analytic poetry and his "public" poetry become increasingly interdependent and must be read in light of each other.

Half of this book is devoted to *Near the Ocean* and *Notebook* (1969, 1970 versions), partly because they unite the public and private dimensions and thus extend the possibilities of the American long poem, and partly because they succeed in marrying the visionary—or prophetic—and the realistic modes of writing, which tend to remain discrete in Lowell's earlier work.

While essentially a thematic study, this book can also be read as a commentary or guide to much of the poetry. The author never simplifies the extreme complexity of Lowell's work and in fact sees ambivalence as a key to his thinking and his sense of form. Mr. Williamson works close to the text and offers detailed readings of the major poems from the collections treated.

Alan Williamson, assistant professor of English at the University of Virginia, is a poet and has published in *The New Yorker*, *Poetry*, and other magazines.

Pity the Monsters

PITY THE MONSTERS

The Political Vision of Robert Lowell

Alan Williamson

New Haven and London, Yale University Press, 1974

Library of Congress catalog card number: 73-93614

International standard book number: 0-300-01734-0

Designed by John O. C. McCrillis
and set in Baskerville type.
Printed in the United States of America by
The Colonial Press, Inc., Clinton, Massachusetts

Published in Great Britain, Europe, and Africa by Yale University Press, Ltd., London.

Distributed in Latin America by Kaiman & Polon, Inc., New York City; in Australasia and Southeast Asia by John Wiley & Sons Australasia Pty. Ltd., Sydney; in India by UBS Publishers' Distributors Pvt., Ltd., Delhi; in Japan by John Weatherhill, Inc., Tokyo.

For My Mother
and
To the Memory of My Father

Contents

Acknowledgments

My thanks are due, first, to my teachers who read and criticized this manuscript at an earlier stage in its development. I would like to thank David Perkins for his care and attentiveness, his almost ideal combination of high standards as to form and argument, and open-mindedness as to critical method. I would like to thank William Alfred, for an immense amount of information and encouragement, and an energetic opposition to prematurely absolute judgments; and Joel Porte—though I worked with him more briefly—for some very valuable comments.

I have appreciated, and learned from, all the existing books on Lowell. But since they are not generally much concerned with the poetry since *For the Union Dead*, or with politics, they have not greatly influenced my own work. The exception is Patrick Cosgrave's *The Public Poetry of Robert Lowell*, which I read with great interest. But Mr. Cosgrave's work is framed by very strong moral and aesthetic premises that are so opposite to mine as, finally, to make him of little use for my purposes. He is constantly censorious toward the radical side of Lowell's thought; and he asserts, at one point, that Lowell is necessarily inferior to Pope in moral vision because Lowell's age lacks a coherent, universally accepted moral system. To my mind, some of the intellectual qualities of our age—its uncertainty and openness, its skepticism about ideas of order that amount to national or class self-ratification, its hesitation to exclude anyone from the bounds of empathy, having seen the terrible results of such exclusions—are advantages, not impediments, to moral wisdom. I can imagine no better text for this contention than Robert Lowell's poetry, and I would gladly set him against Pope (as a moralist, that is; between true poets, as William Blake said, there is no competition).

The first piece of criticism I ever read about Lowell still seems

to me the best and the most suggestive: Randall Jarrell's "From
the Kingdom of Necessity." Two other essays, also excellent, Irvin
Ehrenpreis's "The Age of Lowell" and Gabriel Pearson's "Robert
Lowell," have partly influenced, partly anticipated, my own
thinking. I also learned much from Norman Mailer's *The Armies of
the Night*. By far the closest treatment to mine in spirit is an
unpublished Harvard doctoral dissertation by Richard Tillinghast, *An Introduction to Robert Lowell's Recent Poetry*. It was written
after my own first draft; but it has suggested many lines of
thought to me, consciously and—doubtless—unconsciously, during the process of revision.

But my strongest debts by far, though the most difficult to pin
down precisely, are to conversations with friends. I would like to
thank Richard Tillinghast; my wife, Anne Winters; Frank Bidart,
David Guisso, Stephen Kurian, and Richard Wertime; and the
graduate students at the University of Virginia who have
participated over four years, more and less willingly, in my
preoccupation.

I would also like to thank the two assistants provided me by the
Work Study program at the University of Virginia, who have
saved me incalculable amounts of time: Frances Garrett and
Penelope Schmidt Harpold, for typing the final manuscript;
Penelope Harpold, in addition, for solving an unexpectedly
difficult and time-consuming research problem.

Finally, I want to thank Robert Lowell, for his encouragement
and for the respect for criticism as an activity which led him
(while giving much useful advice, mainly about *my* style and
values) to avoid providing "right" answers that would restrict my
interpretive freedom.

                                                                A.W.

Note: Half a year after this book was completed, Mr. Lowell
published a third version of *Notebook*. The bulk of the poem, with
additions, is now called *History*, while some, but not all, of the
personal poems have been sequestered into another volume, *For
Lizzie and Harriet*. I have decided against reworking my final
chapter into a commentary on the new version. The earlier two

*Notebook*s have been before the public for several years, and they have a different structural intention than *History*; they cannot be regarded as mere drafts. I do not think any of my major arguments will be useless to the reader who knows only the new version, though some will undoubtedly seem stronger now, others weaker—even ironical. Except for "Long Summer i," none of the poems I discuss at length has been changed beyond recognition; and a detailed analysis and criticism of Mr. Lowell's revisions, while it would interest me, would not be germane to the purposes of this study.

1

Introduction
Robert Lowell and the
Discontents of Civilization

Let me begin by qualifying. When I use the word *political,* in the title and henceforward, I do not mean it in the topical sense, but in a sense almost as wide as civilization, or the collective shaping of human destiny—ranging from the pressure of a family on an anarchic individual to the cumulative action of almost the entire human race in the current crisis of technology and ecology. Robert Lowell is a poet of politics in this largest sense; as such, he is now commonly and, I think, justly acclaimed as the best, the most inclusive, the most deeply intelligent American public poet of his time. He is *the* poet of our advanced—or late—industrial civilization: of the iron bestiary of Victorian Boston fading into the pure geometries of New York; of the manic energy of presidents, and the obscure sadness of the citizen coddled and threatened as never before; of the intelligent mind enmeshed in institutional commitments that no longer automatically justify themselves as right and human, or even as harmless. In Richard Poirier's words, Lowell is "our truest historian." [1]

Lowell's preeminence can only partly be explained by those external enabling factors he shares with many narrower writers: his close personal involvement in politics, both Establishment and non-Establishment, at several crucial moments in recent history;

1. Blurb on the paperback *Life Studies* and *For the Union Dead,* there credited to *Book Week.*

his gifts as a poetic realist, his eye for detail, his historian's grasp of the past. What gives life to these events, these faculties, is the complexity of mind and personality that "sees" the world by means of them; a complexity which—even if we ignore its personal side for the moment and speak only of ideology—is rather unusual. Lowell harbors within himself an Eliot-like conservative's insistence on forms of integrity lost in historical "progress"; a revolutionary's vision of apocalyptic community and hunger for poetic justice; and a liberal's sharp, impersonal scruples (blunted to an essentially conservative *laisser aller* in so many lives, but not in this one). By his faithful recording of himself (or his selves) responding to history, Lowell records a history that is never easy, one-sided, or blinded by the temper of his times. But neither does it conduce to quietistic withdrawal; Lowell continues, almost desperately, to seek images of ethical action, even when the world he perceives gives a compelled, impersonal, and guilty shape to almost every emphatic action it contains.

Lowell's vision of civilization—being a product both of the man he is and of the time he lives in—is particular, painful, and dark. It is redeemed neither by an Eliot's faith that an adequate, if authoritarian, utopia may have existed in the past, nor by a revolutionary's faith that one can be abstractly yet accurately designed for the future. Consequently, Lowell must necessarily leave more questions of value, of cause and responsibility, of fundamental "human nature," open to poetic inquiry than did his nearest predecessors. But it is this very appalling fundamental-ness of Lowell's questions, combined with his honesty about historical terror, that make him a modern epic poet, and (to my mind) a more satisfying poet of history than Eliot or Pound, Auden or Berryman or Olson.

In his later work in particular, Lowell's questioning of civiliza-tion most closely resembles that of Freud in *Civilization and Its Discontents*, and that of the later, radical Freudians, Herbert Marcuse and Norman O. Brown. Like Freud, Lowell is concerned with the cost of civilization to instinctual satisfaction and even instinctual awareness; with the nature of the almost universal human sense of discontent and incompleteness, the possibilities and the illusions of a remedy. He is obsessed with outbursts of aggression and brutality, with their relation to civilized structures and/or to man's fundamental, biologically evolved nature; and with the question of whether this essential nature permanently precludes any realization of man's moral ideal of himself. Finally, Lowell—like Freud—asks whether the whole project of civilization is worth the cost, being the best of the alternatives, or whether, on the contrary, it is—by an internal necessity—suicidal.

To none of these questions does Lowell give a single, unequivocal answer. Ultimately, he seems to share Freud's pessimism as to whether, at this point in time, more pleasant alternatives to civilized life really exist except in an impoverished imagination. On the other hand, like the radical Freudians, he is sometimes disposed to question Freud's later assumption that human aggression is an instinct, growing out of animal greed or out of Thanatos, and to search out causes for aggression, as far as possible, in neurotic and social distortion. Like the later Freudians, Lowell possesses (though he does not altogether trust) a vision of complete instinctual satisfaction as a narcissistic, almost a contemplative, fullness, where Freud tended rather to imagine the unlimited specific greediness of the father of the Primal Horde. Thus, Lowell's thought belongs—as I think a specific examination of his work will demonstrate—somewhere between Freud and the radical Freudians: with the latter in seeing a certain openness in human nature, with the former in testing it against a large and realistic view of history.

Of course, Lowell thinks about these questions not, primarily, as a philosopher but as a poet, in poetry. That is to say, he does his thinking through the picture of environments and epochs that comes to him intuitively, in association and metaphor; through the power and brutality, the discontent, the helpless participation in sweeping historical forces that he knows about concretely and can give a particular artistic shape. His concern is not with the doctrines or truisms of metapsychology in themselves, but with the process of their happening in particular experience; in a sense, he vindicates them as imaginable or believable orderings of the confused interaction of the individual consciousness and its world. Hence, there is no dividing Lowell into a "personal" and a "public" poet; he is almost continuously being both, and more and more deliberately so as his work advances.

And hence, too, comes the most striking—though largely intuitive—similarity between Lowell and the radical Freudians. For Marcuse and Brown, the processes of civilized life can be interpreted by an exhaustive analogy with the dynamics of individual neuroses, the basic forces and contradictions being the same. For instance, sublimation—the channeling of sexual energy into objectively nonsexual activities—might be seen in the need for progress, the desire to live in a technology full of concealed sexual symbols rather than an ecology full of actual sexual beings, animals and plants. Ultimately, historical and cultural change, and historical repetition, are given a logic derived from the study of the development of neurosis in the individual. There is a cultural return of the repressed, a need for continuously stronger defenses, a constant, subtle interaction between Eros and the death instinct.

In Lowell's work, the same analogy develops in a gradual and intuitive way, as Lowell uses his intense self-exploration in *Life Studies* as a source of metaphors for understanding aspects of the public world. Perhaps the moment of crystallization comes in "Memories of West Street and Lepke," where Lowell attempts to find out what his own political vision is by moving analogically from himself, the fragile, complexly cushioned, unhappily social-ized ex-mental patient, to the "lobotomized" Czar Lepke, and finally to the "tranquillized" America of John Foster Dulles's rhetoric. In the succeeding books, Lowell's use of personal analogy extends itself first to the irrational behavior of public men, the great heroes and villains of history; then to similar configurations in the collective behavior of classes, communities, and nations of the apparently normal, in poems like "For the Union Dead" and "Central Park." In *Near the Ocean*, the adaptation of *Prometheus Bound*, and *Notebook*, Lowell's concern extends to the essential nature or essential project of all civilization, in terms similar to Freud's. In *Near the Ocean* and *Notebook*, Lowell develops new forms of the long poem in order to multiply the possible connections between interpretations of the public realm and a personal "confession" more searchingly, more philosophically introspective than ever before. With these books, it becomes reasonable to speak of Lowell's "system" as one would of Yeats's; for the personal-public analogy *is* the overriding structure of the poem, and by following out its implications one arrives at a metapsychology as integrated, and as complex, as those of the prose theorists. In some cases, Lowell's theoretical insights are, as far as I know, unique—particularly in *Notebook*, where Lowell envisions the possible response of contemporary man to the cumulative pressures of civilization in terms of a schizophrenic dissociation of faculties and realities, accompanied by an unleashing of violent but depersonalized impulses.

I hope it is not necessary to apologize for taking a psychological approach to Lowell's work, or for using Freudian terminology. In the largest sense, one cannot defend (or attack) a Freudian approach in exclusively literary terms, since it is a matter of conviction, involving the sum of one's experience and intuition of life. On the other hand, if one is both a Freudian and a formalist—that is to say, if one cares primarily about art, and believes the art to reside in the minute particulars—one can ask whether a piece of criticism concerns itself with what is embodied in the poem, at whatever level of statement or suggestion, or with motives merely presumed from the writer's life. And, of course, one may ask whether both the art and the life are handled in crude and sweeping terms, or delicately, and with a concern for the mysteries of individuality.

But, quite apart from these general principles or personal ideals, Robert Lowell clearly presents a special study. He is the first important poet to take an explicitly psychoanalytic view of his own history, in a long sequence; and the concern with metapsychological speculation in the work after *Life Studies* is equally direct and inescapable. In a more subtle but equally important sense, Lowell's habits of mind are intrinsically psychological; he is intensely self-observant, and always inclined to connect conscious thought processes with the dreamlike, the

infantile, the anatomical. Hence, the greater part of my psychological interpretation will have to do with central themes,
consciously intended by the author; while the remainder will, I
hope, confine itself to what a sensitive close reading will sustain.
One further clarification is perhaps necessary. When I compare
Lowell to any specific psychological theorist, I do not intend to
imply a total harmony of positions, or even, necessarily, an
influence. I simply intend to clarify Lowell's poetic thinking at a
particular moment by juxtaposing it with the prose thinking it
most closely resembles.[2]

There is, as I have said, no dividing Lowell into a "public" and
a "private" poet. Long before there is any systematic effort to
unify the two spheres, the same categories of human experience
preoccupy Lowell in both, and constantly overflow from one to
the other. For this reason, I have given myself the freedom to treat
personal or religious poems at considerable length when they help
to define or enrich our picture of these fundamental categories.
The categories I have in mind are, in some cases, specifically
Freudian; in other cases, perhaps the most interesting, they
already halfway belong to that metapsychological realm they will
ultimately so crucially illuminate.

One such category or theme is the fear of death (a very
powerful emotion in Lowell's work from the beginning), leading
to a self-protective fear of the living-in-time that moves one
toward death, leading to the love of death or a deathlike stasis—a
paradoxical triangular relationship. An equally complex and
crucial nexus of relations involves the will-to-power over others,
the wish for poetic justice, and the temptation to live in a
solipsistic inner reality of fantasy or hallucination. Out of the
ambiguities of this nexus grows the conflict between Lowell's
religious impulse—which centers around a desire to live in
apocalyptic moments when all energy is liberated and the self and

2. In one case, Mr. Lowell told me that he disapproved of a theorist with whom
I had compared him. Since I continue to think that certain of this theorist's
formulations (*not* the ones that Mr. Lowell objected to) describe the intellectual
vision of certain of Mr. Lowell's poems better than any others I have encountered,
I have let the comparison stand.

the world are no longer distinct—and his rationalistic fear that this desire is obscurely married to the worst elements in himself, to a primitive destructiveness. These seem to me the crucial motives and problems behind Lowell's poems from the beginning, though in *Lord Weary's Castle* Lowell is probably unconscious of them, or else thinks them resolved by the leap of Catholic faith. After "Memories of West Street and Lepke," the conscious awareness of them becomes a precious tool in the struggle to understand his mind and the world in their mutual relation.

My division of space and emphasis among Lowell's various books is partly dictated by my concern with public themes. But it also reflects my personal taste and my dissatisfaction with certain extreme distributions of praise and blame which, it seems to me, spring partly from extra-literary feelings surrounding a very famous poet, and detract from a unified or evolutionary view of his work. I feel that such excess is visible in the current disesteem for *Lord Weary's Castle*, though the reasons for it are not difficult to understand. *Lord Weary's Castle* is a youthful, Phaeton-like book, grappling to itself a cosmic or even divine perspective for which neither Lowell's knowledge of himself nor of poetry yet fits him. Consequently, it seems confusing in its ideology and excessive in some of its anger; at times it betrays the heavy and willful strain of the artist convincing himself. On the other hand, its ambition is an accurate indicator of the scope Lowell's work will ultimately earn and hold with confidence. It sets forth Lowell's adherence— sometimes submerged but never wholly abandoned—to a bardic conception of the poet as an Adam-like namer, who reveals and almost creates the inward and essential forms of those things he sees with his imagination, sees "through" rather than "with" the eye. In short, it places Lowell in the tradition of visionary political poets descending from Blake and Shelley through Whitman and Crane.

But in more immediate and poetic terms, *Lord Weary's Castle* has its own unsurpassable power and precision in the dramatic rendering of certain psychological and religious states, particularly a melancholic and repetitive pressure and an inwardly experienced apocalypse. To this dramatization all the possibilities of the book's formal and orchestrated technique contribute, with a wild onomatopoeia in the portrayal of outward violence, a sculptural slow tension in the representation of an inward kind. Only the most diehard anti-formalist could fail to respond to the sensuous power, and the perfect harmony of form and content, in the book at its best (William Carlos Williams himself admired it). In terms of the surrealists' ideal of a direct rendition of the flow of thought, conscious and unconscious, *Lord Weary's Castle* often succeeds brilliantly, where the later "confessional" writing often chooses to view psychological processes more remotely, in rational afterthought.

In its successes, *Lord Weary's Castle* is a powerful opening statement of almost all the symbols, all the tonalities of atmosphere and inward experience, that appear in Lowell's work. In its failures and confusions, it is a kind of photographic negative of the ethical concerns that will obsess that work. For both these reasons (as well as for its intrinsic merit) it deserves an extended treatment in a study emphasizing the evolutionary unity of Lowell's poetry.

No doubt I should apologize for excluding *The Mills of the Kavanaughs* from my survey of the Lowell canon. The reason is not a lack of admiration for some of the poems included in it. Rather, Lowell's authorial stance toward the issues that would most concern me—the vicissitudes of power in New England, religious experience, the balance of subjective and objective perspectives on a person in an extreme psychological situation—seems to me a transitional one, perfectly defined earlier in a poem that I treat at considerable length, "Between the Porch and the Altar." The one truly political poem in *The Mills of the Kavanaughs*, "Falling Asleep over the Aeneid," is a masterpiece, and foreshadows the ethical commitments of "Beyond the Alps" and "Florence"; but, partly because there is a parallel with later poems, it did not seem worth while to create an additional chapter simply to discuss this poem.

Life Studies is regarded by most of Lowell's contemporaries as his best book. I sympathize with this judgment, for I find it his most emotionally moving book, in its treatment of the love and hate in close relationships; the rich color and threadbare texture of outworn day-to-day living; family, childhood, and class. It is moving as the great novels are moving, and on subjects the novel chooses more often than poetry does. Technically, its supreme achievement is the incorporation of anecdotal material, documentation, and the complex humorous tone of accomplished prose, into an order which remains that of poetry, manifesting itself most keenly in the subtlest areas, in echoes, submerged metaphors, altering rhythms. (My strongest regret about the public emphasis of my book is that it does not allow me to explore how this is so, in poems like "Man and Wife" and "Skunk Hour.")

The importance of Lowell's technical accomplishments in *Life Studies*, for his own future work and for the younger personal poets, can hardly be underestimated. And yet—for reasons I can only summarize here but shall present in detail later—this great book does not seem to me to embody Lowell's complete voice, his largest possibilities as a poet. The closeness to prose involves a loss as well as a gain. It restricts the verbal and, at times, the emotional concentration possible in the writing; it augments an already present tendency toward a somewhat too settled, too (compensatorily?) objective and rational manner of self-presentation. As the poet struggles to attain an objective view of himself, public judgments become more difficult and relativistic for him, and the prophetic dimension is less in evidence. This problem is at once confessed and dealt with in the poem that is in so many ways the watershed of Lowell's career, "Memories of West Street and Lepke."

For me, the most fully satisfying period of Lowell's career—the major phase, if there must be one—begins with *For the Union Dead* and continues through the latest additions to *Notebook*. With these books, Lowell returns to the bardic or prophetic view of the poet standing above history and perceiving its essential pattern—a view for which, it must be said, *Life Studies* laid the necessary groundwork, in self-knowledge and in a rich, realistic vision of social interaction. In the later books, public subjects of epic dimension return, and are placed in closer and closer juxtaposition to private "confessional" themes, until—in the two long poems, *Near the Ocean* and *Notebook*—there emerges the controlling psychopolitical vision whose broad outlines I have tried to sketch. As Lowell's ambition reaches an epic scale, his poetic voice becomes less ironic, more passionate and authoritative. A conscious grandeur of tone, the use of a compelling meter to dramatize the synthesizing vision, are once again included in his poetic range. There is a general return to a more richly orchestrated sound, as well as to iambics; there is also a flowing, songlike quality to lines and whole poems that one seldom finds in either *Lord Weary's Castle* or *Life Studies*.

Perhaps the most important technical developments in the later poetry are those which affect Lowell's representation and interpretation of his own psyche. Without losing the advantages of colloquial diction, Lowell has gradually freed himself from too close a bondage to the syntax of prose, or of speech; he has allowed himself the concentration and ellipsis that make possible a montage-like rendering, rather than a rationalized description, of consciousness. The later poetry immerses itself more and more in the flux of immediate experience until, in parts of *Notebook*, Lowell comes close to the pure free-association of surrealism. The poem is no longer, as in *Life Studies*, controlled and shaped by a detached, rational insight into the self; in consequence, the insight expressed indirectly becomes more complex, suggestive, and speculative, as well as more feelingful, less severe. In *Near the Ocean* and *Notebook*, we are once again aware of a transcendent or religious dimension to Lowell's experience, though it is handled without any allusion to traditional theology. In all these ways, Lowell has moved toward a fuller, more dramatic representation of his inner self, at the same time as he has used that self as the measure of his world.

A concluding discussion of Lowell's vacillations concerning form and meter will be useful, since these considerations influence any judgment of the relative merit of his different periods or phases. (Certainly many of those who elevate *Life Studies* far above both the earliest and the most recent books are influenced by an assumption that free form necessarily entails a free attitude toward experience in general, a spontaneity and suppleness, whereas fixed form is a breath from the dead past, an artifice, a forcing of the content.) I myself believe that fixed form and free form are, for Lowell, highly charged psychological and metaphysical categories, with equal and opposite attractions. Lowell himself has said, "I can't understand how any poet, who has written both metered and unmetered poems, would be willing to settle for one and give up the other." [3] But this, of course, depends very much on the temperament of the poet; Richard Wilbur and Denise Levertov, for instance, have made more or less absolute choices with no visible agony.

Iambic meters and rhyme, in Lowell, tend to produce, not neat rational statements, but a kind of trance, in which powerful feelings overflow easily, and symbols arrive with such intensity that they threaten the usually strong tension between symbolic thought and the real world. Here, Norman Mailer is Lowell's subtlest critic:

> Even if much of his poetry could be seen as formal incantations, halfway houses on the road to hypnosis and the oceans of contemplation beyond, . . . yes, even if Lowell's remarkable sense of rhythm drew one deep into the poems, nonetheless hypnotic they resolutely were not, for the language was particular, with a wicked sense of names, details, and places. . . .
>
> Lowell's poetry gave one the sense of living in a well, the echoes were deep, and sound was finally lost in moss on stone; down there the light had the light of velvet, and the ripples were imperceptible. But one lay on one's back in this well, looking up at the sky, and stars were determinedly there at night, fixed points of reference; nothing in the poems ever permitted you to turn on your face and try to look down into the depths of the well, it was enough you were in the well—now, look up! The world dazzled with its detail. [4]

3. Robert Lowell, "On Freedom in Poetry," in Berg and Mezey, *Naked Poetry* (Indianapolis and New York: Bobbs-Merrill, 1969), p. 124.

4. Norman Mailer, *The Armies of the Night* (New York: New American Library, 1968), p. 144.

What militates against the hypnotic flow, as Mailer perceives, is Lowell's love of particularity, his desire to remain anchored in the real world. The agents of this desire within the line are the penchant for proper names that Mailer mentions; the offhand, even deflating, effect of some of Lowell's favorite colloquial constructions; and an almost Anglo-Saxon emphasis on harshly alliterative, heavily consonantal words, words that stick out of the line as if they were the objects they name. These penchants are to be found in all of Lowell's poetry, but they give the poem its dominant shape only in the "unmetered" work, where there is little hypnotic undercurrent. It seems to me no accident that Lowell, in general, has turned toward traditional form when he has turned toward passionate political statement, toward a bardic view of the poet standing above history and penetrating to essential truths through his symbols. Lowell's refusal to make a binding choice between poetic modes significantly parallels the other ways in which he is self-divided: between mystical feeling and tragic rationalism; between the poet as imaginative creator and the poet as ironic witness; between angry, idealistic radicalism and scrupulous, pessimistic conservatism. As has been remarked, "ambivalence is the key to Lowell's poetry"; and the formal ambivalence, like other kinds, has been a source of breadth, energy, and continued inventiveness.[5] It is possible, perhaps necessary, to make some choice between Lowell's two modes, and the metaphysical positions they embody, on the basis of personal taste; but one will not understand the whole man, or the whole achievement, if one excludes either side of the dialectic.

5. Richard Tillinghast, "An Introduction to Robert Lowell's Recent Poetry" (Ph.D. dissertation, Harvard University), p. 27.

2

Vision and Violence

Lowell's politics during the period of his Catholic conversion and conscientious objection have puzzled many, and understandably so. Even his outward actions in this period were often striking for their double significance. His conversion itself seems a radical gesture in the Bostonian context, involving *déclassement* and the repudiation of his ancestors' most cherished beliefs. But in the context of American literary history, it places Lowell in the shadow of Eliot and among the hated enemies of fashionable Leftism (merging into Americanism as World War II approached). It was accompanied by an apprenticeship to the self-proclaimedly "reactionary" Southern Agrarians; but later, it brought Lowell into contact with the Christian socialist *Catholic Worker* group, and with the writings of the millenarian E. I. Watkin. In his open letter to President Roosevelt on his conscientious objection, Lowell condemned the firebombing of Dresden on moral and pacifist grounds, but also brought in a pragmatic argument based on fear of Soviet Russia. He also repeatedly drew attention to the eminence of his family, whose historical religious fanaticism and militarism his poems had condemned.

To see how far Lowell in fact belongs to the "reactionary" tradition in modern American letters, and how far his own temperament separates him from it from the very beginning, it will be useful to compare his early work (in *Land of Unlikeness*) with the work of the writer who most influenced him, Allen Tate. I have chosen two anti-war poems, written at a time when Lowell and Tate were living in the same house, and were jointly exploring the satiric possibilities of intricately rhymed short-line stanzas out of Drayton and other Elizabethans.[1]

"Ode to Our Young Proconsuls of the Air" is not one of Tate's most deeply thoughtful poems. It sprang from a more personal animus than simple disapproval of public policy. Using the slogan "The Irresponsibles," Van Wyck Brooks and Archibald MacLeish had attacked Tate's generation of writers for their ivory-tower and apolitical (or theoretically reactionary) stances, and held them partly to blame for the rise of fascism. To Tate, this was to expect from the artist a foresight and sureness of purpose in which the statesmen themselves had failed; worse, it was to ask him to give up his honesty and universality, suppressing his full vision of his country's problems when praise for its acts seemed expedient. Like Lowell, Tate is haunted by the pejorative *Hun* (both use it as a rhyme-word) and the patriotic demand for a coarsening of moral and cultural awareness that it implies. He asks what the war is *for* as well as what it is against—and the answer seems to him to be a *Pax Americana* in which all other nationalities are squelched and a covert, bureaucratically administered dehumanization replaces direct repression by terror:

> Well-milked Chinese, Negroes who cannot sing,
> The Huns gelded and feeding in a ring.
>   ["More Sonnets at Christmas," II]

Looking back from 1970, we might be inclined to excuse the indifference to Nazi horrors for the sake of this prescient fear. Still, the last step in Tate's argument is unfortunate. Tate certainly shows no sympathy for fascist governments; and yet—perhaps because they are at least nominally on the side of religion, blood-loyalties, and tradition—he comes to allegorize America's war against them as the war of secularism against the traditional society:

1. Interview with Robert Lowell by Frederick Seidel, *Writers at Work: The Paris Review Interviews, Second Series* (New York: The Viking Press, 1963), p. 343.

> Take off, O gentle youth,
> And coasting India
>   Scale crusty Everest
>   Whose mythic crest
> Resists your truth;
> And spying far away
>
> Upon the Tibetan plain
> A limping caravan,
>   Dive, and exterminate
>   The Lama, late
> Survival of old pain.
> Go kill the dying swan.

Because of such passages, when Tate uses the word *Hun* one feels, among the other ironies, a sort of snobbish outrage that America should dare to equate older, more religious societies with barbarism. Lowell's use of the word in "On the Eve of the Feast of the Immaculate Conception 1942" is an instructive contrast:

> Freedom and Eisenhower have won
> Significant laurels where the Hun
>   And Roman kneel
> To lick the dust from Mars' bootheel . . .

Lowell's tone is equally haughty, but his stress is on the mindlessness of the hate-word, not its taste. The people who hate "the Hun" happen to love a general named Eisenhower, whom they equate with "Freedom." In the next lines, the American is identified with the Romans' own classical god of war. Clearly, cultural and moral differences are being dismissed rather than emphasized; the real victor in every war is War itself. One feels here a sense of universal guilt—Original Sin—which is not, as with so many classicist writers, a smug excuse for existing evils, but a fact that has seized and horrified the poet. Elsewhere in the poem, Lowell (by interpreting a cliché literally) virtually equates the act of programmatic thought with the act of violence:

> Bring me tonight no axe to grind
> On wheels of the Utopian mind:

> Six thousand years
> Cain's blood has drummed into my ears,
> Shall I wring plums from Plato's bush
> When Burma's and Bizerte's dead
>   Must puff and push
>   Blood into bread?

A striking and disturbing aspect of this passage is its fusion of religious and blasphemous meanings. The idea that the soldiers are dying to serve the ends of capitalism expresses itself as a frightful parody of the Eucharist ("Blood into bread"). Elsewhere in the poem, the Virgin Mary is addressed as a military conqueror ("another Nimrod") and a Hollywood star ("Celestial Hoyden"); her "burly love" will "improve / On the big wars." To a degree, this is simply satire in the manner of Donne: Lowell points up the blasphemous opposition between the world and God by expressing each in the other's terms. Still, the invocation of a heavenly violence—even if it is only the inward violence of Lowell's own conversion—to overcome the world seems seriously meant, and is disturbing in a poem which, where the secular sphere is concerned, is impartially, totally pacifist. Further, it is not only in Lowell's social poetry that we encounter violent, erotic, victimized, or ambivalent supernatural beings:

> O mother, I implore
> Your scorched, blue thunderbreasts of love to pour
> Buckets of blessings on my burning head
> Until I rise like Lazarus from the dead . . .
>   ["A Prayer for My Grandfather to Our Lady"]

This might partly be attributed to the tradition of sensuous and violent expression in Catholic mysticism. But the imagery seems far more independent of any doctrinal explanation in Lowell than in earlier writers, especially in its quality of ambivalence (for instance, the equation of the Virgin's milk with a thunderbolt). It reminds one of Jung's description of a very early stage in human religious development at which the most ultimately good, and ultimately evil, qualities are united in the same divinities—a stage which, Jung says, often resurfaces in a neurotic's conception of parental figures.[2] At the very least, it shows that Lowell's imagination is preoccupied, to the deepest level, with the violence whose outward manifestation he totally condemns.

Lowell's deeply inward Catholicism, with its stress on universal human guilt, is clearly incompatible with Tate's more programmatic trust in the ethical virtues of tradition and order. In *Lord Weary's Castle*, Lowell abandons even the rhetoric of conservatism, for a rhetoric and underlying myth of apocalyptic liberation, with at least a vague hint of Christian socialism. At this point, I can do no better than quote Randall Jarrell's brilliant account of the "one story and one story only" behind these poems.

> The poems understand the world as a sort of conflict of opposites. . . . Into [a] realm of necessity the poems push everything that is closed, turned inward, incestuous, that blinds or binds: the Old Law, imperialism, militarism, capitalism, Calvinism, Authority, the Father, the "proper Bostonians," the rich who will "do everything for the poor except get off their backs." But struggling within this like leaven, falling to it like light, is everything that is free or open, that grows or is willing to change: here is the generosity or openness or willingness that is itself salvation; here is "accessibility to experience"; this is the realm of freedom, of the Grace that has replaced the Law, of the perfect liberator whom the poet calls Christ.

And, elsewhere in the same essay:

> Lowell reminds one of those heretical enthusiasts, often disciplined and occasionally sanctified or excommunicated, who are more at home in the Church Triumphant than in the church of this world, which is one more state. . . . In his poems the Son is pure liberation from the incestuous, complacent, inveterate evil of established society, of which the Law is a part—although the Father, Jehovah, has

2. Cf. C. G. Jung, "Psychological Aspects of the Mother Archetype," in *The Basic Writings of C. G. Jung* (New York: Modern Library, 1959).

retained both the violence necessary to break up this inertia
and a good deal of the menacing sternness of Authority as
such, just as the poems themselves have . . . the authority of
Mr. Lowell's Christ is sanctified by his rebellion or liberation.[3]

"The First Sunday in Lent" is not one of the best poems in *Lord
Weary's Castle*, but—perhaps for that very reason—its first section
provides a usefully bald illustration of the paradigm. The false
tradition of New England has corrupted the speaker into an
acceptance of war and retributive justice:

> This is the fifth floor attic where I hid
> My stolen agates and the cannister
> Preserved from Bunker Hill—feathers and guns,
> Matchlock and flintlock and percussion-cap;
> Gettysburg etched upon the cylinder
> Of Father's Colt. A Luger of a Hun,
> Once blue as Satan, breaks Napoleon,
> My china pitcher.

This tradition is not only violent but joylessly self-restrained ("a
scolded, sober mob"), snobbish, and humanly isolating. Its whole
stance toward life is a spiritual in-growing which, in an obscure
relation with its violence, seals its doom: "we / Burrow into the
lion's mouth to die." The grown speaker must repudiate such
regression (symbolized, for him, by the attic and its hoard) in that
movement from "closed" to "open" experience that Jarrell finds
characteristic of the book. The speaker anticipates the violence of
the Father ("Lord, from the lust and dust thy will destroys") and
his own subsequent redemption in a collective "unblemished
Adam"

> who will see
> The limbs of the tormented chestnut tree
> Tingle, and hear the March-winds lift and cry:
> "The Lord of Hosts will overshadow us."

3. Randall Jarrell, *Poetry and the Age* (New York: Vintage Books, 1955), pp.
188–89; 192 (hereafter Jarrell).

This Adam very closely resembles the Son as described by Jarrell. He also resembles the redeemed collective heroes of Blake and Shelley—Albion and Prometheus—who, in their apocalypses, perceive and create a world where trees and winds burst their material bonds and become pure forms of living energy, sympathetic to man's. The only real difference is Lowell's stress on submission, on being "overshadowed" by God—but this, too, seems to Lowell an "open" experience, at least in contrast to the Bostonian's preoccupation with his ego and its powers.

Other poems from the series on religious holidays draw the same contrasts, with an even sharper reflection on the State and the Church of this world. In "The Holy Innocents," the forces of redemption are whatever is childlike, passive, ignorant, oppressed. Christ is "a king of speechless clods and infants," a newborn child helplessly "choking in the air"; while the drooling oxen are presented as analogues of his patience and unworldly sorrow. In contrast to him, Herod, "the sorrow of this world," is terrorized and roused to "vengeance" by the mere image of innocence, of passivity combined with liberation—a psychological reaction akin to a father's jealousy of his infant child. The poem expresses at least an implicit revolt against the established church, as well as political authority. The oxen are climbing "St. Peter's Hill," but this ascent becomes identified with the progress of fallen history, a purgatorial mount:

> the year,
> The nineteen-hundred forty-fifth of grace,
> Lumbers with losses up the clinkered hill
> Of our purgation . . .

And when the oxen reach the top, "the worn foundations of their resting-place" are not Peter, the rock on whom the Church is built, but the original manger where the Child shared the sleep of cattle.

It is interesting how unvaryingly Christ appears in these poems as a child—but also as a judge, his very passivity and helplessness constituting the most unanswerable standard. In "Christmas Eve Under Hooker's Statue," Christ returns as a child at the Second

Coming. It is noteworthy, too, how often this child is identified, pantheistically, with natural objects. In "Christmas in Black Rock," his "lips are lean and evergreen" in hedges and Christmas trees. In "New Year's Day," Christ's circumcision—a painful sacrifice under the old Law—finds its analogue in the death of a kitten:

> While we live, we live
>
>> To snuff the smoke of victims. In the snow
>> The kitten heaved its hindlegs, as if fouled,
>> And died. We bent it in a Christmas box
>> And scattered blazing weeds to scare the crow
>> Until the snake-tailed sea-winds coughed and howled
>> For alms outside the church whose double locks
>> Wait for St. Peter, the distorted key.

The kitten, who dies because "fouled" by the world (as Jesus chokes in the air), seems to arouse all nature to call for an inclusive and apocalyptic salvation. This idea of salvation contrasts bitterly with the double-locked church, which has become involved in the property-owner's paranoia, and therefore misinterprets its power to loose as applying only to the afterlife. As Lowell finds Christ in the kitten, so he finds Joseph in a member of the *Lumpenproletariat*, a squatter fisherman living through the winter in a "burlap shack." In the vision that ends the poem, this Joseph

>> relives the wrack
>> And howls of Jesus whom he holds. How sharp
>> The burden of the Law before the beast:
>> Time and the grindstone and the knife of God.
>> The child is born in blood, O child of blood.

Here, the antinomies of the poems are drawn up with greater clarity than ever: on the one hand, Law, the God of duties and sacrifices, sanctified violence, and the pattern of fallen history; on the other, the poor man, the "beast" (here meaning, in part, the innocent physical body), and the Child.

In these poems the "kingdom of necessity," natural and social, is always New England. Yet one notices a good deal of filial ambivalence in Lowell's attitude toward his native region; like a son, he reviles absolutely, but on the basis of an absolute presupposition of the parent's power and importance, which he never doubts that his hearer shares. If the parent is not God, at least he gets to be Satan. (There is also a rather mawkish direct patriotism that comes out when Lowell seeks a good past to contrast with the evil present: "And fought the British Lion to his knees.") A subtle instance of this ambivalence can be seen in a line from the second part of "The First Sunday in Lent": "Who can remember what his father said?" In one sense, this is a cynical and rebellious line: fathers say nothing worth remembering. But it is also very conservative in the judgment it implies: fathers have failed their true function, the transmission of authoritative sayings; sons, therefore, have the right to rebel, but are probably doomed, because unable to acquire any values (the preceding line prophesies that "the racing world . . . must die").

Lowell seems very uncertain that man can dare to live without the authorities he justifiably rejects. This is reflected in the ambiguous politics of his early public gestures: his method is to let one strict authority trounce another (in the interests of a radical goal), rather than to side directly with rebellion. It is reflected, too, in the religion and the poetry themselves; and to this extent Jarrell's view must be qualified, though I think he is entirely right in perceiving that the ideological implication of the most cogent poems in *Lord Weary's Castle*, poems like "New Year's Day" and "Where the Rainbow Ends," is Christian radicalism, or at least Catholic Blakeanism. But the way in which violent action is distanced from the speaker of the poem and made at once ultimately radical and ultimately authoritarian by being placed in the hands of an omnipotent God; the way in which absolute religious submissiveness is made a passionate and liberated characteristic because it contrasts with the often defensive self-as-sertiveness of the bourgeois—these have the air of psychological compromises, though of deeply felt ones. We will see, in later

poems, how they come to be crucial points of moral and aesthetic
difficulty.

II

To turn from Lowell's attacks on modern secular Boston to
those directed against the Puritan past is to do more than unveil
another instance of excessive adolescent hatred. It is to get a
premonitory glimpse of Lowell's conception of spiritual evil—not
a petty, mercantile evil, but a grand, metaphysical, Satanic
variety, involving large passions and persuasive thoughts not easy
to defeat, even inwardly. This spiritual evil is itself a form of
religious experience, centered on devouring time, predestination,
God's anger, the unreality of this world and the despicableness of
the human body and human motives. The horrified fascination
with which Lowell depicts this religious experience—especially
through the persona of Jonathan Edwards, whose biography he
once intended to write—suggests that it may be a possibility in
himself which he is eager to exorcise. The poems themselves make
a brilliant argument for the diametrical opposition of Catholic
and Protestant religious experience; but beneath this opposition
we shall eventually discover certain thematic unities, which are
important keys to the later Lowell's more complex analysis of
other forms of evil. But first, it is necessary to define the
opposition. This, none of the commentators of Lowell's Edwards
poems have yet done with sufficient intellectual clarity; most stop
at the insight that Edwards is abominably insensitive or cruel, a
few even think Lowell agrees with him.[4]

Lowell's Edwards poems, like certain passages in Eliot and
Pound, follow original documents with such an archaeological
closeness that only a few phrases can be attributed solely to the
poet's imagination. Thus, Edwards is allowed to speak very much
for himself; it is only by the subtle effects that usually betray the

4. For other treatments, see Jerome Mazzaro, *The Poetic Themes of Robert Lowell*
(Ann Arbor: University of Michigan Press, 1965; hereafter Mazzaro), pp. 65–71,
and Dallas E. Wiebe, "Mr. Lowell and Mr. Edwards," *Wisconsin Studies in
Contemporary Literature* 3, no. 2 (Spring-Summer 1962): 21–31.

poet's hand in such poems—arrangement, changes of context, the building of image-patterns—that we can sense Lowell leading us toward interpretations of his own, beyond those that Edwards draws. I must therefore request the reader's patience with some laborious quotation, in places where a minor change seems major in its implications.

The sources for "Mr. Edwards and the Spider" are "Of Insects," a treatise Edwards wrote at the age of twelve, and the sermons "Sinners in the Hands of an Angry God" and "The Future Punishment of the Wicked Unavoidable and Intolerable." "Of Insects" addresses itself to a scientific problem: how spiders can "fly" for long distances between trees in apparent defiance of gravity. In a "Corollary," Edwards gives the phenomenon a moral:

> Coroll: We hence see the exuberant Goodness of the Creator Who hath not only Provided for all the Necessities but also for the Pleasure and Recreation of all sorts of Creatures and Even the insects and those that are most despicable.[5]

Further reflection, however, suggests a deeper purpose, and a deeper morality:

> One thing more I shall take notice of before I Dismiss this Subject Concerning the End of Nature in Giving Spiders this way of flying Which though we have found in the Corollary to be their Pleasure and Recreation, yet we think a Greater end is at last their Destruction and what makes us think so is because that is necessarily and Actually brought to Pass by it. . . . I say then that by this means almost all the spiders Upon the Land must necessarily be swept first and last into the Sea for we have Observed already that they never fly except in fair Weather and we may now observe that it is never fair weather neither in this Country nor any other except when the Wind blows from the Midland Parts and so towards the Sea, so here in newengland [sic] I have Observed

5. Jonathan Edwards, *Representative Selections*, ed. Clarence H. Faust and Thomas H. Johnson (New York: American Century Series, 1962), p. 7.

that they never fly except when the wind is westerly . . .
their Chief time here in newengland is . . . towds the Latter
part of Aug, and the beginning of Sept, and they keep flying
all that while towards the sea must needs almost all of them
Get there before they have Done . . .

    Coroll: hence also we may behold and admire at the
wisdom Of the Creator and be Convinced from Prvd
[Providence] there is exercised about such little things, in this
wonderfull Contrivance of Annually Carrying of and bury-
ing the Corrupting Nauseousness of our Air, of which flying
insects are little Collections in the bottom of Ocean where it
will Do no harm . . .[6]

Lowell's first stanza comes almost directly from the essay, but with
a few significant heightenings:

> I saw the spiders marching through the air,
> Swimming from tree to tree that mildewed day
>   In latter August when the hay
>   Came creaking to the barn. But where
>   The wind is westerly,
> Where gnarled November makes the spiders fly
> Into the apparitions of the sky,
>   They purpose nothing but their ease and die
> Urgently beating east to sunrise and the sea;
>
>   What are we in the hands of the great God?

Lowell's use of words like *mildewed* and *creaking* points up
Edwards's morbid imagination, his preoccupation with inevitable
decay in the very height of harvest. But Lowell goes further, and
makes the whole passage a foreshadowing of the adult Edwards's
view of the divine purpose behind human action. The apparently
weightless "swimming" of the spiders (as aesthetically pleasing to
the young Edwards as to us) might well correspond to man's
apparent "free will," which also seemed to Edwards a logical
contradiction demanding a hidden mechanism and cause. The

6. Ibid., pp. 8–10.

spiders' actions seem to them a search for "ease," for the good as it appears to their natural understandings; but their motion is in fact compelled from without by the wind, the instrument of their destruction in the hands of a God who sees them as "the Corrupting Nauseousness of our Air, of which flying insects are little Collections."

Some of Lowell's added phrases seem to broaden the comparison to man in quest not only of "ease" but of salvation. "The apparitions of the sky" suggest the hallucinatory experiences many people went through during the Great Awakening; while the movement "east," which is also a movement toward "sunrise," places two Christian symbols traditionally associated with hope and salvation among the ways by which man draws himself closer to damnation.

The first line of the second stanza makes the allegory absolutely clear, in words from "The Future Punishment of the Wicked." The stanza's dominant metaphor comes from the same source:

> It is in vain to set the briers and thorns in battle array against glowing flames; the points of thorns, though sharp, do nothing to withstand the fire.[7]

The metaphor in Edwards expresses the main point of the sermon, the folly of the sinner's belief that the stoicism that enables him to bear misfortune on earth will still be available in hell. But Lowell's altered context makes us think of "thorn and brier" as the instruments, the "lacerations" used by earlier ascetics to purify themselves of sin, "the fire / And treason crackling in your blood." In Edwards's predestinarian Calvinism, such outward and willful struggles would be totally vain. Lowell's transposition of the image has the effect of equating the Puritans' outward hell with an inward experience of helplessness and self-disgust that their doctrines might be expected to produce:

> Your lacerations tell the losing game
> You play against a sickness past your cure.
> How will the hands be strong? How will the heart endure?

7. Ibid., p. 151.

It is easy to feel that this is not only Edwards addressing his congregation, but Lowell addressing Edwards, pointing to the quality of laceration in Edwards's own rhetoric, drawing tight a loophole Edwards had to leave in his system to preserve his own sense of purpose.

The third stanza advances another of Edwards's arguments, the ease with which a man can be killed as evidence against an excessive estimate of his dignity and power, especially in comparison with God's. Again, Lowell first quotes directly, then begins to rearrange:

> Edwards: Thou canst not stand before a lion of the forest; an
>   angry wild beast, if stirred up, will easily tear such a one
>   as thou art in pieces. Yea, not only so, but thou art
>   crushed before the moth. A very little thing, a little
>   worm or spider, or some such insect, is able to kill thee.[8]

> Lowell: A very little thing, a little worm
>   Or hourglass-blazoned spider, it is said,
>   Can kill a tiger. Will the dead
>   Hold up his mirror and affirm
>   To the four winds the smell
>   And flash of his authority?

By identifying the tiger with man rather than man's enemies, Lowell again suggests questions Edwards might not be prepared to answer. The tiger, if only by its literary associations (Christ in Eliot's "Gerontion," the fearful symmetry of energy in revolt in Blake), bestows a certain dignity on man; unless we are prepared to admire spiders more than tigers, we cannot love or worship God for his power to destroy alone. It is unclear whose "flash" "the dead" is supposed to affirm, his destroyer's or his own; by Edwards's logic it would have to be the latter, but there is some suggestive indirect evidence that the former reading (and the questioning of God's grandeur and justice it entails) has occurred to Lowell. Elsewhere in the sermon, Edwards compares a

8. Ibid.

lightning-flash to the power of God; he also uses a mirroring image to explain why the damned soul will be so publicly abased at the last judgment—God "intends to magnify himself." [9]

These overtones sufficiently undercut Edwards's conception of the divine nature that when he, shifting his own metaphor, says that "It's well" for God to treat us as if we were the only spiders, the reader can take a critical attitude, as he can toward the anecdote which follows.

> Edwards: You have often seen a spider, or some other noisome insect, when thrown into the midst of a fierce fire, and have observed how immediately it yields to the force of the flames. There is no long struggle, no fighting against the fire, no strength exerted to oppose the heat, or to fly from it; but it immediately stretches forth itself and yields; and the fire takes possession of it, and at once it becomes full of fire, and is burned into a bright coal.—Here is a little image of what you will be the subjects of in hell [10]

> Lowell: As a small boy
> On Windsor Marsh, I saw the spider die
> When thrown into the bowels of fierce fire:
>   There's no long struggle, no desire
>   To get up on its feet and fly—
>   It stretches out its feet
>   And dies.

Lowell's changes not only connect the anecdote directly to Edwards's childhood, but draw a specific contrast between this passive acquiescence and the self-entrapping act of flying in the first stanza. To Lowell, this seems to suggest a more ambiguous moral than Edwards's simple argument against stoicism in hell:

> This is the sinner's last retreat;
> Yes, and no strength exerted on the heat

9. Ibid., p. 152.
10. Ibid.

> Then sinews the abolished will, when sick
> And full of burning, it will whistle on a brick.

Contrary to Edwards, Lowell sees the possibility of a "last retreat"—a state of *acedia*, Sloth-Despair, in which the soul has lapsed beyond moral struggle and concern with its own fate, but has also found a kind of escape or resting-place. For Edwards, there was no such "retreat"; God's magnification depended on the soul's passionately repenting, passionately desiring release and salvation, even in hell. Lowell suggests a final stalemate between the soul and God—whether in this life or afterward hardly matters—which reveals less God's glory than the horror and sterility that can result from a predestinarian view of Him.

In the last stanza, as in the second, Lowell uses Edwards's evocation of a literal hell primarily as a metaphor for the static despair of the wholly lapsed soul.

> But who can plumb the sinking of that soul?
> Josiah Hawley, picture yourself cast
>   Into a brick-kiln where the blast
>   Fans your quick vitals to a coal—
>   If measured by a glass,
> How long would it seem burning! Let there pass
> A minute, ten, ten trillion; but the blaze
> Is infinite, eternal: this is death,
> To die and know it. This is the Black Widow, death.

The last sentence has no source in Edwards; by it, Lowell broadens the vision of death far beyond the physical torments of hell, and makes the reader connect it with the many meanings the spider has had in the poem. On the one hand, there is man delighting in sensuous "ease," man entrapped into destruction by his illusory freedom, man as a loathed victim in the hand of God, man's "last retreat" into despair; on the other hand, there is the death-dealing power of God, working inexorably through time (the "hourglass" on the Black Widow's stomach becoming the "glass" of the last stanza). The omnipresence of the symbol makes us feel that Edwards's thought is solipsistic and tautological—a

figurative web, in which all paths lead to death: the inward death
of the soul in a total and impotent disgust with its own nature,
and the final death of the active relation with God in the
stalemate of the last retreat.

"After the Surprising Conversions" portrays a man in exactly
this state of dying and knowing it. The Josiah Hawley addressed
above, Edwards's uncle, cut his throat at the height of the Great
Awakening, in a fit of melancholy such as Edwards's sermon
might be expected to produce (but actually did not, as it was
preached several years later). In the earliest version of the
Narrative of Surprising Conversions, a private letter justifying the
Northampton revival to a rationalistic Boston clergyman, the
incident comes as a brief, shattering postscript; in the later version
Lowell draws on, the causes and consequences of the act are
examined at length, but the fact that Hawley's "melancholy"
family was also Edwards's own is (one presumes deliberately)
elided. I italicize the phrases closely paralleled in Lowell:

> *In the latter part of May, it began to be very sensible that the spirit of
> God was gradually withdrawing from us,* and after this time *Satan
> seemed to be more let loose,* and raged in a dreadful manner. The
> first instance wherein it appeared, was a person's putting an
> end to his own life, by cutting his throat. He was *a gentleman of
> more than common understanding, of strict morals, religious in his
> behavior, and an useful, honorable person in the town; but was of a
> family that are exceeding prone to the disease of melancholy, and his
> mother was killed with it. He had,* from the beginning of this
> extraordinary time, *been exceedingly concerned about the state of his
> soul,* and there were *some things in his experience,* that *appeared
> very hopefully,* but he *durst entertain no hope concerning his own good
> estate.* Towards the latter part of his time, he grew much
> discouraged, and melancholy grew amain upon him, till he
> was wholly overpowered by it, and was in a great measure,
> *past a capacity of receiving advice, or being reasoned with* to any
> purpose. The devil took the advantage, and drove him into
> despairing thoughts. *He was kept awake nights, meditating terror,*
> so that he had scarce any sleep at all, for a long time

together. And it was observed at last, that he was scarcely well capable of managing his ordinary business, and *was judged delirious by the coroner's inquest.* The news of this, extraordinarily affected the minds of people here, and struck them as it were with astonishment. After this, *multitudes* in this and other towns seemed to have it strongly suggested to them, and *pressed upon them,* to do as this person had done. And many that seemed to be under no melancholy, *some pious persons, that had no special darkness or doubts* about the goodness of their state, nor were under any special trouble or concern of mind about anything spiritual or temporal, *yet had it urged upon them, as if somebody had spoken to them, Cut your own throat, now is a good opportunity. Now! Now!* So that they were obliged to fight with all their might to resist it, and yet no reason suggested to them why they should do it.[11]

Most of Lowell's minor alterations in this narrative are stylistic, part of the tour de force by which Edwards's economical, rather mechanistically beautiful prose enters unscathed into a rigid and delicate eighteenth-century poetic net. But in some cases, they serve more specific purposes. Some of them exacerbate the familial tangle and Edwards's implicit guilt: Edwards is made to project onto Hawley a mad "uncle" rather than a mother, to mention his own sermon, and to ponder Hawley's "estate in heaven," suggesting a weird kind of reversed inheritance. Elsewhere, the element of cool logic within unquestioned premises that prevents Edwards from seeing the suicide as a reflection on the kind of experiences the Great Awakening encouraged, is built on until it reveals patrician contempt ("a noisome stir," "the multitude, once unconcerned with doubt"), love of mastery ("kicked / Against our goad"), and sheer incapacity to respond to the events on an appropriate emotional scale ("Good people, but of too much or little wit," "All the good work was quashed").

Lowell's larger additions to the narrative are all related to the

---

11. Jonathan Edwards, *A Narrative of Many Surprising Conversions in Northampton and Vicinity* (Worcester: Moses W. Grout, 1832), pp. 74–75.

themes of nature and theodicy. One of them is borrowed from another of Edwards's conversions:

> He
> Would sit and watch the wind knocking a tree
> And praise this countryside our Lord has made.

The original convert was a girl who, when sinful, had reproached her parents for living far from the center of town, but who later (after becoming incurably ill) preferred to "see the wind blowing the trees, and to behold in the country what God has made." [12] The moralistic sentimentality of this passage forms a rather glaring contrast to the view of fallen nature as a machine of mutual destructions, which we encountered in the spider passages. Lowell reminds us of that view by his use of the harsh verb *knocking;* he also specifies "this countryside," perhaps to remind us that the Puritans often viewed the wild American landscape, and its original inhabitants, as an expression of the Devil rather than of God. Thus, a subtle contrast is established between Edwards's system and Hawley's original spontaneous trust in God's goodness as revealed in His works.

As Hawley's religious experience progresses, "this countryside" becomes a Garden of Eden in earnest: "a thirst / For loving shook him like a snake." Hawley's Fall, it would seem, lies in a melancholic alienation from his own loving impulses, which grows stronger the harder he struggles to make himself feel. Such an alienation, however, would practically be encouraged by the doctrines of Edwards's *The Nature of True Virtue*, a work that reduces all the motives of fallen man to self-interest.

Edwards's view of God, as well as of man, is pushed to a point of final paradox and bewilderment in Lowell's reshaping of the narrative, as Edwards confronts the assumptions necessary to maintain a supernatural explanation of the events in Northampton: an almost total complicity between God and Satan, a willingness on God's part to see his own best work "quashed."

> At Jehovah's nod
> Satan seemed more let loose amongst us: God

12. Ibid., p. 62.

> Abandoned us to Satan, and he pressed
> Us hard, until we thought we could not rest
> Till we had done with life.

Even for Edwards, the Puritan God's inscrutability seems to take on a slightly Manichaean coloration here.

The poem ends with a dense imagistic parable, subtly recapitulating all of its major themes and concerns. There is no source for these lines in Edwards, except perhaps the remark that Hawley "was scarcely well capable of managing his ordinary business," and the indignant denial of a rumor that the same was true of all Northampton.

> September twenty-second, Sir, the bough
> Cracks with the unpicked apples, and at dawn
> The small-mouth bass breaks water, gorged with spawn.

With the "unpicked apples," Eden is again invoked, but rather ironically; for it is the converts' futile effort to undo Original Sin by an absolute religious dedication that has turned them destructively against the demands of their own natures, and of the nature around them. They have turned bounty into rot, in their minds and then in reality. In the last line, Edwards perpetrates a misenvisioning that would fascinate a psychoanalyst: he sees the spawning bass as having swallowed its own offspring. But one need not invoke Freud to see that the genital-oral confusion repeats a larger process in the poem: the distortion of impulses which are both self-gratifying and outpouring or creative (such as Hawley's when he watches the tree) by Edwards's system, which reduces all motives to their selfish components, and by Hawley's melancholy, which quite literally devours his feelings before they are born. The contrast is mirrored in the two images of God: Hawley's God who expresses Himself in His Creation, Edwards's God who detests it and abandons it to Satan, to the devouring principle. Thus, the last line, like that of "Mr. Edwards and the Spider," shows the Puritan system reducing itself to an ingrown stasis or stalemate.

It is noteworthy that the alternative to this, the true, healthy (and, implicitly, the Catholic) vision of God, is expressed through the fecundity of the American land. The symbolism is not unique to this poem. Throughout *Lord Weary's Castle*, plants and animals often appear as vehicles of religious experience or embodiments of Christ—the kingfisher in "Colloquy in Black Rock," the evergreens in "Christmas in Black Rock." In "At the Indian Killer's Grave," King Philip speaks of "the hunter's gashed and green perfection"—a natural mystery recalling the spiritual mystery of the Resurrection. In this poem, the Indian himself becomes a religious figure; and concurrently, the Pilgrims' crimes against him become the inclusive type of Calvinism's spiritual aggression against the redeemable wilderness of human nature. King Philip is compared to John the Baptist, and is given a triumphant speech against the Puritans on Judgment Day. He assails them for their hatred of the land and their preference for idealist, self-referent worlds of their imagination ("your puns / And verbal paradises"). He perceives their repudiation of temporal experience as a terrible psychic violence:

> Your election,
> Hawking above this slime
> For souls as single as their skeletons,
> Flutters and claws in the dead hand of time.

The concluding line is a grim joke on the irrelevance of the Puritans to modern Boston, but it is more than this: it repeats the central device of "Mr. Edwards and the Spider," expressing all aspects of a situation by the same metaphor, so that the reader feels trapped in a world of mirrors. In short, it dramatizes Philip's accusation of solipsism.[13] The connection between solipsistic thinking and cruelty (manifest, too, in Edwards's attitude toward his congregation) is an important one, looking back to the early

13. Lowell's concept of Puritan solipsism bears so close a resemblance to Allen Tate's view of post-Cartesian solipsism in his essay "The Angelic Imagination" (which, however, was written later), that one wonders which was the direction of influence. Perhaps the influence of Jacques Maritain on both writers is the explanation.

line, "Bring me tonight no axe to grind," and forward to the
major portraits of political tyrants.

Perhaps the most extraordinary aspect of "At the Indian
Killer's Grave" is the final religious vision:

> John, Matthew, Luke and Mark,
> Gospel me to the Garden, let me come
> Where Mary twists the warlock with her flowers—
> Her soul a bridal chamber fresh with flowers
> And her whole body an ecstatic womb,
> As through the trellis peers the sudden Bridegroom.

Unless I wholly misread the overtones of that last line, Lowell is
taking the Puritan's worst fear—the Indian raid on the village,
the rape of white women—and making of it a symbol for central
Christian mysteries, the Annunciation, the marriage of the soul
with Christ. The intense sexuality of the passage in itself
demonstrates the total involvement of the bodily human condition—which the Puritans reject—in truly religious experience.
But the element of violence suggests that the soul's complete
subjection, its feminine helplessness before God—experiences akin
to that "sinking of the soul" which Edwards associated strictly
with damnation—are the necessary prelude to mystical ecstasy.
Thus, all that the Puritans reject as evil, in their paranoia, in the
willfulness which, despite their disbelief in the will, haunts their
religious search, becomes in Lowell's vision a possible means of
grace. Beyond it waits a receptive participation in the total
creative aliveness of God: "her whole body an ecstatic womb."
The baroque excess of fertility tellingly resembles that which
disquieted Edwards at the end of "After the Surprising Conversions."

In sum, Lowell associates the Protestant and Catholic principles schematically with the "closed" and "open" experience we
have discussed, and with the sometimes strange set of dualistic
categories that accompany them—categories we have also noted
in the purely Catholic poems, but which we may now, for the sake
of clarity, list in parallel columns:

Open	Closed
Nature	Abstract Thought
Body, Sexuality	Mental Withdrawal, Disgust
The Oppressed	The Oppressor
Primitive Cultures	Technological Cultures
Wise Passivity	Willful Certainty
Symbol, Sacrament	Allegory
Catholic	Protestant

III

Nevertheless, certain problems are raised in the New England poems—nature's cruelty, man's guilt, the conflict between God's love and His justice or violence—which cannot be solved simply by a rejection of one mode of religious thought. In the most ambitious poem in *Lord Weary's Castle*, "The Quaker Graveyard in Nantucket," all the themes we have noted so far recur, but the cultural ones are ultimately subordinated to the more metaphysical.

"The Quaker Graveyard in Nantucket" is an elegy for Lowell's cousin Warren Winslow, who died when his ship sank as the result of an accidental explosion "in these home waters." [14] The poem has been explicated in terms of the conventions of the elegy, and compared with "Lycidas," a number of times.[15] While these conventions were quite clearly in Lowell's mind as he wrote, it seems to me that they become less and less applicable or illuminating as one becomes involved in the inner life and problems of the poem. Where is there another elegy which concludes that its subject died partly because he deserved to? I

14. Critics have offered various accounts of the catastrophe, none of them documented (the ship was torpedoed, or it disappeared mysteriously at sea). My work-study assistant, Penelope Schmidt Harpold, uncovered the truth after a long search through *New York Times* microfilms and a correspondence with the Department of Defense. Lt. Warren Winslow died on Jan. 3, 1944, when his ship, the U.S.S. Destroyer *Turner*, sank as the result of an accidental explosion in the Ambrose Channel of New York Harbor.

15. See particularly, Hugh B. Staples, *Robert Lowell: The First Twenty Years* (New York: Farrar, Straus & Cudahy, 1962; hereafter Staples), pp. 45–52.

shall therefore treat the poem as a complex moral and religious
meditation, creating (in the most important ways) its own form,
and I shall mention the traditional elements only as they seem
relevant to this.

The central moral theme is set forth in the epigraph:

> Let man have dominion over the fishes of the sea and the
> fowls of the air and the beasts and the whole earth, and every
> creeping creature that moveth upon the earth.
>
> [Genesis 1:26, Douay version]

This passage forms the basis for the theological doctrine of
stewardship, according to which man (like the ideal feudal noble)
holds his authority over those beneath him only conditionally, as
a trust from his lord, and is required by God to govern, not to
exploit. This epigraph is crucially important, for it is the failure of
stewardship that provides the subtle link across time between the
three great instances of human wrongdoing Lowell is concerned
with: the exploitative Quaker whaling industry of the nineteenth
century; Captain Ahab's revengeful hunt in *Moby Dick*; and the
technology of modern war, which has killed Lowell's cousin.

The Quakers, of course, were not Puritans, but they probably
inherit some of Lowell's disapproval of Puritans, since they, too,
rejected a sacramental relation with God and preferred a more
willful and moralistic variety which left them prey to their own
self-righteousness. Like the Puritans, they were notoriously hard
bargainers (one remembers Captain Bildad in *Moby Dick*), a fact
that would bear out Weber's theory of the relation between
capitalism and Protestantism—a theory that influenced Lowell,
according to Jarrell.[16] Like the Puritans, too, the Quakers were
irresponsible toward nature; though pacifists in their human
dealings, they were greedy and cruel in their fishing methods, and
nearly exterminated whole species of whales.

Captain Ahab's revenge on a single animal is also, in its way, a
case of bad stewardship. Ahab's quest has often been interpreted
allegorically, as a type of Western man's Faustian drive to know

16. Jarrell, p. 190.

and control the fundamental causes of the material world. It has also been interpreted (notably by Lawrance Thompson) as a deliberately Satanic blasphemy, the whale being a mere surrogate for an inscrutable and unjust God; Ahab says at one point that he wishes to drag "the judge himself . . . to the bar." [17] I think it will become clear that Lowell leans toward both these interpretations (he refers to the White Whale as IS, his own personal translation of the I-AM-THAT-I-AM). As a Faustian questioner, and a monomaniac, Ahab provides a link between the solipsistic thinking of Protestantism and that of modern technology. As a blasphemer, he enacts the spiritual meaning already implicit, for Lowell, in his fellow Quakers' unlimited greed: a total aggression against IS.

From these motives, greed and Faustian inquiry, we proceed to the horrors of global technological war as from cause to necessary effect. Though written before Hiroshima, the poem foresees (particularly in the last two lines) an escalation of destructive power possibly leading to the suicide of the human race. And one cannot escape the fact that Lowell sees a certain amount of poetic justice in this possibility; after all, it is our own persistent violation of our proper relations with nature and God that has brought us these quasi-divine powers we are incapable of using wisely. And yet, if man were allowed to destroy himself totally, it would violate one of the oldest of biblical promises, the covenant of the rainbow with Noah; man's extremity of sin would have changed what we regard as unchangeable in God.

It is understandable that Lowell's fears would give him a Jeremiah-like (some would say an Edwards-like) confidence in the rightness of his prophetic rage, and at the same time deeply shake his faith. Doubtless the unexpectedness of the death "in these home waters" that is the occasion of the poem gives weight to the darker side of these speculations; man is nowhere at "home" in the universe over which he seemingly has such power, and nature itself might be credited, animistically, with rebellion

17. Herman Melville, *Moby Dick*, chap. 132 (p. 535 in Rinehart paperback edition). Thompson develops his view in *Melville's Quarrel With God* (Princeton: Princeton University Press, 1952).

against its misruler, perhaps as the agent of a now vengeful God.

In the first lines of the poem, nature in its mystery appears as the almost military antagonist of military man: "Night / Had steamed into our North Atlantic Fleet." In the ensuing description of the finding of a drowned body, Lowell stresses how the sea has reclaimed it, reducing it to a kind of primal matter, serpentine, heavy, bloodless, an indeterminate "blotch" of colors. The comparison of the body to a ship makes it seem microcosmic (one thinks of the medieval *Narrenschiff*); Winslow, hereafter addressed only as "Sailor," will stand for all mankind as a voyager through the temporal world.

The sea is the most important symbol in the poem, if it can be called a symbol at all. Scientifically, it is the source of all life; "seaward" is "whence it [the body] came" in the ultimate as well as the immediate sense. The sea is powerful, enveloping, seemingly infinite and eternal, and therefore often represents—as in Hopkins's "The Wreck of the Deutschland"—God or His will. But as anthropologists have pointed out, the sea, sea monsters, ocean serpents, both in Judaeo-Christian tradition and in earlier mythologies, are often symbols for primal chaos, hell, death, a devil (or, what is often the same thing, a displaced chthonic or nature-divinity). The sea is thus sacred in a double sense, divine and demonic, as it becomes in Lowell's poem.

In this first section, we see more of the second aspect. The body thrown back into the sea is a "hell-bent deity," and its future is envisioned in the unpleasant image of the "heel-headed dogfish" nudging "Ahab's void and forehead." This line, I suspect, makes a punning reference to God's words to the serpent in Genesis 3:15 ("it shall bruise thy head, and thou shalt bruise his heel"), commonly interpreted as a Messianic prophecy, and thus introduces the idea of the reversal of God's covenants. Of course, in so far as Winslow stands for aggregate mankind, his manner of death itself calls into question God's covenant with Noah. For all these reasons, the body is a "portent" which should terrify the pride of life, the "dreadnaughts", and Lowell prophesies

> When you are powerless
> To sand-bag this Atlantic bulwark, faced

> By the earth-shaker, green, unwearied, chaste
> In his steel scales: ask for no Orphean lute
> To pluck life back.

Poseidon the "earth-shaker" is made, like "night," a military figure, punishing man's military blasphemy; but the steel scales also suggest the ocean serpent or Leviathan; while the quality of superhuman energy and purity in the words "green, unwearied, chaste" makes one think of Lowell's God. The nature of the numinous power opposing man remains ambiguous; but it is clear that man is in danger of losing permanently the contrasting power or grace once available to him—Orpheus, tamer of nature, raiser of the dead, symbol of poetic imagination, and anthropological prototype of Christ. But man is oblivious to his danger, and does not even employ the lute—rather a "hoarse salute" of guns, force against force.

Part II replaces the traditional elegist's Lament of Nature with a kind of rhapsody on the violent interchanges of matter. Here begins a pattern of imagery that runs throughout the poem, in which all natural interactions become acts of violence, and all elements are both victimizer and victim.[18] The wind heaves against the pier, beats the stones, wrings the sea's neck; even the "lubbers" fishing "lash / The heavy surf." Later in the poem the sea is often a devouring mouth, but the land, too, at ebbtide is an "enormous snout / Sucking the ocean's side." Part II is full of cries, screams, expressions of ambiguous portent: "The terns and seagulls tremble at your death"; "The wind's wings . . . scream for you"; "the bones / Cry out in the long night for the hurt beast / Bobbing by Ahab's whaleboats in the East." The impossibility of fixing a meaning on these cries—whether penitence, exultant hatred, or sympathy and lament—corresponds to the ambiguity of victim and victimizer. (It also gives the elegist's idea of natural sympathy a ferocious double-edge: with what human impulses does nature sympathize?)

The one conspicuous island of peacefulness in this section is

18. This pattern was pointed out to me by Richard Wertime.

provided by the sea-gulls that "blink their heavy lids / Seaward."
The image should remind us of the sailor's "staring eyes . . .
Heavy with sand" in part I, which also look seaward in death;
both images convey a sense of inscrutability, of immersion in the
heaviness of matter, of inward or remote, as opposed to ordinary,
seeing. The image becomes more richly resonant later. But even
here, it is a kind of still center, around which the whole world of
violent motion seems to revolve, due to the use of bird-imagery as
a connecting link: "The Pequod's sea wings," the "winds' wings."

In part III the emphasis becomes historical, focusing on Ahab
and the Quakers. Winslow's death epitomizes all deaths at sea;
and their futility, like the ocean itself, separates us, the moderns,
from "castles in Spain"—here not just a romantic never-never-
land, but the more secure feudal world and religious attitude that
formed the ideal of stewardship. In this section, the sea is
explicitly God's immanent will, his "hand" in which the warships
are rocked and cradled like infants. As God's hand, the sea is also
time, which "blues" (forgives or obliterates?) "Whatever it was
these Quaker sailors lost / In the mad scramble of their lives."
Their time, according to Lowell, was "open-eyed"—both innocent and ignorant, in contrast to the modern world of spiritual
terrors associated with the "heavy lids." Lowell mocks the
Quakers, since, like Puritans, they equated success with a state of
grace, and used quasi-predestinarian ideas to create a tautological
justification for their cruel mercantilism:

> In the sperm-whale's slick
> I see the Quakers drown and hear their cry:
> "If God himself had not been on our side,
> If God himself had not been on our side,
> When the Atlantic rose against us, why,
> Then it had swallowed us up quick."

Yet the irony of their fate is a tragic one, for it reflects on all
human efforts to know God's nature and purposes from temporal
vicissitudes; it foreshadows our complete and conscious estrange-
ment from the "news / Of is" we have misused.

Parts IV and V reenact the last scene of *Moby Dick*. One

commentator, Jerome Mazzaro, has equated this "end of the whale-road and the whale" with the death of God at man's hands, the coming of the post-Christian era.[19] This interpretation seems valid as far as it goes, but it hardly accounts for the strangeness of the new apocalypse Lowell imagines, or the continuing ambiguity of the imagery. At the beginning of IV, the *Pequod*'s sailors are the Ship of Fools, and the whale is, appropriately, the punishing God who will send them "packing off to hell." But later, the wounded whale is identified with the crucified Christ as well, "Spouting out blood and water"; while a phrase in the next line, "Sick as a dog," recalls the dogfish of part I and, thus, the demonic aspect of Leviathan. One might recall, too, from part III the phrase "IS, the whited monster," suggesting "whited sepulchre"—a disturbing and blasphemous collocation, even if, as is possible, it is intended to refer only to Ahab's false vision.

Curiously, the same ambiguities attach to the sailor himself as to the whale. At the end of part IV, Lowell asks:

> Who will dance
> The mast-lashed master of Leviathans
> Up from this field of Quakers in their unstoned graves?

In the plot of *Moby Dick*, this "mast-lashed master" would be the drowned lookout, Tashtego; but outside this context he would clearly be the crucified Christ. In the former context, the question is sardonic and pessimistic; in the latter, it appeals, if poignantly and almost in desperation, to the Resurrection, and suggests that even Ahab's sailors are potentially Christ-like.

Part V begins:

> When the whale's viscera go and the roll
> Of its corruption overruns this world . . .

This may be taken as the death of God, the revolt of abused nature, or the dominion of Antichrist, depending on which aspect of the whale symbolism one chooses to emphasize; but clearly the Second Coming is at hand, brought on by the sins of greed and violence both merchant and soldier have committed.

19. See Mazzaro, pp. 41–42.

> Sailor, will your sword
> Whistle and fall and sink into the fat?

On the Day of Judgment, "In the great ash-pit of Jehoshaphat," the sailor's bones "cry" for the whale's blood, and the cry is still ambiguous, perhaps vengeful, perhaps, if "blood" stands for the salvific power of the Eucharist, pleading. Ahab's harpoon becomes the "death-lance" that pierced Christ's side; it "churns into the sanctuary." But in the very same lines Lowell's left hand, as it were, is showing us the whale as Leviathan and Antichrist: like the sea in part I, it is a war-machine with a "gun-blue swingle"; it is also primal matter, a serpentine, "coiling life," like the sailor's "coiled . . . muscles." The end of part V brings forth the literal Apocalypse, and draws, appropriately, on God's reproach to Job out of the whirlwind ("Where the morning stars sing out together" comes from Job 38:7). But even here there is ambiguity, for the phrase suggests Lucifer's revolt as well as the Creation; in Blake's "The Tiger," it is echoed ironically, with that in mind. The last lines of the section are a kind of prayer:

> Hide
> Our steel, Jonas Messias, in Thy side.[20]

This line has been compared to a Metaphysical conceit, but I certainly know of no seventeenth-century line so far sunk in unresolved and blasphemous paradox.[21] To begin with, although a prayer, the line bears some kinship to the defiant last words of Captain Ahab: "*Thus,* I give up the spear." Read in its simplest sense, the line is a supplication to the whale as crucified Christ: it might be paraphrased "take on our guilt, O Lord, even the guilt of Thy death." But the introduction of the biblical parallel between Christ's descent into hell and the story of Jonah complicates matters enormously, for it revitalizes the whole infernal aspect of the whale symbolism. Further, it would seem to equate Ahab's spear with Jonah (and hence, Christ), since both enter and are hidden in the body of the whale. Thus, this line

20. According to Mr. Lowell, the comma after "Hide" is a persistent misprint.
21. See Staples, p. 50.

culminates that confusion of the divine and the Satanic, the aggressor and the victim, which has haunted the poem, without giving us much further indication of its intellectual or religious purport.

We may turn with some hope of enlightenment to the explicitly devotional part VI, "Our Lady of Walsingham," which is based on a passage in E. I. Watkin's *Catholic Art and Culture*. Watkin is a gentler thinker than Lowell, but of similar Christian utopian inclination. He rejects both the liberals and the reactionaries (the latter, "forgetting the Lord's Prayer and St. John's prophetic vision, . . . confine the kingdom to heaven") and hopes for "the kingdom of a deified humanity" through the Holy Spirit.[22] Watkin dwells on the shrine of Walsingham because of a Catholic proverb, "when England goes to Walsingham, England will return to the Church." But Watkin interprets this return to Walsingham as a return to the type of silent contemplation, "beyond emotion and thought," and therefore almost beyond specific belief, which the "expressionless" face of the Virgin expresses.

Lowell's vision remains darker than Watkin's, as his alterations of Watkin's language show. The "cows" and the "munching" lane imply a certain contempt for the too easily consoled worshiper, which the phrase "the castle of God" (replacing Watkin's "city," and echoing "castles in Spain") extends onto the anthropomorphic or societo-morphic aspect of medieval Catholic theology. Lowell's stream, unlike Watkin's, is not wholly an emblem, "the water symbol of the Holy Spirit." It has "whirlpools," as if it came underground from the South Pacific and the *Pequod*'s vortex; and it flows under a "druid tree," a different kind of symbol in a pre-Christian propitiatory worship of the destructive aspect of nature. What the sailor is instructed to "see" will go beyond his superficial gladness and foretell his eventual fate.

The ending of the section, too, is considerably darker than its source. I quote both:

22. E. I. Watkin, *Catholic Art and Culture* (New York: Sheed and Ward, 1944). The relevant section, from which all my quotations come, is pp. 212–15.

Watkin: That expressionless countenance expresses what is
beyond expression. It is the countenance of one whose
spirit dwells in a region beyond emotion and thought, in
that centre of which mystical writers speak. Mary is
beyond joy and sorrow. For her spirit is in God, and she
knows as He knows, receiving His knowledge. No longer
the Mother of Sorrows nor yet of the human joy of the
Crib, she understands the secret counsel of God, to
whose accomplishment Calvary and Bethlehem alike
ministered. Therefore her peace, the central peace of
God, is beyond the changes of earthly experience. And
the inscrutability of that illegible countenance is the
inscrutability of the Divine Will made known to her.

Lowell: Our Lady, too small for her canopy,
Sits near the altar. There's no comeliness
At all or charm in that expressionless
Face with its heavy eyelids. As before,
This face, for centuries a memory,
Non est species, neque decor,
Expressionless, expresses God: it goes
Past castled Sion. She knows what God knows,
Not Calvary's Cross nor crib at Bethlehem
Now, and the world shall come to Walsingham.

In Watkin, God's purpose includes but transcends Calvary and
Bethlehem; in Lowell, it has left them behind ("Not . . . Now"),
and therefore no return on the world's part could possibly bring
them back. Lowell's last two lines still leave open the possibility of
God's punitive withdrawal; at the very least, they imply that man
is absolutely prevented from approaching or understanding God
through the traditional terms.

Yet in many ways Lowell's vision remains the same as
Watkin's. The privation of anthropomorphic conceptions and
symbols is akin to the privation of "thought and emotion," "joy
and sorrow," and so is assimilable to a traditional Way of mystical
development. The description of the statue, in both writers,
contains an allusion to Isaiah 53:2, the passage on the Messiah as

man of sorrows ("he hath no form nor comeliness; and when we shall see him, there is no beauty that we should desire him"), and thus warns us that salvation may come under forms outside our notions of aesthetic and ethical order, and that we may therefore be blind to it. Finally, Lowell's application of the familiar "heavy eyelids" image to the Virgin (while it may have other meanings) at least suggests that her contemplation is closer to modern man's gaze into the blankness and mystery of matter than to the "open-eyed" Quakers' straightforward, bargaining, or—at best— moralistic conception of their relation with God. Interpreting this way, one might detect at least a faint echo of Watkin's optimistic prophecy: "the contemplation expressed by her . . . image . . . is the womb in which Christ's Mystical Body will be born again to a new and a vaster life from the death of historic Christendom."

In part VII, Lowell seems to achieve some of the traditional elegist's reconciliation to the destruction around him: "It's well" (though the echo here of the words of Lowell's own Edwards is disturbing). At the end, human violence seems to be subsumed, through evolution, into the natural chaos of the sea, and thence into God's will; man, in effect, becomes his own Flood.

> You could cut the brackish winds with a knife
> Here in Nantucket, and cast up the time
> When the Lord God formed man from the sea's slime
> And breathed into his face the breath of life,
> And blue-lung'd combers lumbered to the kill.
> The Lord survives the rainbow of His will.

In this new stress on Darwinian inevitabilities, however, God's purpose remains extremely obscure. The last line has the same ambiguous sense as the ending of "Our Lady of Walsingham": it may mean that God is no longer bound or expressed by his covenants, and so might permit man's self-destruction; or the emphasized fact may be that God *survives*, is still available to faith no matter how many traditional conceptions are abandoned.

There are at least three different kinds of religious vision in the poem. Two of them, the harsh moral fable of the withdrawal of God's mercy occasioned by man's persistence in evil, and the

Christian Existentialist, contemplative faith that the privation of temporal interpretations of and demands on God may be the paradoxical opportunity for the rebirth of a living relation, have already been illustrated at length. The third vision I can only call animistic, or pantheistic. We see it in the use of the sea as an inclusive image, containing, at one end, man, at the other, the hand of God; we see it, too, in the panoply of pagan gods and demigods, druids, Christian emblems, Ahab's whale—a bizarre Olympus whose effect is, in part, to set the true God far beyond all human representations of Him, but also, in part, to give nature some ambiguous participation in divinity. More profoundly, I feel pantheistic implications in the poem's strange linking images, which identify so many forces and beings with their natural enemies, with Satan and Jehovah, and with Christ; and in its vision of a formless primal matter, conjured up by science, but identified through the image of the heavy eyelids with the expressionless expression that knows God's will. These pantheistic linkings make me think of another apocalyptic writer I have previously compared with Lowell, William Blake, who sees the reduction of the material world to its ultimate chaos in the wars of the Apocalypse as the precondition for its coming together as the *disjecta membra* of a universal, mystical body of Christ. Lowell's own Apocalypse (in part V) has the thunder "dismember" Ahab's flag, and ends by seemingly blending the identities of all the protagonists in "Jonas Messias."

But to conceive of the Apocalypse in this manner is to welcome rather than fear it; and so, if a real end of the world is at issue, we are once more brought up against the problem of violence. We encounter it, too, if we try to bring the three levels of the poem together. For a violence that is both revengeful and completely liberating is possible in neurotic fantasy, or (some would say) in revolution; but to make it an attribute of an omnipotent and volitional deity (as Lowell has done before, in "The First Sunday in Lent" for instance) is neither very reasonable nor, if one thinks about it closely, tolerable. Perhaps it is unfair to Lowell to take his Apocalypse so literally; perhaps one should take the whole process of imagistic blendings as a purgation of apparent oppositions and conflicts, the Apocalypse as an allegory of Lowell's irradiated sense of beings "beyond joy and sorrow," as he moves into the contemplation of is.

But the relation between vision and violence has been a problematic area in all these poems. It appears in the military image of the Virgin in the earliest poems; in the figure of the Child, who is at once utterly passive and a terrifyingly pure judge; in a negative and repudiated form, in the fanaticism of Edwards; and in all closely described moments of personal ecstasy, from "A Prayer for My Grandfather to Our Lady" to "At the Indian Killer's Grave." It seems probable that Lowell's profounder meditation on this problem, and the arousal of his humanistic conscience on the occasion of Warren Winslow's death, played some part in the shift in his attitude toward religious figures from a strongly emotional identification (or, at least, a directly emotional relation), to Existentialist uncertainty and contemplative quiet. The immediate result is a poem that seems at once more profoundly religious, more mystical, and far more self-contradictory than its predecessors. But in the longer view, so much of Lowell's Catholicism seems involved in the desire to see the world reshaped by the force of his visions, and in the tension of that desire, that one wonders if the move toward the greater abstractness of Christian Existentialism was not in fact the beginning of deconversion.

IV

There is one remarkable poem in *Lord Weary's Castle* that treats both the Catholic and the Protestant experiences, both Edwardsian melancholy and apocalyptic imagination, in a context of contemporary personal problems that are, presumably, in part autobiographical. It is also the first poem to hint at Lowell's disillusionment with Catholicism. "Between the Porch and the Altar" represents a break with earlier work, too, in its overt use of Freudian insights, and in its multiplication of perspectives: it employs the first-person voices of two of the characters, and, in the first section, an authorial third person that can modulate into and out of the consciousness of the obsessed protagonist.

This section, "Mother and Son," begins with a direct, analytical account of the son's regression, his feeling of the unreality of his adulthood:

> Meeting his mother makes him lose ten years,
> Or is it twenty?

With the question, or revision, we move into the son's mind, which, we find, speaks to itself in violent yet abstract, iconographic images:

> Time, no doubt, has ears
> That listen to the swallowed serpent, wound
> Into its bowels, but he thinks no sound
> Is possible before her, he thinks the past
> Is settled.

The connection of time and the serpent occurs elsewhere in *Lord Weary's Castle*. In "Where the Rainbow Ends,"

> The Chapel's sharp-shinned eagle shifts its hold
> On serpent-time, the rainbow's epitaph.

Time is a serpent, here, because it is cyclical and endlessly repetitive. It is "the rainbow's epitaph": visually, for the same reason that Yeats says eternity is where "all the serpent-tails are bit"; spiritually, because it struggles forever under God's punitive law, the eagle, but is unable to attain His covenant of liberation. By applying this parallel passage (along with the obvious reference to the serpent in Eden), we see that the son has translated into religious terms his awareness that the guilt and suffering of his childhood persist, and tend to repeat themselves in some form, despite his conscious belief that, whether by virtue of growing up or of conversion, "the past / Is settled." But to paraphrase thus is to ignore the anatomical savagery of the image; and given the context of filial regression, what suggests itself is an unpleasant fantasy of the embryo as both a parasitic worm and the swallowed prey of its mother, both devouring and devoured. Later images in the poem reinforce this interpretation, which gives a Freudian substructure to the ideas about time, cycles, predestination, and guilt with which the protagonist wrestles throughout.

The son struggles to hold onto a conscious rationality, even if it is superficial ("It is honest to hold fast / Merely to what one sees with one's own eyes"), but the difficulty of separating seeing from vision becomes clear as the mother's "red velvet curves and haunches" blot out "the pretty driftwood fire's / Façade of welcome." Then the son's only defense is the child's morbid withdrawal

> Into the sack and selfhood of the boy
> Who clawed through fallen houses of his Troy,
> Homely and human only when the flames
> Crackle in recollection.

The allusion is a vivid symbol for the impact of the parents' unsteady marriage on the child. The son now desires, or feels most himself in, this old fantasy, now fed by classical learning, in which, though utterly regressed and withdrawn, he can dramatize his anger and fear. Both he and his environment are "homely and human" only in flames. The bourgeois respect he is expected to show his mother, by contrast, "shames" him, presumably because of the sexuality of the red velvet curves, which is serpentine ("uncoiling"), but also—like the prettified New England atmosphere—somehow fraudulent, a "counterfeit body." His internal balancing-act now shifts to sadistic counterattack, depersonalizing (but also deifying) the mother with references to the Whore of Babylon:

> It
> Is something in a circus, big as life,
> The painted dragon, a mother and a wife
> With flat glass eyes pushed at him on a stick;
> The human mover crawls to make them click.

Of course, there is insight in the sadism: the mother is a clicking social façade, with, no doubt, a desperate and self-debasing person struggling behind. The son's wife appears in the poem for the first time as, it seems, she will always appear to her husband: a mere extension of his mother.

At the end of the section, though still caught in a regressive "schoolboy" fantasy, the son sees the more attractive traditional figure of his grandfather, calling him forward into adulthood and responsibility:

> The forehead of her father's portrait peels
> With rosy dryness, and the schoolboy kneels
> To ask the benediction of the hand,
> Lifted as though to motion him to stand,
> Dangling its watch-chain on the Holy Book—
> A little golden snake that mouths a hook.

But it is a sinister kind of adulthood, governed by the Holy Book and, still worse, the family watch-chain—Time ruled by the cycle of guilty desire and punishment, snake and hook.

Part II, "Adam and Eve," written in the first person, shows us the same protagonist with his mistress. Its setting, Concord at midsummer, contains both the truest glories of his tradition and an overly fecund nature like that in "After the Surprising Conversions." The Minuteman's column is an emblem of moral uprightness, but also extremely phallic; and it is soon (quite literally) deflated in the speaker's imagination.

> The Farmer sizzles on his shaft all day.
> He is content and centuries away
> From white-hot Concord, and he stands on guard.
> Or is he melting down like sculptured lard?

The violent crudeness of the sexual element makes one suspect that the speaker is, again, defending himself through aggressive burlesque; later, he describes his feeling for the statue as "awed contempt." Finally, he lashes out at the Puritans (and, of course, at his own family) for the vanity and pretense behind the tradition they have passed down to him, reinforced by their own self-sacrifice:

> They lied,
> My cold-eyed seedy fathers when they died,

> Or rather threw their lives away, to fix
> Sterile, forbidding nameplates on the bricks
> Above a kettle. Jesus rest their souls!

Possibly Lowell, like Hawthorne, thinks of the elders who wore
out several wives by the number of children they begot; clearly,
these "cold-eyed seedy fathers" had the strength and virility the
speaker doubts in himself, but their "sterile" achievements of
possessive egotism just as clearly deny the sexual in its fullest, most
humane implications.

An alternative form of traditional salvation presents itself in the
Irish Catholic Church of St. Patrick; it once dealt with the
serpent in a gentler, magical way, but now itself has a "puritani-
cal façade." The speaker doubts that even the original Patrick
could overcome his vision of his own energy and life as Satanic,
"the red dragon of my nerves," except by annihilating him.

Even the speaker's love affair seems to him no more than a
warfare of nerves, an "unrest of terror" in which he is again
required "To while away my life," to play the same submissive,
self-sacrificing role as with his mother and wife. This, and guilt
about his adultery, make him accept the identity of sex, sin, and
death ("Man tasted Eve with death") and reach the Sophoclean
conclusion, "Never to have lived is best." At the end, a call for
help from the girl rouses the speaker to a spectacle which indeed
repeats the Garden of Eden:

> Your market-basket rolls
> With all its baking apples in the lake.
> You watch the whorish slither of a snake
> That chokes a duckling. When we try to kiss,
> Our eyes are slits and cringing, and we hiss;
> Scales glitter on our bodies as we fall.
> The Farmer melts upon his pedestal.

But the snake (whorish, so presumably feminine) choking the
duckling also reechoes the speaker's earlier fantasy of being
devoured in his mother's womb. Afterwards, not surprisingly, the
nervous sexual desire of the speaker and his mistress seems to him

as rapacious, degraded, and snakelike as that of the "cold-eyed
seedy fathers." As they "fall" into lovemaking, all the images of
heat, light, of a passion potentially mystical in its intensity
("white-hot Concord") are absorbed into the serpent image. But,
as in the Edwards poems, we feel that the protagonists have really
fallen by bringing their exacerbated nerves and sense of sin into
the Garden, by not accepting "the hunter's gashed and green
perfection." Indeed, the similarity between the speaker's dominant Freudian terror and Edwards's vision of the bass deserves
pondering.

"Katherine's Dream" follows, and its dream-logic develops
undertones we have already sensed in the relationship (whether
the facts it gives are actually true of the lovers' waking reality we
cannot know, but do not need to know). Thus, the dream places
Katherine in a lower-class atmosphere, and makes the affair seem
like slumming on the man's part—weekend parties with beer
"brought in cases" and so forth. But this is appropriate to the
man's feeling that the relationship is degrading, and that sexual
liberation is a betrayal of his family's code. Katherine, too, seems
to feel their connection to be a mutually destructive war of nerves,
airless as a repeated dream:

> The dangling telephone receiver rasped
> Like someone in a dream who cannot stop
> For breath or logic till his victim drop
> To darkness and the sheets.

The dream, or delirium, continues:

> I must have slept,
> But still could hear my father who had kept
> Your guilty presents but cut off my hair.
> He whispers that he really doesn't care
> If I am your kept woman all my life,
> Or ruin your two children and your wife;
> But my dishonor makes him drink. Of course
> I'll tell the court the truth for his divorce.

It is hard to see this rather biblical family relationship as literal, and the last line with the ambiguous "his" suggests a dream-blurring of the identities of father and lover. The lover is certainly a sufficiently superego-ridden figure to seem like a father. In fact, the attitude of at once conspiring with, punishing, and punishing himself for a relationship held at one remove by an incest taboo is, *mutatis mutandis*, a rather apt psychoanalytic description of the lover's feelings about his affair.

Into this atmosphere of circularity and self-defeat, a Catholic episode comes, for once, as a hope of real release. The "Black nuns with glasses," sexless but jolly, represent an agape which the lovers would like to unite with their eros, but cannot because of their adulterous guilt and their compulsion to mutually destructive behavior. Such a fusion, and freedom from guilt, seem to Katherine possible for the "good people" who "go / Inside by twos to the confessor," "forgiven couples" but also "friends." Katherine feels warmed by the generalized love she imagines in them, but soon guilt and the fear of abandonment by her lover return, and the dream again becomes a nightmare of pointless perpetual motion. She runs in circles till she drops "in a yard / Where faces redden and the snow is hard": no longer St. Patrick's yard, but the prison (place of punishment and compulsion) or tenement (place of degradation) that they have made of their love.

"At The Altar" returns to the man's voice.

> I sit at a gold table with my girl
> Whose eyelids burn with brandy. What a whirl
> Of Easter eggs is colored by the lights,
> As the Norwegian dancer's crystalled tights
> Flash with her naked leg's high-booted skate . . .

It is a telling combination of images: voyeuristic sex, costume and artifice, "gold" and capitalism, infernal fire (and how much is conveyed by the usually eloquent speaker's laconic "my girl," linked to all this by such emphatic alliterations and rhymes!). The skater's exhibitionistic performance becomes a perverted reenactment of a child's Easter and Christmas, grown violent as well as grossly sexual, like the Minuteman's column in II:

> The twinkling steel above me is a star;
> I am a fallen Christmas tree. Our car
> Races through seven red-lights . . .

In the ensuing joyride, the lover whispers in the girl's ear the traditional married man's line, but put in an almost comically fatalistic way, that deflects onto her all the questions he is unable to ask himself:

> You know
> I want to leave my mother and my wife,
> You wouldn't have me tied to them for life . . .

The drunken ride ends with the reality, or the fantasy, of suicide, of a head-on crash into the façade of a Gothic church. The ride becomes, for the speaker, the sum of his past, of the inevitabilities of his life, under the aegis of the allegorical Time and the Christmas star become an astrological· fixed destiny: "Time runs, the windshield runs with stars." In the suicide, the joyride and the Church seem to converge and destroy each other in a dream-logic, as apparent opposites bound together on a deeper level; so, in his final baroque vision of himself in hell, the protagonist, like Edwards, sees his God and his Satan become identical.

> Here the Lord
> Is Lucifer in harness: hand on sword
> He watches me for Mother, and will turn
> The bier and baby-carriage where I burn.

Both the bier and hell turn out to be the womb: having received the desired, dramatic punishment for his sexual sin, the protagonist is free to return to the regressive, passive state that has haunted him from the beginning. But, really, this hell is equivalent to his entire life, in which his Lucifer and his God, burning desire and self-punishment, have turned him in repetitive circles, allowing the ultimate control to rest with the mother.

This protagonist resembles Lowell's Protestant figures, Edwards and Hawley, in more ways than simply by being of Calvinist descent and guilt-ridden. For both, nature (and for the modern man, sex) is at once a paradise and a hell of mutually devouring monsters, and one may be damned either in accepting it or in rejecting it. Both are determinists, the one seeing human history, the other his own life, as a pattern of repetitive situations bringing inescapable guilt. But in both, this determinism is related to an image of total regressive withdrawal and weakness which both fear but half-desire (in Edwards we can sense this only obliquely, in his fascinated description of the "sinking" of the soul in hell, but Lowell's later poem on Edwards in *For the Union Dead*, to be discussed in the next chapter, deals with passivity in Edwards's own personality). All three figures are preoccupied by the idea of a Last Judgment, and Hawley and the modern protagonist are tempted to bring it on themselves by suicide. But all are cut off from a positive vision of liberation or grace, and are left in a condition of spiritual stalemate by the tautological, incestuous Jehovah-Satan system we have described.

It should be clear by this point that this constellation of motives is not as remote from Lowell's Catholic vision as his schematic oppositions might make it seem. There, too, we find an intense concern with the cruelty and violent self-interest in nature and man; with an intense experience (though mystical, not infernal) of submission and "sinking"; and with the remoteness and power of God. If we detect a Freudian theme of infantile regression in the Puritans' picture of hell, we might also find it in the image of a newborn baby, "choking in the air," as the judge of this world. In the Catholic's yearning for immediate Apocalypse, we might find a significant inversion of the Puritan's fear of the onward rush of time toward death and judgment.

I have suggested that Lowell, like his fictionalized Edwards, confronts a certain amount of guilt when a portion of God's destructive power is transferred to the performing preacher's modern analogue, the vatic poet; and we observed in him a similar difficulty (except perhaps in "The Quaker Graveyard") in going beyond rather febrile vision to the contemplative "center" usually considered the highest form of Christian experience. It is doubtless significant that in the poem where Lowell first treats the Protestant experience as an enduring part of a modern sensibility close to his own, he has also begun to question the absolute validity of the Catholic experience. He has also, it would seem, begun to question his own method of working reality into poetic structures. His protagonist's habit of constructing baroque and violent allegories in his mind in order to make tolerable a pain he cannot understand or communicate in ordinary social terms—his sensibility of necessary exaggerations—seems almost a parody of the way the more typical and less inspired *Lord Weary's Castle* poems, poems like "The First Sunday in Lent," operate.

But to recognize Lowell's criticism of his early techniques should not blind us to what those techniques have achieved in psychological portraiture. Few writers give us so vivid or dramatic a sense of that interpenetration, or confusion, of the personal with the archetypal which Jung holds to be characteristic of extreme neurotic experience. And no style in literature, I venture to say, captures so well the process of formalization by metaphor: the disturbing object becoming still as it becomes impersonal, yet suffused with a violent—almost a caricatural—emotionalism, as the buried feelings assume control over reality. (This may, I suppose, be an element of emotional appeal in the static violence of all baroque art, which would explain certain of Lowell's baroque affinities—for instance, the agitated heaviness of his meters.)

We have seen all these qualities in "Between the Porch and the Altar," but we might look at a particularly remarkable passage in "The Death of the Sheriff," where the speaker uses his classical learning to escape from his (rather obscure) family troubles into a self-induced madness—and then recoils, in terror, when the madness starts to come too easily.

> Now I can let my father, wife and son
> Banquet Apollo for Laomedon:
> Helen will satiate the fire, my Lord.
>
> I search the starlight . . . Helen will appear,

> *Pura per noctem in luce* . . . I am chilled,
> I drop the barbless fly into my purse

The lines speed up, with wild exhilaration, as the speaker translates his family more and more completely into his fantasy of the Trojan War, with a more and more open display of murderous feelings. Then they slow, with a kind of drugged intensity, as the fantasy begins to turn into hallucination. At this point, the quality of self-hypnosis is wonderfully conveyed by the technique: the emphasis given the word *will* by its slightly extra metrical stress, its repetition, and its reinforcement by consonance ("*Hel*en" and "chilled"); the quality of incantation, almost of lullaby, which the Latin possesses, partly because we understand it somewhat more vaguely than English, partly because of the repeated *p-r*'s and *u*'s. The Latin, in fact, represents the entry into hallucination (as allusion often does in early Lowell and, to a degree, in Eliot); it is immediately followed by the "chilled," and, I think, frightened reversion that expresses itself in very specific, corporeal perception.

The unsympathetic reader might, of course, admit these dramatic merits in Lowell's baroque style and still find *Lord Weary's Castle* existentially inauthentic, in that it claims to be a Christian book yet often uses Christian terms as counters—even, perhaps, as coloring—for what are essentially issues of family and personal identity. But to argue thus would be to beg a question about the general relation between personal and religious experience which is well-nigh unanswerable—Erik Erikson's *Young Man Luther* is the classic book on this subject. Finally, it is no shame to Lowell—rather, a tribute to the fineness of his objective correlative—that we can find aspects of the religious emotion in *Lord Weary's Castle* adolescent, and yet be delighted, illuminated, enthralled by the novel of adolescence that we then discover.

Ultimately, *Lord Weary's Castle* seems to me as deeply and rewardingly personal a book as *Life Studies*. In a sense, they divide Lowell's world between them, for the one has only the barest points of reference in an unmythologized reality, while the other, despite its "confessional" content, has almost no element of recaptured mental flux, or free association. The ultimately greater achievement of the more recent books is to unify the two realms. Until this fusion is attained, Lowell oftens seems to regret the loss of belief, and of its absolutely accepted order of archetypal symbols. In "For George Santayana," from *Life Studies*, he compares the suppression of an impulse to believe to the repression of sexual impulses, and sees the consequences of both choices for Santayana's philosophy as a deeply paradoxical victory-in-defeat.

Finally, it is just as important to say—and just as often overlooked—that *Lord Weary's Castle* is very closely related to the later work, indeed probably necessary to it, as Yeats's early commitment to courtly love and Irish legend—equally willful, equally slow to exhaust itself in the face of problems it could not encompass—was necessary to his later meditation on all visionary commitments. In Lowell's case, the ensuing secular themes are the anatomy of the will to power and the will to apocalyptic destruction, the value and danger of absolutism, the complex triple relation of sanity, madness, and imaginative transcendence. With "Between the Porch and the Altar," Lowell comes to agree with Wallace Stevens that "now both heaven and hell / Are one, and here, O terra infidel." [23] But what heaven and hell have meant—a Blakean entrusting of oneself to the imagination of a wholly living universe, that brings with it dangers of egomania and violence, as against a melancholy holding-back from the life-process and one's own motives, that brings the danger of self-violence—remain crucial categories in Lowell's treatment of his own discontent and the discontents of civilization.

23. Wallace Stevens, "Esthétique du Mal," *Collected Poems* (New York: Alfred A. Knopf, 1954), p. 315.

3

The "Tranquillized Fifties" and the Self-Analytic Poet

I

The importance of *Life Studies* for the development of American poetry makes it somewhat difficult to discuss as a part of Lowell's own development—one phase, one voice among several. Lowell has stated as well as anyone the sense of impasse among intellectual poets in the preceding period, the handicaps of the too thorough near-science of putting together traditional poems that was the legacy of the New Criticism:

> But there's another point about this mysterious business of prose and poetry, form and content, and the reasons for breaking forms . . . it seems to me we've gotten into a sort of Alexandrian age. Poets of my generation and particularly younger ones have gotten terribly proficient at these forms. They write a very musical, difficult poem with tremendous skill. Yet the writing seems divorced from culture somehow. It's become too much something specialized that can't handle much experience. It's become a craft, purely a craft, and there must be some breakthrough back into life.[1]

Life Studies was a conscious attempt at such a breakthrough, by the infusion of apparently arbitrary personal detail, suggestive but less reducible than traditional symbolism, and by the elevation of private honesty to an aesthetic criterion, not the opposite but the

1. *Writers at Work: The Paris Review Interviews, Second Series*, p. 346.

creative contrary of craft. Older poets, including, it is rumored, Allen Tate, were largely predisposed against this break with Eliot's Impersonal Theory and the tradition that rested on it (Eliot himself, interestingly, seems to have admired the book and to have given Lowell a much-needed word of praise).[2] But a whole generation of younger poets seized on Lowell's method of escape, and, understandably, newer critics have arisen to exalt *Life Studies* (sometimes at the expense of Lowell's more recent work), and to surround it with a new aesthetic terminology and doctrine.

My purposes in this study will not allow me to do justice to *Life Studies*'s human and, as it were, novelistic richness; I must ask the reader to believe that this omission does not spring from lack of appreciation. I shall be concerned with *Life Studies* as a political book, in the sense that it deals with the socialization of the individual by family, class, and law. I shall also, however, be concerned with the relation of the *Life Studies* voice to the other voices of Lowell's career—a relation which, to my mind, has a crucial bearing on the judgments Lowell can or will make about politics in the more usual sense. To this latter end, the term "confessional poetry" is less helpful than it is when used to connect Lowell with those he has affected. As I have suggested before, in some ways *Life Studies* confesses less than *Lord Weary's Castle* and *The Mills of the Kavanaughs* do. In so far as insanity is a subject of all the books, the earlier ones give a more vivid sensation of mental loss of control, through their direct presentation of dream, fantasy, and hallucination. Likewise, violent marital conflict, attempted and successful suicide, murder, even parricide and incest, are rendered directly in the fictitious contexts of the early narrative poems. In *Life Studies*, when violent actions seem to be in question, they are summarized after the fact, in brusquely general and analytical terms, or else merely hinted at.

But it is not only such reticences that hold the chaos of experience at a distance in *Life Studies*; it is the pervasive attitude

2. Ibid., p. 365.

and voice of the speaker himself. Most of the poems are reminiscences of the past, but even when the poem is set in the present, the speaker seems an impartial and inclusive observer, peculiarly at a distance from the emotions he is feeling. In "Waking in the Blue," for instance, we get a detailed picture of daily routine in a mental hospital, and of the personalities of other patients, but we must read between the lines to get more than a vague idea of Lowell's own emotional state (the strength of the poem is that it allows us to do so, through the power of imagery and tone).

The *Life Studies* speaker often seems less a whole man than the embodiment of that man's search for objectivity, for acceptance of himself through unsparing self-knowledge. The speaker is a profound and sophisticated ironist, who constantly places his experience in framing perspectives provided, often, by psychological and sociological ways of thinking that lead back to the family, milieu, and culture as determinants of individual personality. As in *Lord Weary's Castle*, learned allusions are fairly common; but the difference in the effects sought through them in the two books is striking. In the early poetry, the allusion, however stiffly introduced, rapidly becomes personalized, even hallucinatory; it is the carrier, if also the disguise, of some excessive private feeling. In *Life Studies* this is partly true, but mainly the allusions (excluding references to New England history that are really part of the plot) serve to lead away from the exclusively personal, toward a shared world of sophisticated discourse which provides methods of analysis, historical and cultural contexts for even the most delicate issues of sensibility.

The cooler tone, the external emphasis, indicate not only a desire for objectivity but a change of values, the creation of a new poetic self. This can easily by seen through a comparison with the dominant voice of *Lord Weary's Castle*. Where that old self seemed to be imprisoned in introspection, and to make other people into the symbols of an inner metaphysical drama, the new self cultivates social awareness, observant responsiveness to the surface of life, a dramatic treatment of people's behavior. Where the old self was absolute, even peremptory, in moral judgments, the new self is more relativistic, more often amused than angry at moral incongruities and human blindness.

On the ultimate level, as we shall see, *Life Studies* is as tragic, and as unsettling to civilized moral complacencies, as Lowell's early work—more so, perhaps, since there is no religious loophole, and there is a new and profound insight into the unhappy patterns of individual lives. But direct assertions of Lowell's despair are sparser and quieter now; much of the time, he prefers to seem to be writing very high, ironic comedy rather than tragedy. Implicit in all of these changes is a renunciation of the special immunity or superiority of bard or ideologue; Lowell now wishes to see himself as acting and acted upon, as a man living among men.

These changes of attitude are intimately related to the technical innovations of *Life Studies*, its open form (or, more accurately, fractured formalism) and anecdotal tone. Conversation, social discourse, becomes a desirable model for poetry, and the resulting casualness gives us the sense of a spontaneous and receptive self, welcoming external perspectives; whereas the early formal mastery suggested—often with good reason—an ego rather tyrannously bent on extending its cherished internal rhythms and orders. In fact, the sound-pattern of the *Life Studies* poems is rich, particularly in alliterative effects and internal rhymes. But it is suggestive that the external rhyme-scheme is usually either cleverly concealed by off-rhymes, or by crucial rhymes placed much farther apart than is customary in English poetry, or else blatantly pointed out by doggerel repetitions, or tag-rhymes that make couplets of conspicuously discontinuous lines. These latter effects go beyond the casual to the violently slapdash; so, at times, does Lowell's use of colloquial English, when he applies "lowbrow" or imprecise slang terms to situations that seem to cry out for emotional heightening. These breaks in style are rhetorical weapons—sometimes satiric weapons against persons, as in the following passage on Lowell's father (the italics are mine):

"Anchors *aweigh*," Daddy boomed in his bathtub,
"Anchors *aweigh*,"

> when Lever Brothers offered to *pay*
> him double what the *Navy paid.*
> I nagged for his dress sword with gold *braid* . . .

But more often, these tactics, both of diction and sound, become weapons against the emotions of the "I," intended to prevent us from taking his poses or actions as seriously as he has. Two examples should indicate what I mean:

> as a gemlike undergraduate,
> part criminal and yet a Phi Bete,
> I used to barge home late.

> I was a fire-breathing Catholic C.O.,
> and made my manic statement,
> telling off the state and president, and then
> sat waiting sentence in the bull pen . . .

Emotion is also held at a distance—but from different motives, and to different effects—by another stylistic penchant, the relentless, documentary accumulation of facts: place-names, dates, brand-names, bits of history, and objects, objects, objects, each one handled with the meticulousness of an Agassiz. Of course, objects bulked large in *Lord Weary's Castle*, too, their bulk standing sometimes for the intransigence of this world, sometimes for the violent intrusion of religious truth. But now, for the first time, a Lowell poem can be constructed of nothing but objects and data, as "Father's Bedroom" is. In these poems, the impersonal declarative sentence, the past tense of the linking verb, are as ubiquitous as grinding, tearing, and howling were in "The Quaker Graveyard."

This tendency may have something to do with the influence on Lowell of prose writers like Chekhov and Flaubert, and of that extremely object-conscious poet, Elizabeth Bishop. But clearly the impulse has deep roots in Lowell's own temperament. In his essay "On 'Skunk Hour,' " he describes how, during the composition of that poem, he was "haunted by the image of a blue china doorknob"—an image which he did not use, and claims not to have understood, but which he feels "started the current of images in [his] opening stanzas," and so enabled him to anchor his "fierce confessions" in the real world.[3] In another statement, Lowell defends Snodgrass for writing about "whimsical, minute, tender, small emotions that most people don't feel but which Laforgue and Snodgrass do." [4] Psychologically, I think one might question whether these feelings and hauntings are really independent emotions, or obsessions—symbolic deflections of emotions that really lie closer to home, to oneself or to other people. Such obsessional thinking is a double-edged advantage for a poet. It can generate symbols, covertly admit the inadmissible, and give the poet an understanding of how people's chosen milieus, in general, reflect their psychic lives. But it can also render the poem sluggish or frigid, too evasive of its own emotional raison d'être (a problem, to my mind, in some of Elizabeth Bishop's work, though not in her best). In Lowell's case we can see both the dangers and the advantages in this passage from "Dunbarton":

> Our helper, Mr. Burroughs,
> had stood with Sherman at Shiloh—
> his thermos of shockless coffee
> was milk and grounds;
> his illegal home-made claret
> was as sugary as grape jelly
> in a tumbler capped with paraffin.

There is emotional depth here, bearing on the boy's feelings about his grandfather; but we must seek it out by reflection on the total context—we are not led to it by any personal or emotional energy in the language. On reflection, the coffee, wine, and illegality seem to suggest a child's fantasy of escape into an unregulated he-man society; that the embodiments are shockless suggests that the ideal of masculinity, coming from old men, is slightly enervated, and the note of outlived military glory confirms this.

---

3. Robert Lowell, "On 'Skunk Hour,' " reprinted in Thomas Parkinson, *Robert Lowell: A Collection of Critical Essays* (Englewood Cliffs, N.J.: Prentice-Hall, 1968), pp. 133–34.
4. *Writers at Work*, p. 348.

This poem, unlike some others, expands and energizes its associations by reusing them in a rarely direct, free-flowing description of fantasy, and in doing so suggests how wildness and sickness become interwoven in Lowell's view of himself:

> I saw myself as a young newt,
> neurasthenic, scarlet
> and wild in the wild coffee-colored water.

Apart from its general merits and demerits, documentary factuality has certain particular advantages in *Life Studies*. In the childhood poems, it brings to life a period when, for all of us, the objects of the environment are newer, more definitive in their relation to ourselves, less distinct from people, than they are later—a state of affairs that often generates those memories that seem to us most tender, most frightening, most fraught with our own inner essence. Few authors, apart from Proust and Joyce, make us experience their childhoods as vividly as Lowell does, and his factuality plays a large role in this. In the adult poems, on the other hand, the factuality serves to steep lives in their meaningless functionality, to show, rather cruelly, how a round of impersonal activities can provide people with the necessary illusion of meaning, coherence, even happiness. In the presence of death, such a use of fact is particularly arresting and appalling; in "Terminal Days at Beverly Farms" and "Father's Bedroom," it gives us the real, numbed pain of the life surrounding a death in a way that no traditional elegiac stance ever could.

Finally, the factuality—though it may seem to lead away into the inscrutably private—actually subserves Lowell's ironic method, his desire to place himself in cultural history. For man-made objects carry their time—its morals, aesthetics, and predominant fantasies—around with them, even (or particularly) in the minutest details; on a level far below conscious thought, they shape the child's expectations of the world and reveal the adult's. (That other facts, such as family anecdotes and idiosyncrasies, do this, need hardly be stated.) Thus, to name one's objects precisely is already to open large areas of seemingly private experience to public and historical methods of analysis.

The discussion of a particular poem will help to give substance and direction to these rather abstract assertions. I have chosen "Grandparents," because it has a relatively uncomplicated plot, yet provides excellent illustrations of many of the traits I have mentioned: ironic detachment from the emotions of the "I," factuality, the sophisticated personal application of historical allusion, the interpenetration of self-analysis and the analysis of values with mutually illuminating effect. The poem begins in reminiscent description, and reaches its essential subject with lines 12 and 13:

> the nineteenth century, tired of children, is gone.
> They're all gone into a world of light; the farm's my own.

The first line invokes the childish fantasy that a parent dies intentionally, to punish the child utterly and finally for persistence in misbehavior. But at the same time it is a sophisticated cultural allegory; by affirming the child, the twentieth century has lost, or killed, the mental and moral security which the Matthew Arnolds of the world preserved by affirming "adult" qualities—self-restraint, reasonableness, social and familial responsibility—over vitality and imagination. The affirmation of the child is both literal, in that families have become more child-centered, and figurative: Freud and Marx, the destroyers of the old order, gave primary importance to the child (that is, the suppressed, the energetic, the disorderly) in the personality and in society. The next line presents an inescapable double reaction to the situation. The Vaughan quotation expresses the feeling that death is preferable to a life from which the protective figures of childhood have vanished, but opposed to this is the adult pride of ownership and self-sufficiency. Both feelings, however, are greatly darkened here: the Metaphysical sentiment persists without the religious framework that made it reasonable and bearable, while the self-congratulation rings hollow for reasons that soon appear.

The speaker spoils "another season," what should be his own zenith of confident mastery and creativity, by regressive desires like those in "Between the Porch and the Altar," though here

they are expressed as a social and material, rather than a
religious, nostalgia.

> I hear the rattley little country gramophone
> racking its five foot horn:
> 'O Summer Time!'
> Even at noon here the formidable
> *Ancien Régime* still keeps nature at a distance. Five
> green shaded light bulbs spider the billiards-table;
> no field is greener than its cloth,
> where Grandpa, dipping sugar for us both,
> once spilled his demitasse.
> His favorite ball, the number three,
> still hides the coffee stain.

Like all ancien régimes, Lowell's childhood milieu was distrustful
of nature (again, I feel we are invited to take his statement in its
widest cultural sense, to think of the different "natures" of
Rousseau, Darwin, Lawrence, and of their ideological potency as
weapons against traditional values and authorities). Its highest
aim was to control nature by pure sublimation or transmutation,
the cloth greener than a field. But the stain (nature conceived as
something merely degrading) takes its characteristic revenge for
such subordination; and the most graceful, quaint, and lovable
act of this ancien régime (or of the speaker's enduring loyalty to
it), the placing of the number three ball, is symbolically a pious
fraud, the appearance of order maintained as a moral necessity by
those who know it to be a lie.

The succeeding description of a billiard game in which the
grandfather shoots for both sides is also charming, and also
implies a dark verdict on families and old orders. The speaker sees
that to accede to his forebears, or to his own nostalgic desires,
would be to gain enveloping security at the cost of a wholly
fraudulent individuality, a life lived out for him in advance by
others. Yet, the calculatedly embarrassing outburst that follows
testifies to the strength of the desire:

> Grandpa! Have me, hold me, cherish me!
> Tears smut my fingers.

The recoil is immediate, and the careful weight of its phrasing betrays the simultaneous presentation and dissociation of emotion I have discussed. *Smut* is the crucial word, conveying the sense of shame, but also of pornography, the deliberate feeding and working-up of an ingrown, masturbatory emotion. It also reminds us of the dirt and decay of the old house, and symbolically rhymes with *rattley, spider*, and *stain*.

The final image both sums up and explains: the speaker holds his *Illustrated London News* (so quintessentially genteel an activity that the rhyme with *cues* must be calculated) and draws a mustache on the last Russian czar, "disloyal still" as he puts it. But we remember what actually happened to Nicholas II, and sense the roots of the man's paralytic inertia in the murderous intensity of the child's rebellious feelings, and his consequent guilt. It is this that keeps the adult independent only in childish, impotent ways, unable to own or disown his tradition; therefore, as he tells us through an apparently casual phrase, he rents his own life. This is indeed an extreme and neurotic "confession"; but to the generation of apartment-dwellers who read it, it is also social history, and Lowell's ambivalence about assuming the old adulthood of ownership and "ritual Friday spins" mirrors their own. Nowhere is the mutual illumination of private and public more evident.

In "Grandparents" it is obvious that psychoanalytic ideas provide the basis for the speaker's understanding of himself, and for many of his witty cultural perceptions as well. Indeed, if any one structure of thought has replaced Catholicism as Lowell's source of methods and values, it is psychoanalysis; his goal is self-understanding, and his principal techniques—the resurrection of early memories, the unsparing objectivity about present behavior, and the increased conscious awareness of interpersonal dynamics—are all common features of the analytic experience. (Of course, there is a more direct dependence on specific Freudian insights in many individual poems, for instance "During Fever" and "Man and Wife.")

But Lowell's commitment to a psychiatric concept of health, though genuine, is limited (like Freud's) by a tragic view of life;

after all, the book's final symbol for the continuing will to live is a foraging skunk. Even in "Grandparents," psychoanalytic understanding is not wholly able to free the speaker from the impasse (though it can point to the most incapacitating personal determinants, such as the association of impulses toward liberation with murder), and one reason may be that psychoanalysis is itself implicated in the conflict. There is no universally accepted answer—indeed, there is heated dispute—on the question of whether analysis can lead only to a livable compromise between the individual and his background, or the reality principle, by the annihilation of immature forms of revolt, or whether it can produce a truly free man, capable of rebelling creatively and without neurotic conflict, against "reality" itself—that is, the neurotic restrictiveness and violence in society.

This is basically the dilemma of "Grandparents," and it is in many ways the dilemma of *Life Studies. Lord Weary's Castle*, of course, represented the paradigm of the immature solution: the choice of a revolt-identity as opposite to the family tradition as possible, and the denunciation of ancestral traits that are latent in the poet himself, more than he dares to realize. Yet, the earlier mood at least had the advantages of ferment and dialectic, which are sometimes clarifying; in "Grandparents," sober understanding seems to lead merely to stasis, and the whole book reflects this quality somewhat, in the poetic slow-motion of its irony-laden, heavily documented lines.

II

Though its style may suggest a diminished rebelliousness, in content *Life Studies* is as much concerned with social oppression as *Lord Weary's Castle* was. But it is not, now, the large-scale oppression of military capitalism, rather the misshaping of individual lives and energies by families, class codes, and, ultimately, civilization itself. Toward the end of "My Last Afternoon with Uncle Devereux Winslow," there is a nasty instance of how far a code will go in managing or ignoring individual feelings—perpetrated, as it happens, by a character whom Lowell, in other contexts, portrays as lovable.

My Uncle was dying at twenty-nine.
"You are behaving like children,"
said my Grandfather,
when my Uncle and Aunt left their three baby daughters,
and sailed for Europe on a last honeymoon . . .
I cowered in terror.
I wasn't a child at all—
unseen and all-seeing, I was Agrippina
in the Golden House of Nero. . . .

The incident seems scarcely less brutal to the young Lowell as witness than to the uncle. He is the "all-seeing," precocious little adult whose childish emotional reactions are quite literally "unseen" as long as he behaves properly; he is, in effect, no more allowed to be a child than his uncle is. But this in itself does not explain why he feels directly threatened, like Agrippina, or why he seems to attribute to his elders the malignity of Nero. Perhaps that is simply a way of saying that the elders, whom he has considered omnipotent, force death into his world by their own helplessness in the face of it. But I hear a more directly personal bitterness in the lines, which recurs in the images applied to the dying uncle:

He was as brushed as Bayard, our riding horse.
His face was putty.
His blue coat and white trousers
grew sharper and straighter.
His coat was a blue jay's tail,
his trousers were solid cream from the top of the bottle.
He was animated, hierarchical,
like a ginger snap man in a clothes-press.
He was dying of the incurable Hodgkin's disease . . .

There is the brushed horse; then the terrible picture of the clothes fitting better and better as the man's face loses its shape, turns to "putty"; and finally, the "ginger snap man in a clothes-press"— which, one remembers, would be put there to lose its shape, by absorbing moisture, and so protect the clothes. Clearly, Lowell is drawing at least an unconscious connection—if not causality—between the uncle's physical death and the appropriation of his inner selfhood by the family, the role, the clothes. On this presupposition, it is very clear why he would identify with the uncle, and fear the same fate for himself. He, too, can be summed up in terms of his clothes:

> I was five and a half.
> My formal pearl gray shorts
> had been worn for three minutes.
> My perfection was the Olympian
> poise of my models in the imperishable autumn
> display windows
> of Rogers Peet's boys' store below the State House

In his little-adult role, he too has "perfection"—but he must "model" himself on a mannequin, and he feels in an autumn rather than a spring of life, too early bound to an adulthood that seems to him only a descent toward death. Throughout the last section of the poem, the young Lowell expresses his as yet inarticulate ("What in the world was I wishing?") desire for escape and, perhaps, destructive revolt, by the significant obsessive act of picking at the anchor on his white sailor blouse.

Life Studies is full of characters whose souls have simply gone underground, with varying degrees of perceptible psychic mutilation, as a result of familial and social pressures. There is Great Aunt Sarah, who, in her youth, refuses an advantageous marriage and tries to become a concert pianist, but is too nervous to appear for her debut—and who then, in old age, is forced to play a soundless dummy piano to spare the nerves of Lowell's tone-deaf grandmother. There is Lowell's father, to whom the phrase "[his] soul went underground" is actually applied.[5] Woman-dominated in childhood and marriage, the father has had one real moment of authority and adventure in his life—"nineteen, the youngest ensign in his class, / he was 'the old man' of a gunboat on the

5. "91 Revere Street," *Life Studies* (New York: Farrar, Straus and Giroux, 1959), p. 16.

Yangtze"—which remains, ever after, the center of his pathetic daydreams.

Though we share Lowell's shame at his father's subsequent failures (to the point that patriarchally minded critics have found the portrait cruel, even indecent), our final emotion must be pity for the man's utter imprisonment within himself, his "dumb depth" which could express itself only in "statistics." The humiliations themselves are almost always the result of accepting someone else's expectations rather than formulating his own; whether in sports (" 'Bob,' they said, 'golf's a game you really ought to know how to play, / if you play at all' "); or in the business career his wife forces on him in preference to his relatively successful military one; or in the marriage, where he is constantly diminished by her ferocious image of the aggressiveness and control proper to the male sex. In the last poem about Lowell's father, we learn that his one moment of triumph sprang in part from an impulse of his mother's, who gave him Lafcadio Hearn's *Glimpses of Unfamiliar Japan*; and that she herself could not accept that triumph without an abiding strain of motherly reproach, annotating the book

> "This book has had hard usage
> on the Yangtze River, China.
> It was left under an open
> porthole in a storm."

Lowell's mother is, in many ways, a far more complicated figure to respond to and understand than Lowell's father. Hers is the stronger intimacy with her son from earliest childhood, when she shares with him her fantasy world of ideally masculine figures: "Mother's hero dove through the grottoes of the Rhine and slaughtered the homicidal and vulgar dragon coiled about the golden hoard." The Freudian imagery might lead one to think that the hoard stands for a reserve of sexuality or personality unexercised in her life; and, a few lines later, Lowell writes, "Her marriage forced her to squander her subconsciously hoarded energies." [6] When the father returns from the distance at which

6. Ibid., p. 17.

he can be turned into Siegfried, the mother casts him as "vulgar dragon," and encourages her son to identify instead with tyrant-slayers like Napoleon, or with her own adored father. A frighteningly overt encouragement of Oedipal feelings is one side of the situation; a premature sense of adult responsibility is another:

> She said, "Oh Bobby, it's such a comfort to have a man in the house." "I am not a man," I said, "I am a boy."

The young Lowell's reactions to his situation are of an anguished complexity, and it is far too simple to say that he loves his mother and therefore entirely shares her contempt for his father. When he bursts out at the dinner table, "Mother, how much does Grandfather Winslow have to fork up to pay for Daddy's carving school?" is he angry because his father has failed to learn to carve, or because the father has accepted a galling dependency for so trivial a goal? It would be hard to say, and Lowell confesses he was "furious for no immediate reason." [7] As his later interest in the figure of Orestes might suggest, Lowell has as much difficulty forgiving his mother's coldness, and her manipulation of his feelings, as his father's weakness. He is able to forgive his mother, in *Life Studies*, in so far as he can see her too as a victim: partly of an unconscious attachment to her father too strong to permit any rivals, partly of the roles and expectations of women in the "old life of decency."

> Born ten years and yet an aeon
> too early for the twenties,
> Mother, you smile
> as if you saw your Father
> inches away yet hidden, as when he groused behind a screen
> over a National Geographic Magazine,
> whenever young men came to court you
> back in those settled years of World War One.
> Terrible that old life of decency

7. Ibid., pp. 23, 33.

without unseemly intimacy
or quarrels, when the unemancipated woman
still had her Freudian papa and maids!

   It is fascinating how many of the adult Lowell's attitudes (even in *Lord Weary's Castle*, but particularly in the books following *Life Studies*) can be seen as reactions to this unusual family romance: the pacifism, yet the helpless fascination with power and violence; the sympathy for fleshly weakness; the love and hatred of perfectionists, revolutionaries, tyrannicides. (Perhaps, too, the sense of distance—sometimes melancholic, sometimes productive —from conventional adult roles and responsibilities, in a range of poems from "Grandparents" to "Memories of West Street and Lepke," stems partly from the feeling of being pushed into a premature adulthood.) The horror of a cold ecstasy of moral strictness, which connects the early Jonathan Edwards poems with "Florence" in *For the Union Dead*, resounds clearly in the description of the mother's family graveyard in Dunbarton. It is Dante's hell of ice, reserved for betrayal in intimate relationships; and the implicitly violent imagery of the passage suggests that Lowell holds his mother's Winslow coldness psychologically responsible for hastening his father's death.

> The graveyard's soil was changing to stone—
> so many of its deaths had been midwinter.
>
> . . . .
>
> The only "unhistoric" soul to come here
> was Father, now buried beneath his recent
> unweathered pink-veined slice of marble.
> Even the Latin of his Lowell motto:
> *Occasionem cognosce,*
> seemed too businesslike and pushing here,
> where the burning cold illuminated
> the hewn inscriptions of Mother's relatives:
> twenty or thirty Winslows and Starks.
> Frost had given their names a diamond edge. . . .
>
>   ["Sailing Home from Rapallo"]

But even in this poem, the mother's destructiveness seems a
helpless result of her family's ethic; or of her class's tendency to
make life a series of formal exercises, through which the
individual is shunted without self-definition, responsibility, or
commitment. "Mother travelled first-class in the hold," Lowell
says, meaning her corpse; and later she loses even a name.

> In the grandiloquent lettering on Mother's coffin,
> *Lowell* had been misspelled LOVEL.
> The corpse
> was wrapped like *panetone* in Italian tinfoil.

Yet the pun on the "love" lost in her marriage and her tradition
seems a poignant epiphany. Indeed, both the mother's and the
father's last days sadly embody the hopeless but never abandoned
pursuit of the dreamed life, the self-created self. The father speaks
of a "buccaneer" and a "king's ransom," referring to the purchase
of a car; the mother dies in a February spring in northern Italy,
effervescent and chilly *"spumante,"* the unreal glitter of the
Siegfried fantasy—with the Dunbarton graveyard pulling, in the
structure of the poem, like a magnet from the other side of the
earth.

Even in the famous mental hospital poem, "Waking in the
Blue," the stress is on social as well as private wounds. Lowell
speaks of the wealthy Brahmin inmates as "thoroughbred mental
cases" (one remembers how the dying Uncle Devereux was
compared to a "riding horse"), and as "old timers" (in America?
in McLean's?). Their insanity is partly the result of an intense
early narcissism, tied to achievements ("a Harvard all-American
fullback," "Porcellian '29") whose value does not carry very far
beyond the confines of Harvard Yard, or of adolescence. Lowell
also regards the mental hospital itself as a social institution, where
sanity and madness are political categories: the aristocratic
inmates are under the power of Irish Catholic attendants, who
now seem to Lowell more stupid than blessed, and even a little
manic, in their acceptance of life. (One "catwalks down our
corridor"—a choice of verb that foreshadows Lowell's manic
"strut," but carries the secondary meaning of crossing a narrow

walkway over enormous depths.) Whether these generalized portraits are snobbish, as M. L. Rosenthal feels they are, does not concern me here; they obviously reflect Lowell's experience, and raise understandable doubts as to whether sanity and madness are absolute categories or forms of social regimentation.[8]

For if the inmates represent over-civilized failure, they also represent fundamental energies. Their exhibitionistic nudity, and the phallic imagery surrounding them (one is a "ramrod," and soaks in a "vaguely urinous" tub, while another is a "sperm whale"), make them powerfully, unsettlingly instinctual. (We see the same instinctual quality, but enormously repressed, in the attendants' "bachelor twinkle.") The inmates are frequently compared to animals, especially to aquatic animals. This body of imagery links them, distantly, to Lowell's victimized, wordless, and nostalgic nautical father; but it also links them, still further back, to a divine victim, powerful to save and to avenge, the whale of "The Quaker Graveyard in Nantucket."

If madness is in one sense the final form of "going underground," a childish regression from civilized life, it is in another sense the defiant assertion of a pre-civilized nature or truth—man the poor, bare, forked thing—which Lowell still holds in an almost religious awe. I believe that the prevalence of animal comparisons throughout *Life Studies* serves partly to keep this nature continuously in our minds; and this nature bursts forth anew, in a paranoid apotheosis, in the book's concluding parade of skunks. Yet its triumph is never complete, or completely positive; and it is constantly confronted with an equal and opposite body of imagery, clothing—man as role alone, the reverse of the nude madmen—which begins so frighteningly in "My Last Afternoon with Uncle Devereux Winslow," and culminates in "Memories of West Street and Lepke." [9]

8. See M. L. Rosenthal, *The New Poets* (New York: Oxford University Press, 1967), p. 54.

9. Here, and throughout this section, I am indebted to the insights of David Perkins, presented in a class lecture at Harvard but not yet formulated in print; and to some suggestive points in Richard Tillinghast's dissertation.

In the last section of the book, the adult Lowell, a released mental patient, faces the question of how to live as a social being. Like many people, but to a more intense degree, he finds that the most clearly visible alternatives are the worst: a depressed adherence to familial patterns and class roles, as against the premature and inauthentically total revolt of his younger self, or the other revolt of mania. (Perhaps the indulgent accommodation that society will make to Lowell as wealthy man and noted poet is itself a third alternative; but, if so, its emptiness of inner grounds of identity makes it nearly the most frightening of all.)

In his difficult search, Lowell can find less than no help in his cultural context. It is "the tranquillized Fifties," that dubious period after the McCarthy persecutions when the temper of intellectuals, as well as of the general public and the government, drew back not only from communism but from all ideologies, utopias, questions of ultimate value, and turned to pragmatics, to faith in the quasi-empirical quasi-benevolence of the American Expert. It was a period of timidity in the personal life as well: of earlier marriages and more stable careers; more artists in the academy, and fewer eminent bohemians; of an "adjustment"-oriented psychiatry, and a popularized existentialism, in which the critique of absolute values appeared without the concomitant emphasis on engaged, contingent choice, and so rationalized an acceptant hedonism. Ecstasy and a self-created life style were considered dubious goals for the individual: the all-important thing was what Adrienne Rich—who, after Lowell, has written some of our best poems of bourgeois intellectual life—has called "difficult ordinary happiness." [10] Rare was the Ginsberg or Mailer who could ignore this ethos, and small (as we know) his chance of getting a serious hearing, except from the very young.

In this bad time, Lowell continued to write some political satire in his early manner, notably "Inauguration Day: January 1953":

> Look, the fixed stars, all just alike
> as lack-land atoms, split apart,

10. Adrienne Rich, "In the Woods," *Necessities of Life* (New York: W. W. Norton, 1966), p. 11.

> and the Republic summons Ike,
> the mausoleum in her heart.

Yet he could not wholly separate himself from his time; for it was
in this time that he had renounced Catholic utopianism and
turned to psychoanalysis and to a relativistic, socially sophisticated irony as the tools of insight and the rationale of form. And
the aspiration of *Life Studies*, though muted and doubtful, was, on
the whole, toward "difficult ordinary happiness." Out of these
conflicts grew the one truly great political poem in the book
(except, perhaps, "Beyond the Alps," which for various reasons
will be treated in the next chapter): "Memories of West Street
and Lepke."

That moral and intellectual relativism is itself an issue in the
poem is indicated, I think, by the dominant imagery of clothing.
Of course, Lowell has used this imagery throughout, to denote
human absorption in roles; but its exaggerated employment here
underlines the fact that Lowell must now perceive people and
situations through these roles and appearances, without the
prophet's confident penetration to spiritual conditions. A further
complicating factor is that the characters in the poem are all
extreme, contradictory, sui generis—all Dickensian solipsists.
Their relation to social processes is obscure and mystified, most of
all to themselves; and taken collectively, they mirror the author's
own confusion about the possibility of interpretive or moral
judgments on society. Indeed, not the least solipsistic among them
is the author.

The opening stanza reveals Lowell's subtle discomfort at his
accommodated position, at the growing distance between his
concept of himself and any of the roles he must or can play. He
sees himself as an underground eccentric, wearing his pajamas
most of the day; but this eccentricity—and the daily load of
laundry—is made possible by a respectable job, though one so
luxurious it hardly seems such: "Only teaching on Tuesdays." He
"hog[s] a whole house"—a residential arrangement quite appropriate to his class and background, but clearly unnatural in terms
of his own feelings. Lowell proceeds to invent a bizarre but
appropriate analogue to his own paradoxical status:

> even the man
> scavenging filth in the back alley trash cans,
> has two children, a beach wagon, a helpmate,
> and is a "young Republican."

(Perhaps this figure deserves to be interpreted more seriously, as Marcuse's vision of the superficially unexploited proletarian who pays for his comforts by a subtle regimentation extending not only to his politics but to his play—"a beach wagon"—and his sexuality—"a helpmate." But the archness of tone suggests that Lowell intends him—for the present, at least—mainly as metaphor.)

Within bourgeois community and responsibility, Lowell has found at least one vital center for his life, his baby daughter: "Like the sun she rises in her flame-flamingo infants' wear." Yet even the daughter's importance is cheapened when it must be expressed through the irrelevant poetry of departure of advertising. This rhetoric bears out a dominant pattern of excess, especially of over-size—in Lowell's house, his teaching arrangements, the age-discrepancy between him and his daughter—a pattern that has some of the terror, if not the moral implication, of Macbeth's "giant's robe / Upon a dwarfish thief." At the very least, Lowell's exaggeration of his contentment is a subtle way of questioning it—of admitting that he is "selling" himself.

One reason, presumably, for Lowell's delayed parenthood is the very different kind of commitment that engaged his youth:

> Ought I to regret my seedtime?
> I was a fire-breathing Catholic C.O.,
> and made my manic statement,
> telling off the state and president, and then
> sat waiting sentence in the bull pen
> beside a Negro boy with curlicues
> of marijuana in his hair.

"Ought I to regret my seedtime?" is the essential question of the poem: has Lowell's present ironic vision transcended, and so gained the right to reject, his earlier committed one? The question, for me, recalls one of Blake's Proverbs of Hell: "In seedtime learn, in harvest teach, in winter enjoy." The proverb is relevant to more than Lowell's occupation, for the Devil is satirizing the conventional life-cycle, claiming that it is merely a mind-forged manacle designed to prevent man from ever enjoying his instincts, ever distinguishing his true self from his society's rationalizations.

Lowell's mature irony does indeed reveal disturbing, incontrovertible truths about his earlier self. His revolt was itself solipsistic, ineffective, merely bizarre, or at least society could make it seem so: the apolitical, Dionysiac Negro he was paired with was no better an objective correlative of his commitments than his fellow professors and Marlborough Street neighbors would be now. The phrase "telling off" makes his argument seem a sloppy emotional catharsis; just as, later, the comparison of the prison roof to "my school soccer court" would reduce his martyrdom to a compulsive repetition of childhood experiences involving authority, violence, and exhibitionistic attention-seeking (assuming that the reader makes the obvious connection with "91 Revere Street"). Of course, this too could be seen as part of society's mystification: prison makes the dissenter doubt his own manhood and judgment, since it reduces him to the dependence of a child.

At times, however, Lowell's irony backfires: the use of a technical psychoanalytic term like "manic" in a subtle descriptive context, however accurate it may be, suggests a complacent patness attained at some cost to richness of feeling and recollection.

In the prison scenes Lowell's vision of anomalies and disconnections becomes still more intense and maddening. The pervasive costume imagery absorbs—though with a grimmer irony than usual—so palpable a reality as the New York slums: "bleaching khaki tenements." The prisoners, defined by garments ranging from "rope shoes" to "chocolate double-breasted suits," are worlds unto themselves, and worlds full of self-contradiction. One, Abramowitz, carries pacifism to a cosmic extreme, yet clearly has his own problems about aggression and masculinity (he is called a "flyweight" and urgently wishes to be "tan"). Lowell can finally dismiss his point of view with a rather sneaky reference to Eden and the Fall. Nor can Lowell feel much common cause with the other war protesters, one of whom belongs to a sect the Catholic C.O. has never even heard of. Still less, of course, is there a feeling of unity among the prisoners in general. Indeed, the prisoners' interactions reveal to Lowell another, equally important kind of disunity; the ethical contradictoriness of our society, which punishes the aggressive conformist for his acquisitiveness while bearing down on the eccentric for his dislike of force, but allows the persecution of the eccentric by the conformist to go on in prison just as it does elsewhere.

Something unanticipated happens in the poem, however, when Lowell focuses on the last prisoner:

> *Murder Incorporated's* Czar Lepke,
> there piling towels on a rack,
> or dawdling off to his little segregated cell full
> of things forbidden the common man:
> a portable radio, a dresser, two toy American
> flags tied together with a ribbon of Easter palm.
> Flabby, bald, lobotomized,
> he drifted in a sheepish calm,
> where no agonizing reappraisal
> jarred his concentration on the electric chair—
> hanging like an oasis in his air
> of lost connections. . . .

One difference is technical. Where, before, hesitancy and the sense of disconnectedness expressed themselves in abstention from eloquence, halting metrics, submerged or doggerel rhyming, now the lines become emphatically iambic, the rhymes prominent, regular, stately; there is a touch of the surging periodicity of *Lord Weary's Castle*.

We are led to look for a reflection of this increased intensity in the moral content of the lines. One insight that becomes very clear is the real power of money and violence cutting across all claims of value and principle in American life. Morally repudiated and condemned to die, Lepke is still czar, still "segregated" into privilege like a Southern white, still given "things forbidden the common man." Further, these things are exactly what the conventionally respectable desire: the American Way of Life, an unexamined jumble of consumer goods, piety, patriotism. As the scavenger earlier identified with these things against his own class interests, Lepke identifies with them against the whole legal and moral tenor of his life; unless, of course, one cynically concludes that the law and public life are themselves so pervaded by this doublethink that their ostensible values are meaningless.

For Lepke, as the citation from John Foster Dulles would suggest, is a symbol of at least one aspect of American public life. He has organized, bureaucratized, depersonalized individual murder; America, in the "tranquillized Fifties," has done the same thing with its power to annihilate mankind. Lepke is "lobotomized," has had certain electrical connections in his brain severed (whether literally or metaphorically is not to the point here). America, too, has "lost connections," between its values and its acts, the fiction and the reality of its motives, the news and the appropriate emotional reaction; it too "drifts" toward its fate, unable and unwilling to change. (Rightly considered, the phrase "agonizing reappraisal" was as grotesque when spoken by Dulles as when applied to Lepke.) America, too, is "calm," "tranquil-lized" as Lepke is "lobotomized"; but in both cases the calm may be merely the psychological effect of an overwhelming, inescapable fear—of execution or nuclear annihilation. And here Lowell's analogy carries an especially frightening implication; for in Lepke's single-minded concentration on death, his attitude seems to change from terror to fascination to love. Death becomes an "oasis," the only escape from fear. A number of radical writers have seen such a *Dr. Strangelove* psychology in the attitude of Americans toward the bomb; and we remember that both Freud and Marcuse predicted a resurgence of the death instinct in very advanced civilizations.

The concluding phrase, "lost connections," seems to reflect not only on Lepke and official America, but on the poet himself. For he too, at the beginning, suffers from an inability to connect his inner identity with his social roles; and an inability to go beyond an inclusive, defensive irony to the patterned vision of social processes that might allow him to locate himself, and reopen the possibility of political engagement. This vision arrives with the symbol of Lepke; and it is important that Lepke is a symbol, while the other characters, because of their obscure or mystified relation to society, remain unbudging, fruitless particulars. The return from observation to symbolism, like the more intense metrics, and like the vision itself, suggests a kind of breakthrough or change of heart in Lowell—one that, I believe, is mirrored in the structure of *Life Studies* as a whole.[11]

It is dangerous to base an important argument on a book's arrangement, but "Memories of West Street and Lepke" does initiate a separate section, one in which each poem deals with a present situation involving existential choices, questions of ultimate value. These poems are spoken in a far more intimate, passionate voice than their predecessors, and they deal directly with more violent subjects—marital conflict, the sensation of incipient manic breakdown. Furthermore, none of these poems is as quiet in diction, as loose in form as, for instance, "Grandparents." "To Speak of Woe That Is in Marriage" is in couplets, "Skunk Hour" in rhymed six-line stanzas; while "Man and Wife" is a masterful blend of the two modes, casual in the reminiscent section, tight and pulsating in the presentation of an immediate crisis.

These poems would seem to bear out my contention in chapter 1 that, for Lowell, formal metrics are associated less with order and control than with a strong flow of feelings, and a trust in feeling. That Lowell chose to end the book with these poems seems to suggest that he saw himself as moving away from detachment on many levels, toward some new accommodation of disrupting energies and experiences. *For the Union Dead* fulfills this promise, with a more immediately involved treatment of personal themes in poems like "Water" and "Going to and fro," and with a wealth of new political poetry.

11. My view of the "architecture" of "Memories of West Street and Lepke" is partly anticipated—or at least complemented—by Gabriel Pearson's in "Robert Lowell," *The Review*, no. 20 (March, 1969), pp. 32–36.

I hope the above argument will not be misunderstood as implying that *Lord Weary's Castle* represents a "good" vehemence or radicalism, to which Lowell returns after a deviation into mere conformity. *Life Studies* is, finally, the more profound book about human life in general; and its politics of everyday victimization and mystification is subtler, more continuous, and probably more influential in human affairs than the grander politics of *Lord Weary's Castle*. Even if political didacticism were the point, the middle-class citizen would more probably be led to reassess the implicit commitments of his life by reading "Memories of West Street and Lepke" than by vicariously sharing Lowell's earlier anger against distant villains. Nevertheless, Lowell's cool objectivity is inescapably a part of the cure that makes him feel "frizzled, stale and small"; a power to see things in their largest bearings, to clarify the real stupidity and horror of the world we must live in, has gone along with the manic fierceness—and we are never so aware of the loss as when it is restored, in the last stanza of "Memories of West Street and Lepke."

III

Before turning to the political poems in *For the Union Dead*, I would like to consider separately one poem from that volume which conspicuously revisits the territory of *Lord Weary's Castle*, in order to show how Lowell's new relativism, rejection of ideology, and self-critical stance have affected his view of history, and of the methods by which it can be made into poetry. In "Jonathan Edwards in Western Massachusetts," the first thing we notice is that Lowell now speaks in his own voice, and that he feels at a distance from Edwards, in need of "relics." The power of identification that enabled the young Lowell to breathe freely, though with fierce antitheticalness, within the very words and cadences of Edwards's mouth, is gone; in its place has come a sense of real historical distance, of the need for evidence and reservation of judgment that would concern a historian. The change reflects Lowell's changed poetic personality, which could be neatly described as an effort to embody the very values the earlier poems put forth by negative implication, in their criticism of Edwards: a belief that the mundane and transitory are significant and demand our respect and love; that man should strive to free his view of himself from intellectual obsessive circles, and at least to imagine himself and others as possessing free will.

The later poem is thus a good deal less absolute and tragic: it gives us a world in which the hellfire sermon that drives one man to suicide may drive others quite calmly to work up a political pretext for demanding the preacher's resignation, and in which the two reactions are equally important. It is also a world in which Edwards himself has many selves—a Berkeleyan pantheist, a lover, a lovable absent-minded professor, a pulpit sadist, a self-pitying, self-dramatizing exile—and in which there is some question as to whether it is possible to fit them all together into a coherent psychological interpretation, let alone one that would justify an ethical judgment on the whole man. It is significant that the poem relies on documents ranging far beyond the sermons and theological writings: "Of Insects," the "Personal Narrative," letters, and a description of Edwards's bride-to-be, Sarah Pierrepont, written when she was only thirteen years old.

Lowell sees himself, as well as Edwards, as having many selves, no one of which he is obliged to make his final choice. He loves Edwards, makes fun of him, merely feels remote from him, or, at times, feels the same moral revulsion as before. The critic who accused Lowell of condemning Edwards too facilely for believing that "people were spiders," on the ground that Lowell himself had clearly entertained the same feeling, was really missing the whole point, which his own insight would only reinforce.[12] Still, it is in the old mode of caustic quotation that the poem opens. In a letter to his cousin, Major Joseph Hawley (son of the Hawley of "After the Surprising Conversions"), who had been instrumental in his dismissal from Northampton, Edwards smugly applied to his enemies Christ's warning:

> If so, then doubtless what Christ said to his disciples takes hold of you. *He that receiveth you receiveth me, & he that despiseth*

12. Herbert Leibowitz, "Robert Lowell: Ancestral Voices," *Salmagundi*, 1, no. 4 (1966–67): 42.

*you despiseth me. . . . And Take heed ye despise not one of these little
ones. —He that offendeth one of them it were better for Him that a
milstone were hanged about his neck & He drowned in the Depths of
the Sea.*[13]

"Edwards's great millstone and rock / of hope": religion served
Edwards less, perhaps, as hope than as a useful millstone; but
considering his effect on such more vulnerable "little ones" as his
uncle Hawley or the child convert Phebe Bartlett, it might just as
well be hung around his own neck. Yet, Lowell will not call the
crumbling of even this kind of religion an unmixed blessing. The
descendants of Edwards's congregation, though no longer a flock,
are still sheeplike and "square" as their houses; leading what
Thoreau called lives of quiet desperation, they unknowingly try to
find religious consolation within their purely materialistic world:

> Hope lives in doubt.
> Faith is trying to do without
>
> faith.

They no longer believe in the end of the world, yet they are the
first people to have the power to bring it about.

But Lowell is far from completely confident that his own ways
of thinking are less tautological than Edwards's, less a form of
damnation in a Dantesque hell: "We move in different circles."
As he thinks the Puritans did, Lowell places his most nearly
satisfactory image of the Promised Land in a dream of the past, a
Renaissance England where body and spirit, nature and grace,
action and ideals were reconciled analogically:

> *Was it some country house
> that seemed as if it were
> Whitehall, if the Lord were there?
> so nobly did he live.*
>
> *Gardens designed
> that the breath of flowers in the wind,*

---

13. Jonathan Edwards, *Representative Selections*, p. 401.

> *or crushed underfoot,*
> *came and went like warbling music?*
>
> *Bacon's great oak grove*
> *he refused to sell,*
> *when he fell,*
> *saying, "Why should I sell my feathers?"*

Lowell underlines the variety of ways in which such an ideal can be betrayed, by paralleling Bacon's worldly fall through venality to Edwards's through severity, and he shows both finally exploiting their deepest values to maintain a rather paltry self-pity.

In the main body of the poem, Lowell retraces the contradictions of Edwards's life a great deal more lovingly than before: the secret prayer in the swamp; the love and hate for the spiders; the more attractive, pantheistic side of Edwards's feeling of total dependence on God, and the projection (despite all doctrinal belief in depravity) of this pantheism into his polyphiloprogenitive love for Sarah Pierrepont, whom he described as follows.

> They say there is a young lady . . . who is beloved of that Great Being, who made and rules the world, and that there are certain seasons in which this Great Being, in some way or other invisible, comes to her and fills her mind with exceeding sweet delight, and that she hardly cares for any thing, except to meditate on him. . . . She will sometimes go about from place to place, singing sweetly. . . . She loves to be alone, walking in the fields and groves, and seems to have some one invisible always conversing with her.[14]

Edwards's cruelty is rendered harder to understand by this lack of constant morbidity; it seems almost more the result of professorial detachment, and an unrecognized enjoyment of power "in your moment of glory," than of deliberation. The only relic Lowell finds, "the round slice of an oak / you are said to have planted," embodies the contradictions: the greenness of Edwards's love

14. Ibid., p. 56.

against the monochromatic unity of his clothes ("White wig and black coat, / all cut from one cloth") and his "design" for human destiny,

> flesh-colored, new,
> and a common piece of kindling
> only fit for burning.

The contrast to the equally "designed" gardens of body and soul in Lowell's idealized Renaissance is clear.

The poem thus centers itself, quite ironically, on the question of the freedom of Edwards's own will, the root of his destructive actions—or, to use modern terms, on the integrity of his identity.

The final vignette Lowell presents, Edwards's vacillation about becoming president of Princeton, involves many modulations of will. It reveals Edwards as fearful and passive, a medical as well as spiritual predestinarian, sensing his own lack of energy and fatalistically attributing it to

> a constitution
> peculiarly unhappy:
>
> flaccid solids,
> vapid, sizzy, scarce fluids
> causing a childish weakness,
> a low tide of spirits.

But in one area, his will appears to be insatiably intense: "All your writing, writing, writing, / denying the Freedom of the Will." This writing itself, of course, willfully rationalizes the passive side of Edwards and converts it to wisdom. Lowell adds to his quotation from Edwards's actual letter an invented last line, a final irony: "these studies / that have swallowed up my mind." The Edwards whose greatest wish was "to be swallowed up in God," and whose dark vision of human emotions revealed itself, in "After the Surprising Conversions," through misapplied oral metaphors, is now shown as having surrendered will and personality to his system, itself an active, ravenous maw.[15] Thus here, as

15. Ibid., p. 60.

in the earlier poems, we are left with the mystery of *acedia:* the will that acts only by deliberately choosing its own negation, out of whatever subtle fear of the eventualities of human life.

Any judgment of value between Lowell's Edwards poems must be personal to an unusual degree. The later poem has a charm and pity in its teasing tone which explication does not easily communicate, and some will find its mature detachment all gain and no loss. Others might find it lacking in power and momentum, self-defeating in its refusal of the risk of personal identification that leads to dramatic art.

It is clear that the later poem is a characteristic product of the same attitude of mind which lies behind *Life Studies.* The balancing of mundane, and humane, considerations against ideological ones, the tentativeness and respect for evidence which approximate the method of the social sciences, the willingness to rest in uncertainty, are all intellectual methods Lowell had tested out on himself before applying them to history. Yet it is noteworthy how alike "Jonathan Edwards in Western Massachusetts" and "After the Surprising Conversions" are in their final diagnosis, their picture of a paralytic melancholy and an orally defined fear of life at the heart of Edwards's difficulties. This continuity, like many in *Life Studies* itself, points forward to a new poetry in which Lowell's deepest and most constant preoccupations will no longer appear on the edges, but at the center of a systematic way of thinking about the world.

4

Pity the Monsters
Lowell's Mature Politics

After *Life Studies*, Lowell faced what was little less than the forging of a new public conscience—a conscience that would have to be resilient enough to encompass such disparate elements as his pacifism, his new distrust of self and ideology, his underlying reverence for dangerous yet vulnerable pre-civilized energies, and something, at least, of his old moral sternness, his clarifying rage. This conscience, as it emerges, is one of the less predictable of our time—given to quirky solicitudes for old orders and evildoers, and to a measure of *laisser aller,* but capable of accepting uncompromising stances and actions if taken with sufficient moral honesty. Yet this conscience has a peculiar authority; both radicals and conservatives have stood in awe of Lowell for his ability to bear mixed sympathies that easily turn into multiplied guilts, and for the sense that his scruples come from the intensest empathy, not from fear of change—which, when he can believe in it, Lowell passionately desires.

A conscience, if it is to be more than a set of negative prohibitions, requires a myth, a central insight into human behavior. Such a myth does not really exist in *Life Studies*, while the myths of *Lord Weary's Castle*, its "closed" and "open" forms of experience, are too self-righteously rigid to serve the later, chastened Lowell. A new myth—built around long-familiar categories of experience but heavily indebted to psychoanalytic thought—emerges in the pages of *For the Union Dead*, particularly in the title poem, "Florence," and in "Caligula." We will be concerned with the ramifications of this myth for the remaining three chapters; but its basic themes are already present in the earlier poem that announces Lowell's departure from the Catholic Church, "Beyond the Alps." Lowell had never entirely shared the belief in orthodox culture as a sufficing social value that informed the work of Eliot and Tate. But he had drawn his values and symbols, and his fragile sense that history is more than a chaos of power-lust and pointless suffering, from a particular orthodoxy; hence, apostasy for him was both a revolt against historical nostalgia and the beginning of a painful critique of all attempts to make history meaningful.

In "Beyond the Alps," Lowell regretfully leaves Rome, the "city of God" and of Mussolini, "where it belongs," and goes to Paris, a city whose associations are more worldly and problematical. The poem takes place on a train, a regulated environment created by modern technology, in which religious ceremony is sadly, emptily recalled by the precariously balanced procession of stewards striking their gongs to announce, not the elevation of the Host, but the dinner hour. Lowell's concern with nostalgia as a political as well as a spiritual force is early established by the focus on Mussolini, the man who thinks that he can conjure up a great civilization by aesthetic trappings, that by holding up Caesar's eagle he can be Caesar, and who is yet woefully vulnerable to Freudian demolitions. Psychologically as well as visually, his desire to unfurl a banner is very much like his desire to tear the clothes off every woman he sees. He is crude, imitative, unimaginative, "pure prose"; worst insult of all, for one of the generation of T. S. Eliot, his conspicuous and wasted affirmations are not terribly different from those of the Victorians, who lived on inherited and diminishing funds of trust which their own intellectual efforts could not augment or sustain, and which held them aloof from the real issues of their time.

Mussolini's pseudo Renaissance is paralleled by the Church's effort to maintain, on a level of aesthetics, the validity and the hold over the human mind which it has lost on the plane of intellectual credibility:

> When the Vatican made Mary's Assumption dogma,
> The crowds at San Pietro screamed *Papa*!

The Holy Father dropped his shaving glass,
and listened. His electric razor purred,
his pet canary chirped on his right hand.
The lights of science couldn't hold a candle
to Mary risen, gorgeous as a jungle bird!
But who believed this? Who could understand?
Pilgrims still kissed Saint Peter's brazen sandal.
The Duce's lynched, bare, booted skull still spoke.
God herded his people to the *coup de grace*—
the costumed Switzers sloped their pikes to push.
Oh Pius, through the monstrous human crush . . .[1]

The elevation of the bodily Assumption of the Virgin to the
status of dogma in 1950 seemed a gratuitous slap in the face of
rationalism; for the event in question is not only irrational, like all
miracles, but uncanonical and of little consequence theologically.
It is, however, congenial to the cult of Mary (a semi-pagan and
therefore doubly tenacious part of European folk-religion) and
important in Christian art, having inspired such works as Titian's
altarpiece in S. Maria Gloriosa dei Frari in Venice, to which the
description of "Mary risen, gorgeous as a jungle bird" is highly
applicable.

The applause-hungry player-pope has elevated a pet canary to
his right hand, the position of Christ with respect to a loftier *Papa*.
But the right hand does not know that the left lives in the inimical
world of rationalistic technology, where it holds the purring
electric razor. The point is not just that the cat will swallow the
canary; it is that a religion whose values have become primarily
aesthetic in its desire to outplay science has committed the same
spiritual vulgarization as the peasant heroine of Flaubert's *Un
Coeur simple*: it has turned the Holy Ghost into a stuffed parrot.
The canary does, of course, tap a desire to return to a "jungle"
freedom and delight in life which a cerebral culture may ignore to
its cost; but, like more open forms of primitivism, it seems a sad,
self-conscious escape-hatch of the modern mind. Aesthetic religion

1. All quotations from this poem follow the text in *For the Union Dead*.

can thrill and be appreciated, but, reversing both terms of Augustine's famous formula, it can neither be believed nor understood. Behind the blind gestures of worship and self-abnegation that tradition can still compel, it is the voice of Mussolini, of secular politics manipulating pomp, that really speaks. In this age, even the traditional image of the Good Shepherd turns sinister: the people are a "herd" in the sense of being anonymous and expendable, and there are few descents of grace that do not take the form of a death-blow for someone.

In the rest of the poem, the scope of Lowell's distrust expands from the hothouse heroic ages of fascism and neo-Christianity to those very pinnacles of human civilization—of belief, power, unified sensibility, artistic fecundity—toward which the nostalgia of the 1920s was directed. The entrance of the pope's Swiss Guards echoes back to a reference to the failure of a Swiss expedition to climb Mt. Everest, a link whose intellectual underpinnings are rather complex. Gaining the summit represents a supreme moment of human control over nature, but also perhaps of religious certainty; both Everest and Olympus are God-inhabited mountains. The similarity of the Guards' pikes to mountain-climbing equipment suggests a less obvious connection between the inert mass of the mountain, which the climbers traverse, and the submissive masses of humanity, whose dulled, deprived, and war-ridden lives bear the burden of all achieved cultures and empires. This metaphor is made explicit in the third stanza; the mountain becomes the Cyclops, a brutal, sensual, and unintelligent monster, yet subject in the *Odyssey* to a divine protection whose violation brings formidable consequences. In the image of the blinding reflected sunrise, Apollo, god of poetry and rational civilization, is identified with the wily and cruel Odysseus, the whiteness of the Parthenon with the white-hot brand that puts out the Cyclops's eye.

The "altitude" represented by this vision, like that of Everest, cannot be reached by buying a ticket, or by the mechanical conjuring tricks Mussolini and Pope Pius employ; but Lowell, by now, questions the desirability of reaching it at all. The height of Hellas, or of the Renaissance, produced Machiavelli's prince,

Cesare Borgia, and the venal, simoniac popes, as easily as Plato; and the Golden Bough, Aeneas's ticket to the supernatural, gave him both an assurance of immortality and divine order and the mission to create civilization by war. The hubris, or hypertrophy of the cerebral, behind Greece can create not only a greater power to kill but a greater desire; for its narrow drive to perfect its own splendor requires an indifferent, or even a Neronic, experimental attitude toward most human individuals. "Pure mind" becomes "murder at the scything prow," Minerva a "miscarriage" (misuse or wrong evaluation, as well as abortion) of the brain.

The extent of Lowell's moral claim on behalf of humanity as a crude, warmth-loving flesh-mass can be seen in his sympathy for Mussolini, the man of "pure prose" who seems somehow better than the idea he follows and renders ridiculous. When "the Duce's lynched, bare, booted skull" appears, it is directly juxtaposed with "Saint Peter's brazen sandal," as though the saint himself had kicked in the dictator's head. The tables once turned, Mussolini is immediately seen as suffering man; those who kill and succeed him now embody the superhuman, anti-human force of the ideal, but still speak with his voice.

The final couplet of the poem presents the alternative to Rome in a tone of rich ambiguity:

> Now Paris, our black classic, breaking up
> like killer kings on an Etruscan cup.

Paris is "breaking up" (disorder, fragmentation, dissociation of sensibility, impending Armageddon) but still a "classic"; and the word reminds us that the Earthly City of avowed hedonism, skeptical empiricism, libertarian or even anarchic politics, is, like the "city of God," an enduring possibility for the social and cultural organization of human life. Even "black" does not have entirely unfavorable connotations, in contrast to the earlier Melvillean horror of white absolutes. The stanza restored in *For the Union Dead* suggests an almost positive blackness, associated with Ovid, whose apolitical "tomcat" ethic had, for Caesar, the menacing force of an apocalyptic beast, and with Lucan, Tacitus, and Juvenal, "the *black republicans* who tore the tits / and bowels of the Mother Wolf to bits." Even Aeneas's bellicose vision of civilization finds its contrary in the Etruscans, the weaker, dispossessed, but, to some moderns, the more interesting classic.

Yet, after all this is said, the content of the barbaric Etruscan vision is still "killer kings." The loss of the illusion of salvation through a religion of culture leaves the poet more defenseless than ever, before the realities of greed, violence, and power-lust that lie behind social structures. Here, the poem's epigraph becomes relevant: it was from Lowell's Earthly City that Napoleon, the first post-Christian political messiah, set out to make the enervated Church a theatrical prop to secular authority. Whatever new Apollonianism is to be seen in the monstrous births of the mountain stanza, whether the science of stanza two or the "red east" of the restored stanza, it is not likely to transcend these conditions; the train, like the Swiss, the Church, and Apollo, is a mountain-climber. Only the inclusive moral consciousness represented by the poet seems destined not to be born to effective life, as he lies kicking in his tight technological womb.

"Beyond the Alps" will be important in American literary history for its rejection of the ideals of a previous generation, on grounds partly of objective truth and programmatic viability, but mainly of vital and excluded moral claims. But it is an equally important turning-point in Lowell's own career, for it is pregnant with the themes and images of the later political poetry: the theatricality and the sexual bases of the drive-to-power, even in idealists; the ease with which even "pure mind" becomes a tool of an irrational impulse to kill; the moral claims to be made for warm, unintelligent animality, whether that of the common man or that of a tyrant. In "Florence" from *For the Union Dead*, we see these themes asserted more universally, and with a greater consciousness of their ultimate implications and paradoxes.

In the modern Florence, the idea of the Earthly City is developed far beyond the hints in the last couplet of "Beyond the Alps."

> I long for the black ink,
> cuttlefish, April, Communists

> and brothels of Florence—
> everything, even the British
> fairies who haunted the hills,
> even the chills and fever
> that came once a month
> and forced me to think.

Florence's color is the black of its ink (associated with cuttlefish ink, and thence, later, with the horseshoe crab). Its politics are Left, but talkatively and ineffectually so, Communists being cataloged among other tourist attractions. It encourages odd tastes in food and sex, extends equal tolerance to fevers and fairies. Its acceptance of sickness and mortality leads to new thought, perhaps to wisdom; it is a kind of Ultima Thule of the world of experience, the world after the Fall:

> The apple was more human there than here,
> but it took a long time for the blinding
> golden rind to mellow.

The implicit contrast here is America, also a decadent country, closer perhaps to the "blinding golden rind" of its heroic age, but less intelligent and "human" in its present compromises with animality and evil. But the full implication of the apple metaphor is that the heroic age is itself the Fall.

The real subject of the poem is the earlier, heroic Florence, "patroness / of the lovely tyrannicides." The tyrannicides are the three statues, subsidized by Florence or Florentines, which dominate the Piazza della Signoria, and all of which portray patriotic young people slaying monsters or oppressors: Michelangelo's *David* with his slingshot, Donatello's *Judith and Holofernes,* Cellini's *Perseus.* But the phrase also suggests the many uprisings, feuds, and purges—some merely political, some religious—which fill the history of Renaissance Florence. In one instance, art and life meshed: the Donatello *Judith* was dragged out into the square, where it has remained ever since, to celebrate Savonarola's expulsion of the Medicis.

Before the tyrannicides enter the poem, Lowell provides a

prototypal image that seems to reduce their motives to a child's
random destructiveness, an excuse to kill:

> How vulnerable the horseshoe crabs
> dredging the bottom like flat-irons
> in their antique armor,
> with their swordgrass blackbone tails,
> made for a child to grab
> and throw strangling ashore!

The image of the child makes us keenly aware of the youth of the
tyrannicides: two boys held back from their rightful positions in
the world, desperately eager to prove themselves against grown
men; a girl sacrificing her chastity to a cause. If none of them
share the child's arbitrariness, they do share something of his
nonchalance, his pride in the potency of his will. In all three,
narcissism, ambition, and a conviction of divine parentage or
favor merge with the sense of patriotic or moral mission; while
their incomprehension and cruelty, like Hamlet's, are directed
against adult figures who live by sensuality and opportunism in a
world without absolute values.

Further, in all three cases the heroism has disturbing Freudian
overtones, either of Oedipal wishes or of closely related sexual
ambivalence. This is most explicit in the Perseus story, where
Medusa, as described by Lowell, becomes a focal point of male
ambivalence toward women and sexuality:[2]

2. Richard Tillinghast has uncovered a passage in Freud (*Sexuality and the
Psychology of Love* [New York, 1963], p. 212) suggesting that this association has a
more or less universal basis:

> To decapitate = to castrate. The terror of Medusa is thus a terror of
> castration that is linked to the sight of something. Numerous analyses have
> made us familiar with the occasion for this: it occurs when a boy, who has
> hitherto been unwilling to believe the threat of castration, catches sight of the
> female genitals, probably those of an adult, surrounded by hair, and
> essentially those of his mother.
>   The hair upon Medusa's head is frequently represented in works of art in
> the form of snakes, and these once again are derived from the castration
> complex. It is a remarkable fact that, however frightening they may be in
> themselves, they nevertheless serve actually as a mitigation of the horror, for

> I have seen the Gorgon.
> The erotic terror
> of her helpless, big bosomed body
> lay like slop.

We see how the hero's disgust with the Gorgon's vaguely maternal body reduces her, in his eyes, to "slop," and reduces sex itself—figuratively speaking—to headless animality. But we also catch an unadmitted note of sadomasochistic pleasure, shared by both parties. What further complicates the story, and makes it supersede David and Judith in Lowell's interest, is the fact that there is more than one monster involved. The killing of Medusa is mainly an initiatory ordeal, but the possession of Medusa's head enables Perseus to attain his real objectives, the deposing or killing of no less than three oppressors: his usurping grandfather, Acrisius; his mother's suitor, Polydectes of Seriphos; and Phineus, the incestuous uncle-fiancé of Andromeda—all, in short, surrogates of the repressing father.

Given this latter fact, and the element of repudiation yet covert indulgence of Oedipal wishes in the killing of Medusa, the Perseus story would seem to resolve the problem of the tyrannicide's motives along the lines of Freudian sublimation and projection. It is from suppressing, decapitating (that is, cutting off from his conscious life) impulses in himself very much like the tyrant's that the hero gets the power of moral energy to depose the tyrant and impose his own ideal order on the world. The Gorgon's power to petrify further suggests that the tyrannicide acts by reifying the tyrant, turning him (mentally) from a person into a thing, in order to place him outside the bounds of moral empathy.[3] The final description of the head bears out the idea of sublimation: the very phrase "severed head" suggests cerebration unnaturally

---

they replace the penis, the absence of which is the cause of the horror. This is a confirmation of the technical rule according to which a multiplication of penis symbols signifies castration.

3. This point was suggested to me by Richard Tillinghast, who draws on R. D. Laing's interpretation of the Perseus story in *The Divided Self* (London: Penguin Books, 1965).

divorced from its bodily sources of life, and Lowell uses it elsewhere as the title of a poem about the widening gap between a hallucination and physical reality. Further, the comparison of the head to a lantern ironically equates its power to petrify with the schematic doctrinal enlightenment the hero claims to bring.

These considerations lie behind Lowell's explicit, and admittedly perverse, moral judgment:

> Pity the monsters!
> Pity the monsters!
> Perhaps, one always took the wrong side—
> Ah, to have known, to have loved
> too many Davids and Judiths!
> My heart bleeds black blood for the monster.

Black blood: a final articulation of the light-dark symbolism, but, literally, vein blood from the area around the genitals, returning to the heart through the kidneys, laden with waste, at the end of its circuit. Middle age, decadence, empiricism, genital sexuality: these are the values Lowell collects together to define a stance that is equally hostile to all efforts to control or see design in history through ideology, which if anything finds the control that only seeks to satisfy personal greed relatively the more innocent. The stance, of course, represents one impulse of a very complex and ambivalent sensibility, and is to be taken with irony; Lowell knows as well as anyone that it is perverse and fatalistic, a recipe for political and intellectual sterility. Elsewhere it is articulated with a comic sense of its paradoxes, as in the mouth of the time-serving clergyman in the play *My Kinsman, Major Molineux.*

> What shall we do with people? They
> get worse and worse, but God improves.
> God was green in Moses' time;
> little by little though, he blossomed.
> First came the prophets, then our Lord,
> and then the Church . . .
>   The Church
> gets more enlightened every day.

We've learned to disregard the Law
and look at persons. Who is my neighbor?
Anyone human is my neighbor. Sometimes
my neighbor is a man from Sodom.[4]

But if Lowell recognizes the problem, the inability to "do" anything with people, he still cleaves to the insight that any effort to pattern history after one's own will, whether "selfish" or "altruistic," has the same psychological dangers, and raises the same moral problems, when it instrumentalizes people. To understand this fully, one must grasp what the impulse to tyrannize means to Lowell, beyond politics, as a psychological configuration.

The tyrant is a recurrent figure in Lowell's poetry, whose traits are remarkably unvarying. He is a manic narcissist, and yet terribly afraid of loneliness, of the criticism, disapproval, or even the independent judgment of others. "That's the law and disease of tyrants—they are more sensitive than we are," says Lowell's Prometheus, speaking of Zeus. "If a friend makes a slip, they see a traitor." [5] The tyrant's cruelty comes partly from this "sensitivity," partly from a need not merely to *have* power, but to experience it, directly and physically—as Louis XVI does when he breaks a dog's back because it has splashed him with tar ("1790"). A related impulse, it might seem, is an immoderate appetite for sexual conquest—sometimes, as with Mussolini, over women, more often perhaps, as with Nero and James I, over men. The tyrant seems to need a superabundance of being, acknowledged but never shared by others—a world of mirrors, such as Lowell's Caligula literally creates when he gives all the gods his own face. This need for excessive being is not merely a motive of outward actions; it becomes a characteristic of the inner life. Caligula lives in a solipsistic mental world, directionless yet hyperactive. He is consumed by insomnia, by feelings of omnipo-

4. Robert Lowell, *The Old Glory* (New York: Farrar, Straus and Giroux, 1965), p. 105.

5. Robert Lowell, *Prometheus Bound* (New York: Farrar, Straus and Giroux, 1969), p. 10.

tence, and by a general inability to stop thinking and planning:
"Your mind burned, you were God, a thousand plans / ran
zig-zag, zig-zag."

But Lowell is acute in dramatizing the terrible truth of the
truism that every victimizer is first a victim, a rejected one. All the
excess seems, finally, an inevitable compensation for an excluded
child's feeling that he does not really have, that others will not
allow him, an identity: having been forced to be nothing, he must
be all. Caligula, repudiated for his physical ugliness and almost
expected to be sexually and morally abnormal, must extort a
universal recognition and communication through his power to
annihilate: "a hand no hand will hold . . . nose thin, thin
neck— / you wish the Romans had a single neck!" Even his
dreams of replacing the gods, of being anointed in the blood of the
slain Adonis, are homosexual fantasies in which his role is
predominantly passive and feminine, though sadism and masochism are deeply intertwined. Caligula kills Adonis, yet the very
spurting of Adonis's lifeblood is the ejaculation which consum-
mates the god's imagined rape of Caligula. The fantasies reveal
that masculinity and power are things Caligula deviously seeks to
incorporate from without, because he feels them to be absent from
his proper being. As he turns to the gods, so he turns to animals,
and animality, to heal the metaphysical terror of his difference
from other humans. But this too fails, for his cruelty is never an
instinctive rapaciousness, rather "the lawlessness / of something
simple that has lost its law."

Caligula is something of a special case, the aesthetically
conscious tyrant, "Cal" Lowell's namesake; but the same characteristics appear in more ordinary, limited, and spontaneous men
of power, notably the President in "Waking Early Sunday
Morning."

> O to break loose. All life's grandeur
> is something with a girl in summer . . .
> elated as the President
> girdled by his establishment
> this Sunday morning, free to chaff

his own thoughts with his bear-cuffed staff,
swimming nude, unbuttoned, sick
of his ghost-written rhetoric!

There is the same animal metaphor, suggesting the almost physical enjoyment of power experienced in the bullying of attendants. There is the same link between the will-to-power and the elation of sexual fulfillment ("something with a girl in summer"), borne out in the homoerotic, or at least exhibitionistic, implications of the spectacle of the President floating naked in a pool while lecturing to a surrounding circle of aides.[6] The overtones of the word *girdled* add to the sense of a hidden femininity in the ostentatious stag-party masculinity of the occasion.

But above all, the President resembles Caligula in the mania that unites narcissism and insecurity: the continuous monologue, the need to be a theatrical spectacle, the need to keep talking and keep being paid attention to, the mind that builds and overextends "a thousand plans" of the world remade in its own image, and then frenetically tries to badger the world to accept the remaking. One thinks, as Lowell perhaps did, of the story of this President forcing the reporters to sit on the ground while he delivered a monologue from a hammock until three in the morning, while his audience, one by one, fell asleep. But the same qualities can be found in a dozen or more political figures in Lowell's work, early and late; and analogous motives—the sense of sexual or ontological inadequacy, the desire for a direct sensation of power and an exemption from common human vulnerability—are even to be found in the behavior of dominant races and classes, notably, as we shall see, in "Central Park."

6. The frequent link between tyranny and homosexuality undoubtedly has complex underpinnings. Psychological views of homosexuality as extended narcissism, or as an attempt to acquire selfhood and strength from another person through incorporation, are obviously relevant. (But perhaps it is only our civilization that would find the link strange to begin with, tending as we do to associate homosexuality with external weakness, effeminacy, passivity. To the Greeks, it was perfectly logical that a man preoccupied with military things, strength, and violence, would love people for related qualities, and despise—even fear—antithetical ones. Cf. Lowell's "Epigram" on Thermopylae.)

Lowell's concentration on this common enough but surely not universal form of the will-to-power suggests that he sees in it a possibility of his own nature, an alter ego of some sort, perhaps related to his own experience of a manic form of mental illness—the "homicidal eye" of "Man and Wife." The likeness, such as it is, is explored in later poems. For the present, it is enough to note that it gives a deeper reason both to Lowell's humility—his injunction to "pity" all monsters—and to his awareness of the dangerous element in the power-impulse, even in seemingly rational men.

The ultimate motive of the tyrannous impulse, in Lowell's vision, would seem to be the denial of dualism, of the distinction between self and world. It is at this level that the tyrant and the tyrannicide are one. In the tyrant, the impulse appears as the desire to create an airtight, planned, egocentric society in which no contingency that might stir up his fears of loneliness and loss of identity can arise. In the tyrannicide, the same impulse appears as a fanatical dedication to an abstract principle, a tendency to dehumanize adversaries, or a suicidal unwillingness to live with any human imperfection.

This configuration, in both its modes, bears at least a family resemblance to the traditional motives of Satan, whom Lowell has characterized (in discussing Valéry's *"Ébauche d'un serpent"*) as "the spirit that insists on perfection." [7] Perhaps this is one reason why Satan appears so often in the pages of *For the Union Dead*, as, for instance, in "Myopia: A Night."

> I see the morning star . . .
>
> Think of him in the Garden,
> that seed of wisdom, Eve's
> seducer, stuffed with man's
> corruption, stuffed with triumph:
> Satan triumphant in
> the Garden! In a moment
> all that blinding brightness

7. In conversation.

> changed into a serpent
> lay grovelling on its gut.

Satan, of course, is first the tyrannicide, the resplendent intellectual questioner who finds the flattery-centered universe of a Puritan God too small. The image for this Satan, "blinding brightness," suggests a manic explosion of energy and a destructive enlightenment, and recalls the imagery in the Apollo stanza of "Beyond the Alps," and the "lantern" and "blinding golden rind" of "Florence." But the Satan of the Garden merely re-creates God's tyranny; he is envious, sexual, a bringer of wisdom yet reducible to a stuffed gut. It is interesting that Satan's degeneration, which occupies several books in Milton, is here a matter of a "moment"; the contracted time-scale shows how unwilling Lowell is to separate the two aspects. There is some resemblance to Blake's cyclical myth of rebellion, the Orc cycle, but this too is of limited applicability, for Blake's rebel becomes like the tyrant only when he accepts the tyrant's world-view in a negative definition of himself. In Lowell's universe, as far from Blake's as Milton's, the Satanic impulse seems so basic that no music of order, human or divine, will transmute its nature; rather all orders, examined closely enough, will reveal themselves as its masks or accommodations.

The oral metaphor applied to Satan deserves further comment. (We remember how important a role oral metaphors play in Lowell's treatment of Jonathan Edwards, a religious absolutist similar, in many ways, to the tyrants and tyrannicides.) In theories of psychosexual development, the oral phase is said to precede the idea of the distinction between self and world; its erotic drive is to incorporate the beloved object into its own body, though initially, of course, this has no sadistic implication. Subsequent perverse sexual behavior, and psychotic behavior, are often interpreted as regression, as an attempt to regain the innocence of this absence of distinctions. We have seen the role that the idea of incorporation plays in tyrannical behavior; and the psychoanalytic perspective may also help us to understand the tyrant's project of omnipotence, and his combined cruelty and overcharged need for emotional assurance in personal relations. Psychoanalysis would seem to lend support to Lowell's belief that tyrannical behavior has universal roots in human nature.

At times, this belief seems so strong as to rule out any political stance except quietism—or, at least, the self-absolving, purely emblematic form of protest chosen by many liberals of Lowell's generation. The depth-psychological basis of the drive to omnipotence, and its intimate connection to the very notion of order, lend new force to the idea that power corrupts—and may corrupt even the most seemingly healthy. Practical politics may often be expected to join forces with the darkest inner impulses. All these fears receive allegorical expression in Lowell's play *Endecott and the Red Cross*. The protagonist, the Colonial Governor Endecott, dreams that he is conducting a religious trial (he is unsure, in the dream, whether he is still a Puritan, or a Jesuit inquisitor). The trial ends in an orgy of slaughter, each individual against all others, like Cadmus's sowing of the dragon's teeth. In the dream, God Almighty stands behind Endecott and confirms his judgments; in the actual situation, Endecott himself must play this role, mitigating or enforcing the judgments of his fanatical assistant, Elder Palfrey. The implication is clear: the man in total power must be his own final sanction, his own God, and so repeat the crime of Satan. The action of the play would seem to bear this out. While still a political temporizer, Endecott judges with humor and humaneness, as when he frees the drunken Indians. But once he has declared himself a revolutionary, he feels he must dramatize the absoluteness of his principles with effective gestures, hence changes his mind and has the Indians killed. The moral seems to be that principled, or even purposeful, politics has an innate tendency to encourage man's worst side.

"July in Washington," a poem about the deterioration of American politicians and of America, displays a similar fatalism; it suggests no persons or forces responsible, but rather ends with a metaphor of gravitation:

> but we wish the river had another shore,
> some further range of delectable mountains,

distant hills powdered blue as a girl's eyelid.
It seems the least little shove would land us there,

that only the slightest repugnance of our bodies
we no longer control could drag us back.

That the image for the Earthly Paradise is not only sexual, but artificial and suggestive of sophisticated Washington society, seems intended as a final reminder that any ideal we project will, in some way, carry along with it the same impulses that have led to our corruption.

Lowell's nearest approach, in *For the Union Dead*, to an image of moral political action is to be found in the title poem. As the title suggests, "For the Union Dead" is in some ways a deliberate reply to Allen Tate's "Ode to the Confederate Dead," which revolves around the same two figures, the poet-outsider and the dead hero. But where Tate suffers so intensely at the lack of a personal release into action that the hero is almost totally idealized, Lowell questions—with similar anguish—whether the active man can ever measure up to the moral completeness of the outsider's vision.

Lowell's active man, Colonel Shaw, is in many ways highly vulnerable to Lowell's usual critique of the disparity between ideals and realities, and of political theatricality. Like Governor Endecott, Shaw is a gloomy, soul-searching man who ends by being wholly committed to a morally dubious, though seemingly idealistic, enterprise. He accepts the command of the Massachusetts 54th, a Negro regiment officered by whites, trained with a hastiness that suggests no high regard for the value of black lives, heavily exploited for Union propaganda, and massacred in its very first battle. Yet Shaw has redeeming qualities. Though he is engaged in a theatrical venture, he—and his father—desire nothing for themselves but "privacy." "When he leads his black soldiers to death, / he cannot bend his back": meaning, perhaps, that he cannot recant his decision—the absolutism of the idealist—but also that he accepts its consequences personally, and will not provide himself with a security that his men do not have. When Shaw's body is thrown (vindictively, by the Confederates) into a mass grave with his troops, Shaw's father recognizes the appropriateness of this end in the light of his son's principles, and the implicit racism of those Northerners who see in the act only an outrage. He wants no other monument but "the ditch."

The dislike of monuments, the fear that abstract images will too effectively distance unpleasant realities, becomes a central theme in the poem. The exemplary contrast to Shaw is William James, who, "at the dedication [of the monument] . . . could almost hear the bronze Negroes breathe," and who seemingly found in this artistic resurrection some sort of emotional compensation for their real deaths. (It may be relevant here that James's one unbookish brother, Garth Wilkinson James, was Colonel Shaw's adjutant, and suffered a wound that left him a semi-invalid for life, in the battle in which Shaw was killed. In spite of his invalidism, the younger James went South during Reconstruction and attempted to run a communal, integrated plantation. William James himself was prevented by poor eyesight from fighting in the Civil War. But even without this information, the contrast between James and Shaw is clear enough.) Later in the poem, the increasing modern romanticization of the Civil War, the "statues of the abstract Union Soldier" that "grow slimmer and younger each year," form a bitter contrast to the country's continuing indifference to racial injustice. Indeed, that indifference is itself encouraged by a distancing medium: the television screen where frightened black faces become, like the cast bronze of the statue, mere "balloons."

It might be said that Colonel Shaw is a bit of a monument in his action, stonelike, unbending. Yet because he knows concretely, and undergoes in his own person, the full consequences of his choice, he remains a meaningful contrast to all the abstractionists in the poem, from William James to the television set; he represents a compromised, but still living, still responsible connection between ideology, or image, and reality.

The central issue of the poem can be stated in another way: given that mere rebellion or dissociation is unsatisfactory, what can man do with his inner monsters—his bear, snake, and horseshoe crab—that will somehow go beyond them and complete his humanity? "For the Union Dead" probably contains a greater

profusion of animal imagery, for its length, than any other poem
by Lowell. Nowhere are the organs, acts, and motives of man, the
shapes and forms of his self-expression, more insistently animal
than here. Yet the simple equation of animal images with
brutality, instinct, and raw power that works in the tyrant
passages is no longer viable here, although the yearning for a
"dark downward and vegetating kingdom" suggesting a subra-
tional unity of consciousness, even a return to the womb, is
certainly akin to Caligula's desires. For, in this poem, gentle and
humane qualities, and even those faculties of rational choice that
seem exclusively human, are seen in animal terms. "The cowed,
compliant fish" suggest an analogous quality of blind endurance
in the Negroes; but Colonel Shaw's own angry vigilance is
"wrenlike," his ability to combine gentleness with discipline,
principle, and readiness for action is "a greyhound's." The
imagery thus serves to remind us how far man is a part of
evolution, his fate the common destiny of living creatures, his
most distinctly human qualities, more refined analogues of traits
that animals, too, have had to develop for biological survival.

This line of thought is the key to the importance of the elegy on
the aquarium with which the poem begins and ends. Imagistically, the passage functions as an overture on many levels, but its
overriding emotional tone is nostalgia: Lowell mourns the loss of a
curiosity about other living beings that made people want
aquariums. Modern men no longer wish to acknowledge their
kinship with the animal world, but prefer the comforts and thrills
given them by machines—cars, televisions, urban centers oriented
around the "civic sandpiles" of underground garages. Here,
Lowell's thought begins to parallel—and may, indeed, be influenced by—Norman O. Brown's in *Life Against Death*.[8] In
Brown's view, man creates cities and technologies partly in order
to identify with them and thereby escape his two greatest fears, his
animal instincts (purged in the cleanness of mechanical processes)

8. See Norman O. Brown, *Life Against Death* (New York: Vintage Books, 1959;
originally published by Wesleyan University Press), particularly the subsections
"The City Sublime" and "Immortality," pp. 281–87.

and animal mortality (denied in the seeming permanence of steel and stone). But, Brown says, in culture as in individual neurosis, what is repressed reappears, and is more pervasive and uncontrollable in direct proportion to the intensity of the repression. This is also Lowell's vision, as revealed in the last stanza of the poem:

> The Aquarium is gone. Everywhere,
> giant finned cars nose forward like fish;
> a savage servility
> slides by on grease.

Denied a fixed locality in the scheme of man's city or his mind, the fish suddenly appears everywhere.

In turning to the seemingly impersonal power of machines, man is condemned to endless repetition not only of animal motives but of animal forms, his final point of reference for both form and purpose being his own biologically evolved nature. The same point is made earlier in the phrase "yellow dinosaur steamshovels," with the added suggestion that the end product of man's self-perfection will be his self-destruction. Protected from the knowledge of his animality and mortality by the spurious permanence and orderliness of the machine-world, man becomes not only more powerful, but also more dangerous, because he is spared direct responsibility: he is so shielded from the horror of reality that he can not only commit the Hiroshima bombing, but then use it to advertise a safe. Or perhaps the meaning is almost the reverse: modern man is so terrified of technological war that he can endure its image only when aided by a further identification with the inanimate permanence of—money! Suspect though the monuments are, their disappearance from the modern city is the sign of something far worse: an almost schizophrenic dissociation of the fact that war happens to living human beings, which, again, liberates man's cruelty.

If Lowell's dark vision of advanced civilization parallels Norman O. Brown's, his image of a hero closely resembles Brown's psychological ideal, not in that ideal's more notorious sexual aspects, but in the conception of a willing self-surrender to time and death. For the portrait of Colonel Shaw provides a moral resolution to the question of animality and death, as to that of political abstraction. Imagistically, as I have shown, Shaw is in touch with his animal nature, and able to draw from it his most heroic qualities; further, his acts are finally justified by his willingness to accept physical suffering and death in a brutal, unvarnished form, to accept "the ditch" of mass burial. The very next stanza menaces mankind with a death of a different order: "The ditch is nearer." This ditch is a many-layered symbol, bringing together nuclear annihilation, the absolute zero of outer space, the blank terror in the faces of the Negro schoolchildren, the hollowness of ideals out of touch with real circumstances, the bubble on which Colonel Shaw suffers, waiting for the "blessed break."

Taken together, the two ditches pose an inexorable alternative: Yeats's "blind man's ditch" of natural birth and death, with its ugliness and uncertainties, as against an abstracted, centerless existence, whose quest for perfection of power easily metamorphoses into pointless and suicidal violence. But what is at issue is more than a restatement of the perverse argument that the tyrant is more pitiable than the tyrannicide, the monster than the abstractionist; for Colonel Shaw provides a pattern of the action that is quintessentially human: "he rejoices in man's lovely, / peculiar power to choose life and die." Man, who alone has rational knowledge of death, alone can voluntarily accept it, philosophically as well as in particular circumstances, for the sake of a complete and life-giving response to existence. It is paradoxical but moving that this act is said to make Shaw rejoice, surely a rare word in Lowell. Shaw's attitude is the diametrical opposite of the effort of the threatened identity to include the entire world in its own being, the effort that unites tyrant and tyrannicide, Satan and mechanized man: that might be called man's less lovely, equally peculiar, power to choose death and live.

The ideal implied in the portrait of Colonel Shaw is explicitly stated in the concluding passage of moral advice in Lowell's translation of Juvenal's "The Vanity of Human Wishes," a passage which Lowell (unlike his source, according to an essay by Patricia Meyer Spacks) calls the portrait of a "hero":[9]

> pray for
> a healthy body and a healthy soul,
> a soul that is not terrified by death,
> that thinks long life the least of nature's gifts,
> courage that takes whatever comes—this hero
> like Hercules, all pain and labor, loathes
> the lecherous gut of Sardanapalus.

This hero, though something of a tyrannicide in his "loathing," has managed to conquer the tyrannous "gut" motives of oral absorption. He finds his basic integrity not in his acts but in the amount of "pain and labor" in his life, the burden of responsibility and moral insight that he is able to bear. And, as with Shaw, his greatest moral success is seen in his triumph, not over worldly temptation, but over the fear of loss of identity in death.

This idea of an only barely activist heroism of insight dominates the political poetry, and to some extent the personal poetry, in *For the Union Dead*. In *Near the Ocean*, Lowell's stance becomes more dynamic and ambivalent, partly because his direct juxtaposition of political and confessional material brings more personal feelings into play, and partly because the issues are timely and pressing ones on which he must take sides: the war in Vietnam, racism, police brutality. *Near the Ocean* both extends the psychopolitical themes of *For the Union Dead* (in particular, toward interpretations of mass psychology and of historical repetition), and partly transcends its bad conscience about political belief and anger.

9. Patricia Meyer Spacks, "From Satire to Description," *Yale Review* 58, no. 2 (Winter 1969): 232–48.

5

The Achievement of *Near the Ocean*

In June, 1965, Robert Lowell refused to attend President
Johnson's White House Festival of the Arts, as a protest against
the war in Vietnam. It was Lowell's most widely publicized
political act since his conscientious objection (later in the anti-war
movement, he again risked imprisonment by joining Dr. Spock
and others in support of draft resisters). Lowell has credited this
refusal with providing the initial impetus for his five-part poem
Near the Ocean, which must therefore have been composed in a
period of intense creative activity, since two parts of it were in
print within three months after the festival.

In *Near the Ocean*, Lowell resumes, really for the first time since
Lord Weary's Castle, the full authority of the poet-prophet. No
longer an isolated observer cautiously and conscientiously locat-
ing himself in relation to intransigent realities, he seems, rather, to
stand above history, grandly placing it at the disposal of his own
thoughts and symbolic structures, and thus implicitly (as well as,
more and more often, explicitly) judging it.

No doubt the temper of the times has something to do with
Lowell's confidence here, as with his reticence in *Life Studies*. The
climate of the middle 1960s tended to confer a bardic selfhood on
politically engaged poets. The anti-war movement, though small,
was fresher, more unified, more hopeful then than later; and it
came, for many, as a philosophical release from the myth of a
benevolent technocracy beyond moral or ideological criticism
which grew up in the Cold War years. The Left had the
advantage, for morale and the symbolic imagination, of being
able to concentrate the powers of evil in a single person—a person

sufficiently complex and myth-conscious that, for a few moments in June, 1965, he conceivably saw himself as engaged in spiritual single combat by Robert Lowell. In the pages of the *New York Review*, coedited by Lowell's second wife, and in the work of Norman Mailer, a new kind of journalism put the author's personal commitments, even his free associations, squarely at the center of attention, arguing that this was more measurably objective than the impersonal style of Establishment writing, in which concealed prejudices could share the dignity of facts. When Eugene McCarthy's candidacy seemed to spring full-armed out of his own moral commitment, without the appurtenances of pragmatic power, the countermyth seemed to have become a reality. It was a good time for the idea of the Word against the world, the prophetic imagination against the reasoning spectre. Allen Ginsberg wrote, "I declare the end of the war"; and Lowell's authoritative tone (though accompanied by continued political pessimism) might be considered a distant echo of the same impulse.

On a more personal level, one might say that, as one cause of Lowell's earlier diffidence was self-distrust, one element in his new authority is an ability to make more radically imaginative connections between public and private experience. For the first time, the same poem can deal intimately with the poet's manias, depressions, artistic and sexual frustrations, and with poverty, assassinations, the war in Vietnam. And the "confessions" themselves seem more inward—more experiential, less factual—than they were formerly. The advantages to both sides of Lowell's poetic endeavor are manifold. The artist's candor places the public beliefs in the context of a whole personality, but without thereby diminishing them, as the second stanza of "Memories of West Street and Lepke" seemed to do; while the "confession" ceases to be an end in itself and becomes an interpretive tool, illuminating by analogy the irrational motives of statesmen and masses.

Near the Ocean also becomes more bardic, perhaps, through an unusually wholehearted return to rhyme and meter. All but one of the five poems are written in tetrameter couplets, three in the four-couplet stanza of Marvell's "The Garden" and "Upon Appleton House." Marvell seems a significant ancestor; the tender irony with which he develops a double ambivalence toward the Edenic vision and the issues of ordinary experience very closely resembles Lowell's. But so, too, does Blake, in whose hands the short couplet could be a fierce instrument of political clarification and attack. Stimulated, perhaps, by these precursors, Lowell achieves a more suave and songlike tenderness, a calmer moral grandeur, than he allows himself elsewhere.

Yet *Near the Ocean* remains an extremely modern poem, in which Lowell's taste for variety and cacophony is given ample sway. In the personal poems of *For the Union Dead*, Lowell had learned—largely, I think, from Thomas Hardy—that a conspicuous, even an inept and thumping rhyme and meter, when set in counterpoint to a strong natural speech rhythm, can produce an extraordinary effect of mental energy, tension, or anguish. In *Near the Ocean*, this is achieved much more delicately; the meter itself is so emphatic, yet so limpid, that a mere inverted foot is a substantial disturbance. A jazzlike syncopation results, turning to wild improvisation when used—as it often is—in combination with heavy internal rhyming, off-rhymes, and conflicting alliterations. If the sound is jazzy, so, too, is the speech: Lowell's use of slang and hip terms is much more daring here than in *Life Studies*, and has little of its earlier derogatory overtone. Lowell seems to enjoy using vocabularies beyond his usual territory, and often makes them the starting point for brilliantly Empsonian verbal games. This new freedom, far from conflicting with Lowell's new high style, gives it the authority of a mind whose receptivity to contemporary experience is not merely intellectual but atmospheric and spiritual, whose speed is commensurate to the modern world's.

Another way one might distinguish *Near the Ocean* is to say that it is more symbolic than the preceding books—in the sense in which the last stanza of "Memories of West Street and Lepke" constitutes a return to symbolism. That is, the symbols seem to arise less from narrative particulars than from the unconscious, and to have an inborn capacity to organize the world of the poem

rather than merely to participate passively in such an organization. This might be attributed simply to the exigencies of a tighter
lyric, or to more daring methods of connecting the personal and
the public. But I think it also suggests a turn toward a realm of
archetypes—both in the sense of more inclusive and autonomous
patterns of thought, and in the Freudian or Jungian sense. This is
reflected, as we shall see later, in the reappearance of a mystical
tendency—but expressed, now, as a pure structure of experience,
not a doctrinal belief.

The themes of *Near the Ocean* remain, it is true, pessimistic. They
have to do with self-annihilating intensities, with processes of
senescence and decay: in the Christian religion, in the American
Dream, perhaps in the human species, certainly in the poet, as he
ages and is forced to recognize cyclical patterns even in creative
and sexual ecstasy. And yet, the sense of new possibilities found in
the style is not missing from the content. Politically, there is an
open expression of just anger which raises—if it never exactly
defines—the possibility of radical action. Lowell's "confession"
seems less clinical, more an utterance of his whole self, than it has
before; and his metaphysical inquiry, too, seems at once to push
toward more ultimate first principles and to rest in a richer
context of inward experience. There is, as I have mentioned, the
hint of a new kind of mystical consciousness. Finally, there is a
quality I can only call tenderness toward humanity, which is
quite new in Lowell's work; his previous poems are often tender,
but always toward a single, indeed an isolated, object, the Christ
Child, a friend, an animal. Lowell's attitude—at once more
searching and more tender—toward his subjects, combined with
the elements of strictly poetic freedom, gives the book a curious
quality of lightness, vitality, and energy of vision which, in my
experience, increases with rereading. Like the Puritans who
continue to fascinate him, Lowell knows very well how to "*sing* of
peace, and *preach* despair" (italics mine).

I

"Waking Early Sunday Morning" is the free-associative monologue of a poet on his Creator's day of rest, inert yet filled with the

foretaste of new creation. At the same time, it is a philosophical meditation on energy and reality-transcending experience— "breaking loose"—in man, a *summa* of its modalities and origins, an agonizing attempt to reach a transhuman perspective from which it is somehow to be judged. In this last respect, it brings out the side of Lowell closest to Jonathan Edwards, a side I have underplayed in treating *For the Union Dead* because I have been concerned with the building up of the image of the hero, in which Lowell consciously stresses the qualities of Freudian or even Norman Brownian health: the acceptance of the body, acceptance of death, vividly corporeal as opposed to abstract imagination. Yet Lowell, like Colonel Shaw, attains such health only through great moral effort: the more personal poems show him filled with physical disgust, violently depressed by the idea of his own individual extinction and the anticipation of nuclear war, driven to flee backward from these eventualities into memory and history, the *recherche du temps perdu.*

These preoccupations lead toward an Edwards-like view of our biological nature: that it is "really" a trap or a mechanism, in which our impulses are organized to lure us on through time in a cycle whose preordained end serves the continuance of the race, but holds no consolation for the individual consciousness that has done the acting and suffering. It hardly needs to be pointed out that, though this view claims a quasi-scientific objectivity, it leads to as extreme a mind-body separation as any religious view. The beginning of "Waking Early Sunday Morning" dramatizes this vision of the life-force, at the very moment that it pleads to be swept away by that force in a Dionysiac release:

> O to break loose, like the chinook
> salmon jumping and falling back,
> nosing up to the impossible
> stone and bone-crushing waterfall—
> raw-jawed, weak-fleshed there, stopped by ten
> steps of the roaring ladder, and then
> to clear the top on the last try,
> alive enough to spawn and die.

The fish, of course, is not a mere allegorical representation of Life, but a complicated symbol. In Christian iconography, it is both Leviathan and Christ; in archetypal psychology, it is both the phallus and the embryo in the womb. In Lowell's earlier poetry, from "After the Surprising Conversions" to "For the Union Dead," the fish has both ranges of connotation: a sexualized violence, and an almost unimaginable innocence and wholeness in natural beings. The arching leap of the fish, the "jumping and falling back," is also a recurrent image. Most often, it suggests the self-consuming nature of energy, the necessity of the Fall: what goes up must come down. But rarely, its arc is equated with the rainbow, the sign of God's will to preserve, the fragment in which is intuited the circle of eternal unity (see, for instance, "The Drunken Fisherman" or, in *Near the Ocean*, "1958"). Here the symbolic link is made explicit in the second stanza, where the fish is called a "rainbow."

"Breaking loose" has, of course, personal as well as metaphysical meanings. It is the oncoming creative impulse, of whose ecstasy the poet is perhaps wary; he fears artistic failure, and, knowing too well his own limits, knows that even success will be disillusioning, for his poetry will express doubt and pluralism rather than the visionary unity such Dionysiac feelings should foreshadow. It may also be a sexual impulse: if the salmon passage is taken as a dream, as its vividness suggests, the Freudian symbolism is clear; and the second, waking stanza is filled with sexual reference, concealed and overt. The "unpolluted joy / and criminal leisure of a boy" suggests masturbation (without necessary contradiction, it can also mean just mischief or playing hooky: in both cases, the child's "joy" is a narcissistic exploration of his own powers, but entails, from the adult point of view, an involvement in destructiveness and guilt). The next lines can be seen as a description of ejaculation, if one pays attention to puns and takes the fish-phallus image literally:

> no rainbow smashing a dry fly
> in the white run is free as I,
> here squatting like a dragon on
> time's hoard before the day's begun.

Aside from their sexual meaning, these lines mark the fall from any kind of ecstatic love of one's own energy, whether artist's or boy's, to a grimly detached view. In one sense, this is the result of guilt and a self-fulfilling prophecy; in another sense, no real fall occurs, for the rift between mind and feeling, criticism and ecstasy, has never really been healed, except perhaps in the first moments of dreaming and waking. The best the poet can now do is to speak in paradoxes: to say he is "free" and a "rainbow" at the same time as he describes himself as helplessly lured to destruction by concealed bait. Now, in his eyes, phallic being or energy is no longer the innocent salmon, the perhaps redemptive "rainbow"; it is the guardian dragon, the Satanic, fire-breathing, paranoid will. One is reminded of "the red dragon of my nerves" in "Between the Porch and the Altar." And time—the moments left him to live, and to write his poem—is seen in the most mathematically reductive and sterile terms, as money.

This, as Norman Brown would be quick to observe, is the misapplication of an anal metaphor to processes more appropriately viewed as genital (the "hoard" itself might be equated with spermatozoa, if one took a graphic view of the dragon-phallus image). We remember that Jonathan Edwards erred similarly, by misapplying oral metaphors. In psychoanalytic literature, such anal preoccupations are associated with consuming fears of loss of self in creative work, sex, or death, and with a compensatory paranoid aggressiveness. But one hardly needs the psychoanalytic gloss to see that such feelings have come to dominate the poem. The poet has moved from a narcissistic delight in energy and in its release to an attitude that at once distrusts and joylessly cherishes it, that is grimly set on deploying it, if at all, to greatest possible effect: "Fierce, fireless mind, running downhill."

Yet, by one of those emotional paradoxes so often encountered in artists of a non-Dionysiac cast, this concept of the self-necessitated Fall, of the way in which ecstatic impulses modulate into destructive ones, itself becomes the fructifying myth, the source of a triumphant symbolic organization of experience, as the ecstasy itself, for Lowell, could not be.

The third stanza, in the earliest published version, was a direct confession about the poet's previous period of artistic sterility and its corrosive effect on his personality.[1] As finally printed, the stanza projects similar emotions through images of nature, a dark pastoral: "vermin," not even a dragon now, go through destructive or completely absurd activities with a skilled yet "obsessive" dedication. They "run for their unstopped holes" in the daylight, as Lowell's energy seeks the fewer and fewer creative outlets open to it. Their violence is not so much a matter of devouring as "grinding"; but even the sun's energy is involved in the same futility, as it begins a "daily remorseful blackout."

Now Lowell moves to the external world, the Maine harbor outside his window, and enters into the more general and historical treatment of energy in decay that will take up most of the poem. He recalls Homer ("the wine-dark hulls"), the Bible ("goes down to the sea in ships"), and the Renaissance explorers' dreams of an earthly paradise ("bound for Bermuda or Good Hope"). In all these periods, men's earthly embarkations and risks seemed—as they still did for Hart Crane—meaningful correlates of spiritual discovery; but, like the poet's own burst of energy, they have ended by revealing the narrow limits of the possibilities,

1. The original version of the poem appeared in the *New York Review of Books*, August 5, 1965. The third stanza then ran:

> Time to grub up and junk the year's
> output, a dead wood of dry verse:
> dim confession, coy revelation,
> liftings, listless self-imitation,
> whole days when I could hardly speak,
> came pluming home unshaven, weak
> and willing to read anyone
> things done before and better done.

Other changes, in the book version, included: the total rewriting of another stanza dealing with artistic difficulties, the ninth, in a more public direction; the rearrangement of the last stanzas for greater momentum; and a general elimination of the word *oh* from the apostrophes. Some of *Near the Ocean*'s hostile critics felt the poem was hurt by these revisions. There is obviously much to be said on both sides. The book version loses some of the sense of intimacy, of humility; on the other hand, the religious themes are more completely articulated, the poem has a tighter and more evident unity, and the cumulative intensity of the ending is overwhelming.

and what is left is only a lesser analogue, numbed by habit, willfully ignorant of desperation—"business as usual in eclipse."

Lowell now presents us with a new symbol of creative and perceptual processes, which is, in a way, his own lesser analogue:

> I watch a glass of water wet
> with a fine fuzz of icy sweat,
> silvery colors touched with sky,
> serene in their neutrality—
> yet if I shift or change my mood,
> I see some object made of wood,
> background behind it of brown grain,
> to darken it, but not to stain.
>
> O that the spirit could remain
> tinged but untarnished by its strain!

We notice several things about this glass: that it is connected, obscurely, to the salmon and the ships, by the overriding image of water; that it is connected to human processes, perhaps to the poet's particular turmoil, through the "fine fuzz of icy sweat"; and that it is a receptive, transmitting medium, conveying both a celestial realm ("serene," if only by the rather nihilistic virtue of "neutrality") and a dark terrestrial "background." The glass would seem to be the image of a disembodied, contemplative consciousness, and of a purely mimetic version of the creative process—a lesser analogue of the image-begetting dream with which the poem began. Implicit in the image is a wish—that the "spirit" could be this calm, precise, immutable, self-sufficient— and a criticism of that wish, since the spirit would then be separated from its own vital flow, imprisoned in its own artifact. In any case, the wish is an impossible one and, not surprisingly, it dissolves into further frustration, a new search for outlets:

> better dressed and stacking birch,
> or lost with the faithful at Church—
> anywhere, but somewhere else!

Of these typical American Sunday-morning activities, church is

treated the more satirically. As in "Beyond the Alps," it is blind to
the implications of its absorption in materialism ("the new
electric bells"); it has shrunk to a social ritual, an escape from
isolation ("lost with the faithful at Church"); it is illiterate with
respect to its traditions ("hymns we hear but do not read"). But,
beneath the satire, we glimpse Lowell's own ambivalence toward
the Christian and the Puritan experience, toward absolute faith.
He is attracted to a system that can acknowledge darkness but
leave "a loophole for the soul," yet frightened of its aggressively
simplistic approach to life, and the darker human qualities that
can lurk in it ("Bible chopped and crucified," "stiff quatrains
shovelled out four-square").

If the church represents a possibility of Lowell's life and art, so
does the woodshed: it suggests the poetry that rejects absolutes
and settles lovingly on trivial, irregular sides of experience not
commonly included among the great subjects.

> No, put old clothes on, and explore
> the corners of the woodshed for
> its dregs and dreck: tools with no handle,
> ten candle-ends not worth a candle,
> old lumber banished from the Temple,
> damned by Paul's precept and example,
> cast from the kingdom, banned in Israel,
> the wordless sign, the tinkling cymbal.

These "dregs" seem to represent not only the commonplace and
useless, but, by their phallic overtones, excluded or sterile sexual
experiences, perhaps the autoeroticism alluded to earlier. In St.
Paul's 1 Corinthians—the epistle referred to throughout this
passage—there is a catalog of sexual sins that will bar one from
the kingdom of heaven.[2] Such sins, or experiences, are the subject
matter of confessional poetry; but they bring with them fears of
impotence and castration (they are "candle-ends," where piety
would be a full candle), and, on the religious and artistic levels,

2. Cf. 1 Corinthians 6:9–10 for "Paul's precept." The passage directly alluded
to in this and the following stanza is 1 Corinthians 13:1–13.

these fears respectively find their equivalents as damnation, and as failure through hollowness and triviality, through reliance on inadequate symbols. (According to Lowell, the pun on *cymbal* and *symbol* is found in St. Paul's original Greek.) Lowell cannot wholly discount these fears, though he hits back at them with the slangy sarcasm "banned in Israel"—suggesting that any theocratic utopia's standards will be as priggish and aggressive as proper Boston's. More subtly, Lowell defends himself through the very figure of banished lumber, which recalls Christ's reference to himself as "the stone that the builders rejected," and which foreshadows the appearance, at the end of the poem, of the Tree of Life.

But, ultimately, the woodshed is no more satisfactory than the church in allaying Lowell's conviction that, contrary to the promise that follows St. Paul's threat, the world and his mind are darkening, receding from rather than approaching the visionary encounter with God.

> When will we see Him face to face?
> Each day, He shines through darker glass.
> In this small town where everything
> is known, I see His vanishing
> emblems, His white spire and flag-
> pole sticking out above the fog,
> like old white china doorknobs, sad,
> slight, useless things to calm the mad.

Here, as before, implicitly, phallic power is equated with religious and political certitude. But, in the imagery, all of these now appear as truncated and impotent as the candle-ends, connected neither to any meaningful absolute nor to the reality of "this small town where everything is known," the "global village" ironically epitomized as a Maine resort. Mankind is therefore as deeply alienated as a psychotic, able to seek virility only in the symbols of impotence, connection and release from self in the symbols of isolation.

The china doorknobs are poignantly relevant in another way because of a personal reference. Lowell has described how this image haunted him for weeks at the beginning of the composition of *Life Studies*, though it was never used in the poems (see chapter 3). This story seems to imply both the mysterious facilitation of new creativity, and its partial drowning in the obsessional and the inarticulable. The image thus expresses the same divided possibilities in Lowell's creativity as the second and eighth stanzas here do, and so helps to cement the connections between Lowell's artistic problems and the general human condition.

That condition has been portrayed, so far, primarily as the frustration of impulse (playful-sexual with the boy, adventurous with the boats, religious with the faithful) under the weight of a knowledge, a mental consciousness, a technical power, that man cannot handle and would like to escape. Lowell suggests in the doorknobs passage that for man, as for himself, there is the danger of insanity in such acute contradictions. The rest of the poem deals with the conversion of dammed-up ecstasy into evil, the outbreak of universal psychosis in spiraling arms-races, wars, atrocities.

> Hammering military splendor,
> top-heavy Goliath in full armor—
> little redemption in the mass
> liquidations of their brass,
> elephant and phalanx moving
> with the times and still improving,
> when that kingdom hit the crash:
> a million foreskins stacked like trash . . .

Many psychological motifs from earlier in the poem reappear: the "hammering" obsessional behavior, the "top-heavy" immobilization of knowledge and technology. The transformation of a hidden narcissistic impulse into paranoid murderousness is implied by the double meaning of "liquidations." The allusion to the slaughter of the Shechemites (Genesis 34) strengthens the Freudian implications, making violence, as in "Caligula," phallic self-aggrandizement or homosexual sadism. It also gives the sense that history is hopelessly repetitive and therefore, with the increase of "top-heavy" power, headed for a nuclear "crash";

while to link a genocide committed for the sake of race honor by
Jews, with the piles of dismembered bodies in Nazi death-camps,
is to give a particularly black view of the universality of the
impulse to persecute.

The flow of angry prophecy is briefly interrupted by a return to
self-analysis.

> Sing softer! But what if a new
> diminuendo brings no true
> tenderness, only restlessness,
> excess, the hunger for success,
> sanity of self-deception
> fixed and kicked by reckless caution,
> while we listen to the bells—
> anywhere, but somewhere else!

Lowell lets us know that he distrusts mere anger as a way of
resolving his poem, that he wishes for "true tenderness." But the
very wish brings on a renewed awareness of the unsatisfied
thrashing about of energy within him: corrosive ambition, manic
tendencies, the alternation between an even keel which he
despises as "sanity of self-deception" and the frustrating visionary / anti-visionary paradox of his creativity, his "reckless cau-
tion." Using the words *fixed and kicked,* Lowell self-laceratingly
compares his relation to either or both states with an addict's
relation to his drug. Lowell is driven back at last to his recurrent
cries of impossible longing: "Anywhere, but somewhere else,"
and, "O to break loose!"

It is worth pausing to note the technical effects in this stanza,
which, though unusually rich and strange, are not atypical of the
method of the poem. The heavy *s*-alliteration, the less prominent
reechoing of other soft sounds (*f-, n-, -ng, u-*) make a kind of
lullaby, or siren-song, of the first two lines. Yet imperfection is
carefully allowed to remain, in the form of unexpected spondees
and inversions ("but what if," "true/tenderness"). As the meaning alters, each line begins with an inversion, and contains an
internal rhyme, so that the lines seem to recoil upon themselves
and each other as the feelings do. The dominant *s*-alliteration

becomes the -*ess* rhyme, but is also blended with more and more dissonant variants (*st-*, *x-*, *k-*, *-tion*), until it seems less to croon than to hiss. Appropriately, the effects become most jazzy as the drug reference approaches. The following line is abruptly smooth and quiet; interestingly, it centers on the word *listen,* which fits the dissonant *st-* pattern for the eye, but restores the pure *s-* sound for the ear. This stanza is the tour de force of the poem for sound, but a comparably meaningful density could, I think, be found anywhere.[3]

The first lines of the following stanza,

> O to break loose. All life's grandeur
> is something with a girl in summer . . .

present special problems of tone. Clearly, some diminution of "grandeur" is intended, and the lines can be read in a cynical spirit, as a mere restatement of the sublimation theme. But the second line (with its concentration of *m-*, *th-*, short *i*, and particularly *s-*) belongs to the wistful music of the previous stanza. The vagueness of the phrase "something with" offers a tantalizing choice of tonalities: banal, fragile, imponderable . . . None of these possibilities can be overlooked; perhaps they all blend in a kind of resigned tenderness at the simplicity-in-complexity (or vice-versa) of human desires, a tone that we have heard before, and will hear again, in the poem. In all their implications, the lines form a magnificent if startling overture to the great scene of the public poem, the appearance of Lyndon Johnson as a character:

> elated as the President
> girdled by his establishment
> this Sunday morning, free to chaff
> his own thoughts with his bear-cuffed staff,
> swimming nude, unbuttoned, sick
> of his ghost-written rhetoric.

3. This paragraph and the following one owe something to the insights of two of my students, Elizabeth Champagne and Kerney Rhoden.

I have discussed this character-portrait already in chapter 4; but in the full context of the poem, and in juxtaposition with Lowell's self-portrait, it becomes less clinical, more pitiably and frighteningly human. The poet's self-analysis provides him with his empathy for the President's manic insecurity, his narcissistic or irregular sexual impulses. But it also makes him see the President as partially helpless, hemmed in by what is predetermined, autonomous, and dehumanized (an "establishment," "ghost-written rhetoric"). Thus, the President's eccentricities and even his extravagant evils seem partly to spring from a desire to be free, to find and give expression to his true sexual humanity, his "own thoughts." The President remains, to be sure, a terrible instance of hubris, a man who wants to be God and has more of the means than any precursor did; but he is still wryly pitied, caught as he is in a spiraling destructive activity ultimately beyond his control, which makes him godlike but then permits "no weekends for the gods."

> Wars
> flicker, earth licks its open sores,
> fresh breakage, fresh promotions, chance
> assassinations, no advance.
> Only man thinning out his kind
> sounds through the Sabbath noon, the blind
> swipe of the pruner and his knife
> busy about the tree of life . . .

The imagery at once recalls events in Vietnam and summons up traditional symbols of moral downfall, spreading disease and fire. It culminates in an ultimate irreligious act against the "tree of life," here meaning both populations and man's innate redeemable nature, Blake's human form divine, "kind" in its old sense. Lowell's "pruner" seems to me to invoke Shakespeare's image of politics as a garden from *Richard II*, much as the earlier allusions to Homer, Genesis, and St. Paul served to frame modern experience in outlived but at least coherent moral perspectives. In Shakespeare, the image makes acts of successful statecraft, even bloody ones, part of a harmonious and life-serving pattern; but here, whether because our ethical sense is no longer shielded by aristocratic ideology, or because our deeds are more out of control, the image seems not only vividly, but purposelessly and indiscriminately, murderous. All these meanings contribute to the sense of a crime repeating, in a worse way, the original one in Eden. Hence, Mr. Lowell's Sunday Morning Service ends with a grim benediction:

> Pity the planet, all joy gone
> from this sweet volcanic cone;
> peace to our children when they fall
> in small war on the heels of small
> war—until the end of time
> to police the earth, a ghost
> orbiting forever lost
> in our monotonous sublime.

The war in Vietnam is made to bear a further bitter lesson: as man's experience has become, in so many ways, "small," he must now either confine his violence to "small" wars or else annihilate himself. Whichever happens, his fate will be no release but (following the ambiguity of the line-break) "war until the end of time." Our knowledge makes the world rather like a manned satellite; but the consequence is that it is as precarious as one, as lacking in an innate, inexhaustible vitality. Depopulated or not, it is a "ghost"; while the direct echo here is Johnson's "ghost-written rhetoric," the word recalls all the forms of mental consciousness and organized activity seen in the poem as cut off from their sources in a full corporeal life. The last line of the poem seems a final abnegation of the possibility of a visionary release: "our" sublime, the infinites of our scientific philosophy, the grandeurs our poetry envisions, are merely monotonous.

It is fair, then, to ask what remains of the positive or redemptive overtones detected earlier—or of those visible in Sidney Nolan's drawings, which fierily identify the forms of phallus, Tree of Life, and mushroom cloud, of fishlike humans and Blakean angels. The drawings at least hint at a return to a reverence for energy, a sexual-religious vision involving an "unpolluted" narcissistic joy, as a possible alternative to the process whereby frustrated energy becomes purely aggressive. In this context, Lowell's poem might be fulfilling a truly eschatological function, building the temple that includes all the banished lumber, that is itself the Tree of Life. But we must balance this suggestion against Lowell's other view of his poetry as the product of a falling process, as lacking in "tenderness" as well as ecstasy. Further, the general symbol of the burst of energy that contains the seeds of its necessary cooling and rigidifying persists all the way to the last stanza: the "sweet volcanic cone."

Like "The Quaker Graveyard" out of Lowell's Catholic period, "Waking Early Sunday Morning" is metaphysically ambiguous, humanly on the pessimistic or tragic side. Yet the differences between the two poems seem ultimately more important than the similarities. Not the least of them is the tenderness, wistfulness, desire to comfort that—despite Lowell's self-doubt—infuses "Waking Early Sunday Morning"'s last stanza, as it infused the line "something with a girl in summer." On the latest of many rereadings, it occurs to me that "Pity the planet" can be taken as a general imperative as well as an individual sigh—an insight strengthening my feeling that the poem would, if it could, teach us a kind of self-love that might, just marginally, save us.

II

"Fourth of July in Maine" seems vulnerable to the criticism that it covers too much of the same ground as "Waking Early Sunday Morning," in the same stanza form and loose free-associative structure. Yet, there are subtle differentiations. The subject of both poems is the vicissitudes of the energy that keeps life going: but where "Waking Early" deals with its grand manifestations for good or evil, religion, sex, art, and war, "Fourth of July" treats the blendings of manic activity and inertia that carry people through the dissatisfactions and self-deceptions of the everyday. In tone, too, "Fourth of July in Maine" is a marked shift; outwardly, it is simple, strident, and hortatory, while inwardly it opens on a labyrinth of Empsonian word-games.

The poem begins with political evils, not on the scale of

Johnson but of a Maine village Independence Day. Theatrical
images predominate: by "children's costumes" and "canned
martial music," the citizens make America what it is not, an
innocent yet irresistible conqueror, and so, they think, "resist / the communist and socialist." The myth of equal opportunity is acted out as a fair in which children compete for ribbons
but every child is assured of winning something. Against the
myth, Lowell sets the harsh reality of the racist poor, whose very
belief in self-help and voluntarism maintains them in bovine
resignation to their lot:

> upholders of the American dream,
> who will not sink and cannot swim—
> Emersonian self-reliance,
> lethargy of Russian peasants!

These paradoxes, inertia disguised in will, mental stupefaction in
rigid opinion, will be a recurrent psychological motif in the poem.
   The scene leads Lowell to bitter reflections on the loss of a more
valuable American dream, that of the "dandyish Union soldier"
who "seems a convert to old age." The effort to comprehend such
elective decay leads Lowell back to the Puritan experience:

> Blue twinges of mortality
> remind us the theocracy
> drove in its stakes here to command
> the infinite, and gave this land
> a ministry that would have made
> short work of Christ, the Son of God,
> and then exchanged His crucifix,
> hardly our sign, for politics.

A complex symbolic history is crowded into this stanza. In the
new Eden, the theocrats not only brought along the Fall but
repeated the Crucifixion ("made short work of Christ") as they
drove in their "stakes." The victims of their crucifixion were, as
the pun suggests, manifold: the wilderness they surveyed and
subdivided; the witches they actually hanged but are commonly
reputed to have burned; their descendant Robert Lowell himself,

who suffers "blue twinges," morbid and predestinarian preoccupations, partly because of their heritage. Rejecting the crucifix as
a graven image, the elders prepared the way for the Unitarians
who eliminated the Incarnation altogether; thus, purged of all
un-American identifications ("hardly our sign") with failure,
poverty, crime, and bodily suffering, religion is safely converted
into a prop of the status quo. The psychology of the rejection of
the crucifix is a sardonic extension of that of the self-reliant poor;
it reminds one of Blake's self-righteous believers who love to
execute criminals but cry, "Look not so merciful upon me O thou
Slain Lamb of God." [4]

Yet, almost in spite of Lowell's belief in historical decadence,
and his resentment of the Puritans, he finds a center of positive
values in the "white Colonial frame house" willed to him by his
cousin Harriet Winslow:

> The founders' faith was in decay,
> and yet their building seems to say:
> "Every time I take a breath,
> my God you are the air I breathe."

This is, for the whole sequence of poems, a rarely wholehearted
evocation of an ideal; one notices how it combines the two kinds
of experience desired in "Waking Early Sunday Morning," a
visionary encounter with God and a loving acceptance of the
everyday. There is also a touch of the pantheism latent in
passages of *Lord Weary's Castle*. Still, Lowell's darker feelings about
New England remain, and his further meditations return interestingly to Jonathan Edwards's image of the spider and its web.

> New England, everywhere I look,
> old letters crumble from the Book,
> China trade rubble, one more line
> unravelling from the dark design
> spun by God and Cotton Mather—
> our *bel età dell'oro*, another

4. William Blake, *Jerusalem*, Pl. 24, l. 59.

> bright thing thinner than a cobweb
> caught in Calvinism's ebb.

As in "Mr. Edwards and the Spider," the symbol has two opposite meanings: the earthly beauty, the earthly home that is so physically fragile, and beautiful or frightening entirely in the eye of the beholder, and the "dark design," the mental system or vision of God that swallows up bright things. The passage delicately sums up Lowell's perplexity at the odd juxtapositions of wholeness and decay in the historical process.

In the next phase of the poem, Lowell's cousin appears as a personal embodiment of the will to live, and of a certain success or beauty in living, in this local and historical context. But Lowell does not enter on this theme without preliminary, framing reminders of the objective grimness of life, the monotonous sublime:

> Dear Cousin, life is much the same,
> though only fossils know your name
> here since you left this solitude,
> gone, as the Christians say, for good.

"Fossils" means "old-timers," but also suggests the dwarfing perspectives of paleontology; "solitude," in reference to this gregarious woman, has an existential force; while "for good" mocks the Christians as people who theologically should believe that all temporal evil serves an ultimately good end, yet who cannot speak of death without euphemisms.

The portrait of Cousin Harriet that follows is tender and gallant, yet almost unwillingly conveys Lowell's darker feelings about such human successes. "If memory is genius, you / had Homer's"—but, since it is not, only Trollope's, is the strong implication. Harriet was clearly an authoritative woman, "majorful," a sender of "emissaries"; and if it is clear that her tyrannical potentialities were counterbalanced by a loving and humorous nature, we are still told that she liked objects better than people, as being more totally manageable, requiring more memory than genius. Lowell is proud of her irreligion, of a sort of Roman

stoicism in her; yet he portrays her as in some ways rather like the
reactionary poor, kept going by a mixture of pointless hyperactiv-
ity and an earthbound imagination. The account of her appalling
final illness, which reinforces the theme of human vulnerability,
also brings out the two sides of Harriet's personality. Her
exhaustive, fussy concern for possessions she can no longer use
makes a vivid contrast to her grandly cheerful way of contemplat-
ing suicide.

So, when Lowell prays that his daughter will resemble her
namesake, we may expect some ambivalence. It shows, even, in
the fervid tone itself, with its evocation of Yeats's "A Prayer for
My Daughter." Yeats's poem is humanly condescending, because
of his belief that women should not have opinions; but Lowell's is
metaphysically condescending, as he himself is ironically aware.
After all, he wants his "blue-ribboned" American daughter to be
happy, yet he is more than half convinced that, in our age,
happiness requires a certain small-mindedness and blindness to
ultimates.

> may your proportion strengthen her
> to live through the millennial year
> Two Thousand, and like you possess
> friends, independence, and a house,
> herself God's plenty, mistress of
> your tireless sedentary love.

We know, of course, that no strengthening of an individual's
character will determine what kind of a millennium it is we are
approaching; but beyond that, the idea of merely living through
one, of whatever kind, suggests a lack of the imagination of the
extreme. Again, the financial-existential ambiguity of "independence" resonates with the ambiguity of the whole Independence
Day. At the end, Lowell's syntax suggests that "love" is an object
to be possessed rather than a spontaneous feeling, and that it can
arise from the "tireless"-"sedentary" dynamic; I think the reader
has reason to be troubled by these implications.

I do not mean that Lowell's prayer is insincere; that its limits
do not spring, like those of Yeats's, partly from his real notion of

wisdom; that Cousin Harriet is in no way the same kind of positive standard that her house is. In a world as menacing as Lowell's, survivor-ship combined with human decency is no mean achievement, whatever its ultimate psychological roots. But Lowell's implicit comparison for both Harriets in the next stanza surely strengthens his darker meanings:

> Her two angora guinea pigs
> are nibbling seed, the news, and twigs—
> untroubled, petrified, atremble,
> a mother and her daughter, so humble,
> giving, idle and sensitive,
> few animals will let them live,
> and only a vegetarian God
> could look on them and call them good.

Rather than turning to his rich cousin for an ethical model of life, Lowell now turns to "man's poorest cousins" for its lowest common denominator. This is the characteristic method of his Edwardsian-Darwinian side, and it leaves him back with the dilemma of the spiderweb: if even as noble and consciously perfected a style of life as Harriet Winslow's can be reduced to blind variations on the struggle to survive, what is one to make of living things in general, those "harmonies / of lust and appetite and ease"? Lowell's tone here is much warmer than Edwards's could possibly be, yet his horror at the cruel and the mechanical aspects of life is strong enough to push him to the edge of blasphemy: the breath of Creation is a "stupor," and "only a vegetarian God"—which, as the story of Cain tells us, ours is not—would really be on the side of the harmless animals.

The meditation, up to now connectable but rambling, suddenly attains an unexpected symbolic concentration. The quick, cold Maine summer nightfall becomes the objective correlative for the poet's double vision, the *bel età dell'oro* and the dark design:

> And now the frosted summer night-dew
> brightens, the north wind rushes through
> your ailing cedars, finds the gaps;

> thumbtacks rattle from the white maps,
> food's lost sight of, dinner waits
> in the cold oven, icy plates—
> repeating and repeating, one
> Joan Baez on the gramophone.

In keeping with his theme of the grindingness of life, its frenetic
arrangements, Lowell converts the mishaps and irritations of a
subsiding holiday into genuinely disturbing intuitions of the
absurd. Yet the details unobtrusively connect with earlier elements in the poem: the "white maps" recall the China trade and
American empire; Harriet's refined, discriminating choice of
"Bach's precursors" is replaced by the endlessly repeated Joan
Baez. It is unclear whether the joke here is against the young—
implying that their life-affirming primitivism is monotonous—or
against the poet, who, like the old gramophone, can only pick up
that aspect.

The scene shifts to the family gathering in Harriet's "converted
barn" (the words themselves suggest "Christianized animality").
Here, we are set between fundamental antinomies, the cold of the
north wind and the fire. Cold, implicitly, represents the objective
grimness of life, and perhaps the state of catatonic isolation and
loss of will with which the poet's vision of it threatens him. Fire, in
turn, signifies the hyperactive energy—always absurd and usually
aggressive, spurred on rather than muted by fatigue—that keeps
us going but, like cold, threatens our stability if we get too close.

> we burn our hands a moment, borne
> by energies that never tire
> of piling fuel on the fire;
> monologue that will not hear,
> logic turning its deaf ear,
> wild spirits and old sores in league
> with inexhaustible fatigue.

Lowell goes back, for contrast, to Eden, the vision of innocent
unity; but, making his own myth out of the anomalies of Genesis,
he actually gives us the image, from "Waking Early," of a
self-contradictory perfection whose nature is to disintegrate. Thus,

when "unmated," man is "still licensed to increase," but mating
brings the Fall, after which sexual energy equals guilt, and the
reasons for continuing the race become questionable. Again,
God's "uncreated Word" is the philosophical Logos, the expression of unity between idea and realization, spirit and matter, only
before it starts to create:

> when God the Logos still had wit
> to hide his bloody hands, and sit
> in silence, while his peace was sung.
> Then the universe was young.

The blasphemous strain in the poem culminates with these lines.
The attribution of "bloody hands" to both the creating God and
the suffering Christ implies that Creation was a murderous and a
suicidal act on God's part. The myth of energy decaying into
outward and inward aggression is projected back into the very
source of energy. And yet, the stanza ends on the naïve, wistful
note familiar from "Waking Early"; perhaps some deep desire to
overcome disunity by mystical paradox is buried here, after all.[5]

In the last stanza, Lowell turns from a religious to a scientific
myth, the ultimate end of life in the explosion or cooling of the
sun. Thus, we are back to the motif of the entrapment between ice

---

5. The ironies of this stanza are, I believe, augmented by three literary
allusions. One is to Marvell's unorthodox views about paradise in "The Garden":

> Such was that happy Garden-state
> While Man there walk'd without a Mate:
> After a Place so pure, and sweet,
> What other Help could yet be meet!

The second is to Blake's "Introduction" to *Songs of Experience*, the Bard

> Whose ears have heard
> The Holy Word
> That walked among the ancient trees.

In the context of "Earth's Answer," this "Holy Word" emerges as a sophistical
tyrant, trying to force the earth to accept the necessity of sexual guilt and
repression. Finally, I would suspect that the Word lacking wit (after the
Incarnation) is a parody of Lancelot Andrewes's Nativity Sermon, made famous to
other purposes by T. S. Eliot.

and fire, which, like Lowell's Eden myth, expresses the total dependency of human life upon ultimate contradictions. Lowell builds on this paradox in the brilliant final apostrophe, which bears the same relation to a Fourth of July family prayer that the ending of "Waking Early" bears to a benediction.

> Great ash and sun of freedom, give
> us this day the warmth to live,
> and face the household fire. We turn
> our backs, and feel the whisky burn.

The questionable freedom of both our country and our wills is invoked as both "ash and sun," "bright thing" and "dark design," energy and its necessary decay. Without this warmth we cannot live, physically or psychically; yet the same warmth, in its overflow, converts the household into a firing-squad, something we need courage to "face." Further, the last line suggests, there is no turning from the battle, no contemplative retreat, that is not, like the escape into literal intoxication, merely another mode of the fire.

Like "Waking Early," though on a different level, this poem works out a unified vision of all the vicissitudes of human energy it invokes. It is still, formally, the more diffuse, haphazard, and uneven poem. In Lowell's own mind, perhaps, the personal judgment-tribute to Harriet Winslow is all the center that the poem needs; and a purely formal precursor might be found in Marvell's "Upon Appleton House," written in the same stanza. There too, within the time-scheme of a single day, a house is described, its family and political history is told, and it is seen as a symbolic organization of life which leads the poet into ultimate religious and ethical questions of value. It even offers prescriptions for the moral education of an idealized young heiress. But we should remember that if Marvell, too, writes of the house and of human activity from a semi-detached stance, it is at least consonant with his position as tutor and patronized poet; Lowell writes as owner and father, and his distance comes entirely from within his own mind. Lowell's house poem strains at its limits because it belongs to an age in which, for better *and* for worse, a house does not provide a man with his absolute location, his "harmonies / of lust and appetite and ease."

III

In "The Opposite House," the Marvellian stanza gives way to a prosy free verse reminiscent of *For the Union Dead.* This is more than a rest for the reader's ear, since it marks the change of setting from Maine to New York, and dramatizes a shift of focus and control from the poet's meditative consciousness to the chaotic multiplicity of outside reality. This is fitting, for while the other poems include political material in their cosmic synthesis, the New York poems are quintessentially *engagé.* As the title "The Opposite House" suggests, we are immediately involved in problems of self and world, observer and observed, like those we encountered in "Memories of West Street and Lepke" and "For the Union Dead." Thus, in daylight, the house is "just an opposite house," perhaps just a geometrical pattern—though there might be food for thought in the fact that an "abandoned police stable" is preserved in a city full of slums, and there is certainly a pleasing sense of liberation in the "ganging" pigeons that remind Lowell of juvenile delinquents. But at night and, perhaps, during a fire, the picture is different:

> Tonight, though, I see it shine
> in the Azores of my open window.
> Its manly, old-fashioned lines
> are gorgeously rectilinear.
> It's like some firework to be fired
> at the end of the garden party,
> some Spanish *casa*, luminous
> with heraldry and murder,
> marooned in New York.

"The Azores of my open window" suggests that looking out is the beginning of an exploratory voyage: the Azores were Columbus's last port of call on the way to America. But what Lowell discovers, as the "marooned" Spanish *casa* suggests, is not the new Eden but an America long since corrupted by the Old World structures of mind left behind in it: class society, the authoritarian passion for order, the quickness to violence. The parallel to the idea of the American Fall in "Fourth of July in Maine" is evident.

All the seemingly casual images of this stanza have a tendency to become sinister on reflection. Thus, the "gorgeously rectilinear" building might stand for the rationalizations of American foreign policy; the "firework" for the hydrogen bomb; the "end of the garden party" for the end of Eden, or the end of the world, which our polite governing classes may precipitate.

These are mere overtones that drift up through the medium of Lowell's free-floating imagination; but the third stanza gives them a local habitation in the sight to be seen, the goal of the perceptual voyage—the veiled intimidation of the watching crowd by the police.

> A stringy policeman is crooked
> in the doorway, one hand on his revolver.
> He counts his bullets like beads.
> Two on horseback sidle
> the crowd to the curb. A red light
> whirls on the roof of an armed car,
> plodding slower than a turtle.
> Deterrent terror!
> *Viva la muerte!*

It is typical police tactics, pre-Chicago style: slow, methodical, insinuating, with no demonstrable show of hate or violence. Yet to Lowell, seeing through and not with the eye, it is a ritual in which the object of worship is the power to kill, valued nakedly for itself (or so the rosary image would suggest). This "deterrent terror," the violence machine that America builds and—because we paranoiacally believe it really is purely defensive—manages to set outside the bounds of human emotion and moral choice, is the common denominator of our national and international "order"; and it amounts to *Viva la muerte*. The allusion is to Unamuno's famous anti-fascist speech during the Spanish Civil War, which was spontaneously prompted by hearing a crippled fascist general shout this slogan at a meeting. This rounds out the pattern of

Spanish images, with their implicit theme of the movement from a fascination with death under religious and chivalric cover to the emergence of pure Thanatos. But it is not too fanciful to think that it also identifies Lowell with Unamuno, the detached man of letters forced into unanticipated political commitment by the strength of a momentary, epiphanic perception. The following poem, "Central Park," begins with the poet in a symbolically more involved position (he is out of his apartment, walking across the park), and the greater imaginative cohesion of his political vision expresses itself in the return to couplets, though not to a fixed stanza-length.

IV

Like the two Maine poems, "Central Park" is delicately framed by a conflict of opposing states of soul in the poet—a vaguely sexual elation ("now light as pollen"), a depressed sense of being used up, mechanized, by the life-process ("now as white / and winded as a grounded kite"). Lowell looks out on a scene of sex-in-nature that might recall the Garden of Eden, but that, to his eye, is as inexorably geometrical as a cubist painting:

> I watched the lovers occupy
> every inch of earth and sky:
> one figure of geometry,
> multiplied to infinity,
> straps down, and sunning openly . . .
> each precious, public, pubic tangle
> an equilateral triangle

This afflicting vision of sameness, of life simplified to mathematics, comes naturally to the Edwardsian side of Lowell; but the real point is that it now comes naturally to all of us, enforced on civilized consciousness by overcrowding, overpopulation, the monolithic architecture of cities. As the painting's pure geometric lines might be overspread with an amorphous gray wash, so, Lowell says, "the stain of fear and poverty . . . darkened every mote of dust" and "each trapped anatomy" (the picture becomes darker still if one remembers *anatomy*'s old meaning, "skeleton").

It is hard to be precise about what this stain-geometry relation means, but one analogy might be a schizophrenic's sense of having a mechanical, active self and a distinct, but immobilized and somewhat formless, inner self.

Under these conditions, Lowell's wistful desire in "Waking Early" for a sexual escape from a devitalized earth, a "sweet volcanic cone," becomes the hopeless wish of mankind:

> All wished to leave this drying crust,
> borne on the delicate wings of lust
> like bees, and cast their fertile drop
> into the overwhelming cup.

This "overwhelming cup" again suggests overpopulation, but, more inescapably, it is a kind of cosmic vaginal symbol, a womb-grave. It implies a regressive nirvana, an escape from individuated consciousness through sexual fulfillment, that leads us back, in a delicate way, to the theme of the death instinct.

The passage of sexual escape leads directly to the picture of the lion in the zoo:

> Drugged and humbled by the smell
> of zoo-straw mixed with animal,
> the lion prowled his slummy cell,
> serving his life-term in jail—
> glaring, grinding, on his heel,
> with tingling step and testicle . . .

Rather obviously, this passage is a social parable on the situation of the poor and the blacks—those people who are "humbled" by living conditions that give them a degrading "animal" image of themselves, treated as criminals a priori, controlled by drugs and a ghetto-cage. The parable shows how society's structures practically compel self-definition through crime and flaunted sexuality —qualities which then "prove" its view of the black man's baser nature. But the very use of the image of a zoo suggests that this is all a kind of theater, fulfilling unconscious, projected desires in the spectator-keeper (a point that Black literature has made repeatedly, from the story of the incestuous father in Ellison's *Invisible*

Man to Cleaver's "The Primeval Mitosis"). But if the lion is an image for black rebellion, it is certainly a pessimistic one; for the energy is seen as purely reactive, chained, like some forms of energy in the poems, to terms of aggression and death.

What follows can be taken as a second parable, in which the oppressed appear not as rebels and criminals but as utterly helpless victims, treated with murderous hypocrisy even by the seemingly benevolent agencies of society:

> Behind a dripping rock, I found
> a one-day kitten on the ground—
> deprived, weak, ignorant and blind,
> squeaking, tubular, left behind—
> dying with its deserter's rich
> Welfare lying out of reach:
> milk cartons, kidney heaped to spoil,
> two plates sheathed with silver foil.

Though Lowell seems to see little hope in revolution, his bitterest satire is reserved for the conscience-salving of reform. "Welfare" is seen as a way of getting rid of the poor, as—in the terms of the metaphor—inappropriate food, so shielded and sanitary (i.e. rotting) that the "animal" couldn't get at it even if he could see or walk. The total picture that emerges from these stanzas is one of complete vulnerability and dammed-up energy on the part of the poor, explicit shirking of responsibility and implicit paranoid cruelty on that of the rich, and something of the inadequacy-om-nipotence dialectic of Lowell's tyrant poems on both sides. We get a very bleak sense of American political possibilities.

The twilight stanza that follows returns to the words *shadow* and *stain,* which now have a more special meaning, the degradation attached to being black. But by the same token, the night the shadows portend is a "jungle hour," the hour of revenge not only for the rebelling black criminal, but for alienated and repressed energy in general. The "mouth of night" is a rather terrifying image, suggesting hell-mouth, Old Night, primal chaos, and other archetypal associations like those of the "overwhelming cup." This image, coupled with that of a failing sun, gives the passage an apocalyptic tone. In this atmosphere, the phenomena of twilight are poignant echoes of the poet's earlier elation and the more innocent sexual escapism: one kite still flies, a "snagged balloon" fails to get much help from "the attraction of the moon," another cosmic feminine symbol.

Lowell now turns to examine the psychology of the oppressor in his moment of peril. But here he uses a direct address, and an angry prophetic tone that carries him farther from the observer stance than he has ventured since *Lord Weary's Castle*:

> Old Pharaohs starving in your foxholes,
> with painted banquets on the walls,
> fists knotted in your captives' hair,
> tyrants with little food to spare—
> all your embalming left you mortal,
> glazed, black, and hideously eternal,
> all your plunder and gold leaf
> only served to draw the thief . . .

The Egyptian imagery springs from the surroundings, Cleopatra's Needle and the Metropolitan Museum, but it is stunningly appropriate, both to the architecture of Fifth Avenue and to an imperial nation with extremes of wealth and poverty and an overextended foreign policy. Lowell sees the American ruling class in much the same way that Eldridge Cleaver does: as people who are essentially, humanly, dead, and driven to seek their lost vitality through simulacra, in their dilettantish art-collecting, and in their sadomasochistic fascination with their social victims. This is the psychology of "Caligula" blown up to a mass scale.

Lowell is also interested in the idea that technology provides a spurious form of transcendence, of immortality. Here, as in "For the Union Dead," his thought parallels that of Norman O. Brown, who holds, in *Life Against Death*, that the city is man's most perfect sublimation; in it, he flees both the body and death by identifying himself with pure geometries, with indestructible, ethereally beautiful metals and stones.[6] But a major thesis of

6. See, again, Norman O. Brown, *Life Against Death*, pp. 281–87; also pp. 100–01.

Brown's book is that the repressed death-instinct, like repressed sexuality, has its "return of the repressed" in a sense of emptiness, death-in-life, and in the breaking loose of aggressive impulses. The theme of an urban death-instinct has been latent in this poem since the line about "the overwhelming cup." At this point, its return seems to have both a homicidal and a suicidal dimension, as the rich become increasingly obsessed with the violence their splendor may provoke.

Whether this fear springs from guilt or secret desire, it leads to a terrible escalation:

> We beg delinquents for our life.
> Behind each bush, perhaps a knife;
> each landscaped crag, each flowering shrub
> hides a policeman with a club.

The syntactical change from "perhaps" to the simple indicative is important. As in a comparable passage in Lowell's translation of Juvenal, the violence of the poor against the rich, though real, is omnipresent only in the rich man's guilty imagination.[7] But society's "deterrent terror" against the poor, on the other hand, has the capacity to be literally everywhere, to fulfill a fantasy of omnipotence.

One can hardly imagine a more scathing radical critique of our class system, extending from its depth psychology to its surface rationalizations. All the same, "Central Park" is not a revolutionary poem, since it offers not the least prospect of a successful and virtuous uprising, but rather, a spiraling release of all destructive tendencies. In another sense, though, it is a radical poem, especially for Lowell, in that it eschews qualification, eschews the "complexity" that can rationalize and blur, and endeavors to see individual human action as at least momentarily identical with the historical or moral force it most deeply serves. It is a poem of

7.   If you take a walk at night,
   carrying a little silver, be prepared
   to think each shadow hides a knife or spear.
   ["The Vanity of Human Wishes," *Near the Ocean*, p. 70]

seeing through, rather than with, the eye, in the tradition of
Blake, of Yeats's "Easter 1916," of Shelley when he wrote

> I met Murder on the way—
> He had a mask like Castlereagh . . .

Perhaps this means that "Central Park" lacks a certain human
depth or human texture in comparison with "Memories of West
Street and Lepke," "Waking Early," or the poem that immediately follows it. Nevertheless, it seems to me one of Lowell's finest
achievements as a poet of moral clarification and urgent, vital
rage.

V

"Near the Ocean" is, for me, after "Waking Early Sunday
Morning," the richest, strangest, and most moving poem of the
sequence. It is easily the most difficult. Since it is both a very
distinct poem and a structural resolution, its own peculiar
themes—sexuality and marriage—constantly open out, in fascinating ways, onto the metapsychological and political concerns of
the entire work. At the same time, the poem is in some ways
inscrutably private. We never really know whether its "they" and
"we" denote different dramatis personae—the poet's first and
second marriages, perhaps—or merely different angles of vision;
whether the incidents in stanzas four through seven tell the story
of a particular relationship, or a much more symbolic history of
all relationships. The privacy works, aesthetically, because the
poem is so free of Lowell's usual need to pin down and localize the
mystery; its surrealistic disjunction and montage lead always
toward the most abstract and inclusive framework.

Thus, the poem plunges us immediately into a free-floating,
dreamlike scene. The opening words, "The house is filled," posit a
theater; but they may also refer to the house of ordinary life,
overfilled with roles, audience, and plots by the inner compulsions
of each psyche. The play appears to be the slaying of Medusa—a
familiar symbol of murderous depersonalization in both the
sexual and the political life. The language of "The last heart-

throb / thrills through her flesh" suggests 'that the primary
context is erotic; death equals orgasm, and a mutual sadomasochistic fulfillment is involved. On the other hand, images of a
stunned hero, petrified, it would seem, before he has even looked
at the head, and a mob, invoke Lowell's fatalistic political vision,
a vision which, in the preceding poems, involves the idea of
politics as theater, as vicarious (and sadomasochistic) experience.

When the protagonist changes from Perseus to Orestes, a
Freudian search for the primal is implied: all sexual aggressions
become the original revenge against the original beloved, the
strong mother who has betrayed both father and son, whose
theatrical-cosmetic "powder" is gunpowder. The symbolic killing
of this mother leads to compulsive sexual repetition, a search for
new mothers:

<blockquote>

He knows. And if she's killed

his treadmill heart will never rest—
his wet mouth pressed to some slack breast,
or shifting over on his back . . .
The severed radiance filters back,
athirst for nightlife—gorgon head,
fished up from the Aegean dead,
with all its stranded snakes uncoiled,
here beheaded and despoiled.

</blockquote>

According to Norman O. Brown, a quest for novelty (sexual or
otherwise) is the inverse reflection of the desire for a lost, or
forbidden, paradise.[8] But this "severed radiance," once recovered,
turns into Medusa's head, and must again be "despoiled" because
of the psychological terrors it resurrects.[9] There is a strong theme
of oral regression here—in the image of the breast and the use of
the word *athirst*—which connects this protagonist with the Caligula figure. The son of the tyrannicidal mother becomes himself a

---

8. See Norman O. Brown, *Life Against Death*, p. 92.
9. According to Freud, the basic terror would be castration. See chap. 4, n. 2.

tyrant, through his insatiable need to be filled with support, love, ardent experience, vital substance. Thus domestic experience, like politics, can become cyclical.

The sense of repetitive instinctual frustration in life leads, once more, to the idea of nirvana, "seas and deserts," the paradise of mere release from individuation.

> Lost in the Near Eastern dreck,
> the tyrant and tyrannicide
> lie like the bridegroom and the bride;
> the battering ram abandoned, prone,
> beside the apeman's phallic stone.

Here, there is an explicit, and two-edged, comparison between sexual and political cycles. We have seen how the sexual warfare of parents may be reproduced in the next generation through patterns of neurotic reaction. But at the same time, Lowell suggests that historical and technological progress be seen in the light of a repetition neurosis, a collective sexual anxiety that drives man to create constantly grander—but never fully reassuring—aggressive simulacra of the phallus. (Again, there is a remarkable resemblance between Lowell's thought and that of Norman O. Brown.)

In the fourth stanza, Lowell turns to the particular unsatisfactory relationship and attempts to understand its failure in terms of specific moments of mutual betrayal. He begins with the sacrosanct "first night"—less sacrosanct already because the phrase has a theatrical meaning, and so, like "backdrop" two lines later, brings the experience into the artificial yet solipsistic world of the first stanza. In other ways, the moment still seems beautiful: the absence of "dogs . . . horse or hunter" suggests a remission of guilt (also, perhaps, of exploitative sexual pursuit), while the water of life seems abundantly present in the nearby swamps. The trees almost radiate darkness—though the odd simile of "extinguished lamps" "watching" might also imply the inverse presence of civilized consciousness and self-consciousness, as the "black sheep," though playful, remind us of repressive family standards and destructive forms of revolt.

Leaving these ambiguities unresolved, Lowell returns to the city, and to the early years of marriage:

> Some subway-green coldwater flat,
> its walls tatooed with neon light,
> then high delirious squalor, food
> burned down with vodka . . . menstrual blood
> caking the covers, when they woke
> to the dry, childless Sunday walk,
> saw cars on Brooklyn Bridge descend
> through steel and coal dust to land's end.

Naïve release has given way to a more willfully maintained, self-consuming intoxication; there is a sharper awareness of the physical, but an element of disgust—appropriately represented by a difficulty with food—has become apparent. The "menstrual blood" and the "childless Sunday walk" emphasize sterility; this marriage will not easily, and perhaps should not, find its further fulfillment in the normal way, by raising a family. The depressing urban imagery has a very subtle function at this point. It is the objective correlative of the lovers' increasingly alienated, mechanistic sense of their own lives; but at the same time it reminds us that, in Lowell's total design, the decay of love and the decay of meaningful community are parallel processes. The "subway-green" flat is a particularly nice detail; it catches a domiciliary impersonality peculiar to New York, and it gives one a sense of rushing through time as though through space in a train, a bewildered sense of displacement and loss.

The third vignette is a meeting "years later"; the lovers have been apart, are perhaps making a last-ditch effort at reconciliation. Instead of being ecstatic, or even manically drunk, they are now reasonable, "cured, recovered": but out of love, they are "out of work," deprived of a comprehensible place in the scheme of things, truly "dead sober." They are cut off from their own life-impulse, symbolized, in keeping with the poem's title, by water (a symbolism subtly maintained even, I think, in the "coldwater flat" of the previous stanza). The setting itself is a sardonic modern version of the exclusion from Eden and the angel's flaming sword: a "gritty green, / all access barred with broken glass."

Brilliantly defined though the episodes are, they yield no single conclusive moment of "betrayal," any more than Lowell's parallel inquiries into his own loss of elation in "Waking Early Sunday Morning" and the decline of New England in "Fourth of July in Maine" do. Hence, the last question is, "Is it this shore?" Is it our total relation to our instincts of sex and nirvana, our "near the ocean" predicament, that insures perpetual dissatisfaction? Lowell elaborates:

> Their eyes worn white
> as moons from hitting bottom? Night,
> the sandfleas scissoring their feet,
> the sandbed cooling to concrete,
> one borrowed blanket, lights of cars
> shining down at them like stars? . . .
> Sand built the lost Atlantis . . . sand,
> Atlantic ocean, condoms, sand.

It now seems to be the mere alternation of hope and despair, of deep communication or insight and disillusionment ("hitting bottom" in looking into each others' eyes) that has finally made the lovers' vision exhausted and nihilistic. The whole setting now seems to offer organic and romantic, or inorganic and abrasive, feelings merely alternately: "sandfleas" are paired against "scissoring," "sandbed" against "concrete," "stars" against "cars." The answer to all the questions is the image of an Atlantis that does not sink cataclysmically, but fades as we perceive its real and only components: the ocean, the dead particulars of the world, our own superfluous sexuality. The "condoms" are important beyond their shock value, for they connect with the earlier references to "abortion" and childlessness, perhaps even with the theme of onanism in "Waking Early Sunday Morning"—all instances of sexuality kept from, or carried beyond, its natural end in man, and all somehow related to the unattainable paradisal vision.

The sense of mere alternation has been suggested earlier in the poem by the "severed radiance," the recurrent image of the neon light mechanically flickering on and off across the walls of the room. It is also analogous to the way in which alternative emotions, with no fully understandable causal connection between them, frame the development of "Waking Early Sunday Morning" and "Central Park." The depth-psychological source of these alternations is perhaps the manic-depressive experience, in which states of affirmation and negation follow each other in a predetermined pattern, more or less independent of objective causes. To make psychotic experience a general symbol of the vicissitudes of human contentment and sense of meaning is a deeply disturbing view—more disturbing perhaps than an unabashed nihilism. Yet, for the poet, after the labyrinthine reasonings and guilts he has gone through in his search for moments of clear responsibility, this insight brings a sense of freedom, however terrible the cost:

> Sleep, sleep. The ocean, grinding stones,
> can only speak the present tense;
> nothing will age, nothing will last,
> or take corruption from the past.
> A hand, your hand then! I'm afraid
> to touch the crisp hair on your head—
> Monster loved for what you are,
> till time, that buries us, lay bare.

In dispensing with the idea of meaningful, or at least knowable, causality, Lowell comes into a radically liberating sense of the unique reality—and therefore the innocence—of the present. If the moment cannot be explained by ideas of prior temporal structure (cycles, repetitions, processes of inevitable decay), it cannot be saved or corrupted by them either; and so existential acts retain their mysterious freedom. Analogously, if we realize that it is impossible to reveal oneself totally, or to know another person in terms of a truth or a category of moral judgment—that only death could be a complete laying-bare—then the fact of relationship takes on an absoluteness, a purity, it could have in no other way. Human beings are monsters, yet are—without self-deception—loved, and there is nothing more to be said.

This mystical acceptance of a paradox takes us back, appropriately, to the very beginning of "Waking Early Sunday Morning," where we saw a unity disintegrate through paradoxes. The reader might be justified in seeing some hope—or at least some transcendence of the pattern of accelerating diminutions and fragmentations—in the fact that where the initial unity was narcissistic, the final one takes the form of an acceptant marital gesture, offered in spite of fear. But it is interesting, too, how much the ethical values of this ending resemble those already offered, for the public realm, in "For the Union Dead": the distrust of abstract interpretations of the nature of reality; the acceptance of death and of the monstrous, in order to accept the present; the willingness to act in uncertainty, and to derive a tentative creativity from seemingly annihilating insights.

VI

The unity of *Near the Ocean*, the incremental repetition of themes and symbols, has been pointed out in context as far as was possible without losing the thread of explication. But it may be helpful, in conclusion, to reexamine some of the most important motifs singly, in the context of the entire poem.

The title of the poem expands in significance as the associations of the ocean do. On one level, the ocean is death, or devouring time, and the central consciousness of the poem feels close to that, certainly, in a number of senses. But the ocean is also the source of life and, symbolically, the life-impulse. We are near to it, in the poem, through the presence of intense creative and sexual energy, through the overriding image of the salmon's leap; but near also in the more dangerous, intellectual sense that modern science, and the poet's devastating intuitions, give us more knowledge and doubt about the nature of life than we are prepared to handle. Finally, the ocean may suggest a religious experience of liberation from, or dissolution of, the self in a total monistic unity, something like Freud's "oceanic feeling." Such experiences, in both their ecstatic and sinister aspects—both the "severed radiance" and the dark nirvana—come close at many points. The possibility of a total mystical experience vibrates through the opening and closing lines of the poem but is never completely realized; we remain "near," not in, the ocean.

We have seen how craftily water imagery is woven through the last poem, and the same is true elsewhere. The salmon's journey itself is a flight from water that ends in water, and still near the ocean; and the salmon cycle is neatly reversed in the last poem, where the protagonist feels the love impulse "inland" and then discovers its true limits in returning to the sea. Again, in "Waking Early Sunday Morning," the linking image gracefully juxtaposes such diverse elements as the "glass of water," the president's swimming pool, and the generals' "liquidations," and reinforces our sense of a "liquid" continuum of human energies.

Similar use is made of some less prominent symbols—for instance, the house as representative of a tradition or an attitude toward life. This is a dominant theme only in the formal house-poem "Fourth of July in Maine." But we note how, in the first poem, Lowell symbolizes his confessional material as "banished lumber," and compares it to the "Temple"; how he modulates into the New York scene through an "opposite house"; how houses (or their false analogues, apartments and theaters) appear in "Near the Ocean." [10]

The unifying power of the psychological themes derived from confession is similarly strong. We have already noted the use Lowell makes of the manic-depressive experience as a source for ideas of the patterned decay of energy and the final relativity of positive and negative attitudes toward life. An equally important theme is the psychoanalytic view of death, which we must consider briefly in the light of the theoretical background. The line of thought begins with Freud's *Beyond the Pleasure Principle*. Its argument, which I greatly oversimplify, is that man has a biological nirvana instinct which always seeks to move from

10. My view of the house theme is indebted to a 1968 Harvard honors thesis by Michael Knapp, "Form and Freedom in Robert Lowell's *Near the Ocean*."

tension or activity to rest, and which consequently, especially under conditions of life where tension is inescapable, ultimately desires death. Freud views this instinct as strong enough to play a dynamic role in masochism and to be converted outward into sadism, just as sexual sadistic feelings, converted inward, become masochism.

Freud's *Civilization and Its Discontents* and Marcuse's *Eros and Civilization* develop the implication that the tensions of advancing civilization must aggrandize the death instinct, a conclusion Lowell approached by a different route in "Beyond the Alps." Norman Brown's unique contribution, in *Life Against Death*, is his analysis of the fear of death (which, again, I greatly oversimplify). He contends that sexual repression prevents man from ever feeling fully alive in the moment, and makes him project fulfillment into the future or some form of immortality; hence, man must in turn repress his Freudian desire to die, which is thereby encouraged to take a concealed aggressive form. I have mentioned Brown's application of this doctrine to industrial societies in connection with "Central Park."

Lowell has possessed these themes, intuitively, from the beginning, and I bring in the theoretical background as a help to understanding rather than as an allegation of source. In "Memories of West Street and Lepke," Lowell shows us a professional murderer at first utterly terrorized by the prospect of his own death, and then unconsciously converting that very terror into a form of love. But in *Near the Ocean* these themes become more dominant, more complex, as we can see by reexamining the opening stanzas. There the poet, under conditions of sexual inhibition and guilt, becomes terrified of the idea that his energy is self-consuming and seeks to die; the result is the transmutation of the aroused energy into two forms, one outwardly aggressive (the dragon image), the other self-lacerating (the impulse expressed in the vermin stanza).

Throughout the poems, we see more or less dehumanized people, usually of the American ruling class or sharing in its ideology (the generals, the president, the policeman fingering his gun, the "Pharaohs") seeking some kind of self-expression or sexual satisfaction through the giving or receiving of death. The last poem deals with murderous feelings in sex and marriage, and the "abortion" theme relates them to civilized deflections of natural eroticism. Even the very last line of the poem can be read as stating the perverse equation of perfect sexual experience and death; though, as I have argued, at this point in the poem Lowell has substantially turned from this mystique toward what Brown conceives of as an opposite, life-serving mysticism, the liberation from time through total immersion in the present. Lowell states this attitude in traditional religious terms earlier:

> "Every time I take a breath,
> my God you are the air I breathe."

Finally, we might consider *Near the Ocean*'s character as a long poem, in relation to the tradition, or traditions, of the personal epic. It has often seemed to me that critics too easily posit a single mainstream of the American long poem, where in fact there are at least two very distinct currents. One is the "open" tradition of Ezra Pound's *Cantos*, the longer works of the Black Mountain School poets, and (with some important reservations) William Carlos Williams's *Paterson* and John Berryman's *Dream Songs*. These poems tend to be very long, and to begin and end casually, almost arbitrarily; except in the case of Berryman, the subordinate units are also long, have no fixed meter, and could almost never be presented as separate lyrics. These poems can contain large sections of almost novelistic exposition and narrative; they tend to develop by loose but openly displayed links, and to make comparatively slight use of hidden symbolic networks. The author's presentation of himself is expansive and many-sided; his intelligence and observation, as well as his imagination, contribute to his authority.

This is the tradition of the personal epic that has received the most theoretical attention and, in general, the most praise in the past fifteen years—a fact that may help to explain the neglect of *Near the Ocean*. (Incredibly, many of the volume's hostile reviewers failed even to notice that it contained a long poem.) But there is another tradition: that of Eliot's longer poems, especially *The*

Waste Land; of Hart Crane's *The Bridge*; Berryman's *Homage to Mistress Bradstreet*; and (with reservations) *Life Studies*. These poems tend to start from intense inward experience, to base their authority on the poet's imagination and symbol-making power rather than his secular self, and to incorporate the larger, public realm by epiphany rather than direct narrative. They center on a few subjectively crucial experiences and fall into short, but distinct and concentrated, lyrical units. Fixed forms and their variation or alternation, symbols and their cumulative associations, are very important to structure, which tends to be subtler and more interesting in and of itself than in the looser form. (None of these remarks, however, is intended to elevate one form over the other, but merely to point out that they have different virtues and powers, springing, ultimately, from a different sense of the important relations between the self and the world.)

Near the Ocean seems to me the one major poem of the last ten years to be written in the second tradition, the concentrated and lyrical sequence. Of all its predecessors, it seems closest to *The Bridge*. Like Crane, Lowell is concerned with the myth of America, the American Eden, and associates it, through his symbols, with an inward religious experience, pantheistic and perhaps (in the tradition of Whitman) pan-sexual, a vision of energy existing in intense harmony. Like Crane, too, Lowell is obsessed with the decline of America, and seeks an explanation for it in the history of consciousness more than in external history: both writers accuse their country of being a mental "convert to old age." Here, perhaps, the thematic similarities end; but the sheer rhetorical energy of *Near the Ocean*, its combination of the bardic and the contemporary, place Lowell among Crane's most direct heirs. (I have wondered, only half-fancifully, if Lowell's use of Crane's central symbols, Brooklyn Bridge and Atlantis, in his concluding stanzas does not constitute an oblique kind of tribute.)

The tendency to dismiss *Near the Ocean* as "an afterbeat of . . . *For the Union Dead*," or some similar phrase, generally comes from critics close to Lowell's own age, who are strongly attached to the realistic vein of *Life Studies*.[11] Younger readers, I notice, often turn

11. The quotation comes from M. L. Rosenthal, *The New Poets*, p. 78.

to the later book with equal, or greater, excitement. I myself am convinced that a work at once so haunting and so enormously ambitious, so profound and so inventive in structure, cannot ultimately fail to be recognized as a major American poem.

6

The Two Walls and the Single Day

I

In Robert Lowell's career, all rising is by a winding stair. After his triumph with the concentrated form of the personal epic in *Near the Ocean* (and perhaps—who can tell?—partly because of its failure to gain wide critical recognition), Lowell immediately plunged into his own version of the enormous, open-ended, omnivorous form of Pound and Berryman. In the most basic sense, perhaps, *Notebook* is a continuation of *Near the Ocean*, for it springs from the same intense effort to fuse public and private visions, high and low styles. Stylistically, in fact, it generally continues the tendency to compression and sonority in the line, with an added synaesthetic richness that looks back toward *Lord Weary's Castle*, or toward Hart Crane. But in other ways, *Notebook* revives and extends the realism of *Life Studies*—in its constant use of anecdote, its wide-ranging yet casual intellectuality, its informal address. The prophetic edge to the voice is, once again, somewhat blunted, partly because of genuine changes of attitude, partly because of a concern for the detailed complexity of living encouraged by the genre itself.

Lowell remains too much of a formalist to choose the most open and unregulated possibilities of the personal epic; his strongest single influence seems to be Berryman's compromise. Like Berryman, he chooses a short, unvarying, traditionally metrical unit, the unrhymed sonnet, which is also intended to suggest a journal entry, as the title implies. This sonnet sequence/diary compromise has both liberating and limiting effects on the possible content of the poem. To begin with the disadvantages, the diary model leads to the partial waste of what might be, in a more objectified narrative, great set pieces: the Chicago Convention, or, to take a private example, the climbing of the volcano in the "Mexico" episode. Also, it encourages the tendency to referential writing, to deadpan catalogs of the factual detritus of history and everyday life, which has long been the Achilles' heel of Lowell's usually invulnerable sense of proportion, of the artistic need to prune and to dramatize. Finally (though this is probably true of all more or less "open" long poems written with deliberate haste), it exposes us to many of the less interesting sides of the poet: his mere opinionatedness, his involvement in the perishable controversies and mannerisms of literary New York, his fondness for bizarrely allusive—and also, oddly, for tenth-grade sexual—humor.

To turn to the advantages, the diary model is almost wholly responsible for the extraordinary freedom and spontaneity of the poem. It permits wildly subjective leaps from topic to topic, and it frees Lowell, in the individual "entries," from Aristotelian expectations of beginning-middle-and-end (or else allows him to redefine them on an amazingly subtle basis). It makes for a perfectly natural-sounding telegraphic style, which helps enormously in the transformation of anecdote into poetry, and also tends to blur the conventional distinction between "rhetorical" and "conversational" writing. Indeed, its greatest advantage, after freedom of subject, is freedom of style. The poet, ostensibly conversing with himself, can modulate within a single line from generalities to the densest introspection, from slang to stately archaism, creating a veritable kaleidoscope of human uses of language. (The blank verse line, having accommodated both the grandest and the plainest writing in English, is a lucky choice in this regard.)

Notebook absorbs a vast amount of Lowell's earlier work into itself, through allusion, parody, or actual repackaging into sonnets. It is equally omnivorous of other people's words: a *Sources and Analogues of Robert Lowell's Notebook* would have to have entries like "Peter Taylor's mother's favorite joke," as well as a literary range from Sappho to Ginsberg. The result is an enormously complex verbal medium that constantly brings together mutually relevant moods and dictions usually kept apart by literary decorum. It is a kind of poetic equivalent of Brecht's dramatic "alienation"; or perhaps one might call it a new definition of Eliot's unified sensibility. In any case, the effect is one of richness and maturity—though any reader will probably object, at times, that an intrusion cuts short greater poetry or thought than it introduces, or that a hybrid style is neither one thing nor the other without quite making up a third. I, for instance, find the last lines of the otherwise superb poem to T. S. Eliot, "Ah, Tom, one muse, one music, had one the luck— / lost in the dark night of the brilliant talkers, / humor and honor from the everlasting dross!" a bit embarrassing in their combination of *East Coker* echoes, early Lowell clottedness, and something very like the impersonal yet keyed-up style of the *New York Review*. (This coterie language plays a larger role in *Notebook* than in Lowell's previous writing, but is rendered less offensive than it might be by the book's verbal omnivorousness, and the thematic concern with the moral possibilities of different kinds of language that has marked all personal epics influenced by Pound.)

Perhaps the most strikingly new quality of Lowell's language is its "surrealism"—a term that Lowell's practice defines much more precisely than his vague "Afterthought" does.[1] Lowell's surrealism is the opposite of much dream- or fantasy-based art (the painting of Dali or De Chirico, for instance), which tends to de-realize experience by artful exclusions, reducing us to the simple relation of a very few sensations, each of them permeated with its symbolic value. Such art often regains in atmospheric unity what it loses in logic, and leaves us with an odd sense of lucidity, even of rest. Lowell's surrealistic poems turn, rather, to the unruliness of the moment, showing us how many separate strands of sensation it contains, how weirdly the mind shuttles

1. Robert Lowell, *Notebook 1967–68* (New York: Farrar, Straus and Giroux, 1969), p. 159. In the 1970 *Notebook*, the term is (unhelpfully, it seems to me) changed to the merely negative "unrealism."

between them and its own equally abrupt and mysterious patterns of fantasy-thought. Lowell struggles, in short, to overcome a monistic fastidiousness that is all but essential to the descriptive process, whether its conventions are realist or surrealist; and to deliver the feeling, if not the literal contents, of a basic mind-flux.

I do not mean to imply that Lowell wishes merely to describe without ordering; rather, he extends the definition of poetic order to meet the new demands of his material. Hart Crane's poems are difficult because he insisted on a "logic of metaphor" of which linear logic is only one dimension; Lowell goes one step further by legitimizing mixed metaphor, allowing metaphor its own inner freedom in the added dimension of time. A rudimentary example of this would be the sudden mingling of idioms or catchwords conventionally unrelated: "the path to death was always under-foot." A more complicated transformation occurs in these lines from "Long Summer":

> Humble in victory, chivalrous in defeat,
> almost, almost. . . . I bow and watch the ashes
> blush, crash, reflect: an age less privileged,
> burdened with its nobles, serfs and Faith.

The verbs *blush, crash, reflect* literally describe the fire, but their figurative meanings fall into an independent pattern under the pressure of Lowell's preoccupation with pride and humility: they wittily sum up the fall of a statesman, and so project the poet (without any intervening explanation) into a meditation on history. We can best see the full possibilities and originality of this method in a complete poem—for instance, the magnificent opening section of "Long Summer."

> At dawn, the crisp goodbye of friends; at night,
> enemies reunited, who tread, unmoving,
> like circus poodles dancing on a ball—
> something inhuman always rising on us,
> punching you with embraces, holding out
> a hesitant hand, unbending as a broom;
> heaping the bright logs brighter, till we sweat

and shine as if anointed with hot oil;
straight alcohol, bright drops, dime-size and silver. . . .
Each day more poignantly resolved to stay,
each day more brutal, oracular and rooted,
dehydrated, and smiling in the fire,
unbandaging his tender, blood-baked foot,
hurt when he kicked aside the last dead bottle.

One notices how the marvelous image of the poodles on the ball persists, giving the "something inhuman . . . rising" a pungently witty specification which counteracts any sense of a question-begging irrationalism, then giving a comic and desperate logic to the harshly visualized marital gestures that follow. Or one sees how the image of the broom (probably suggested by the metaphorical sense of "woodenness") leads to an identification of the people with the firewood, and then to a deeper, more mysterious analogy between human and vegetative existence in the line "each day more brutal, oracular, and rooted." Strangest of all is the almost hallucinatory sweat-oil-alcohol-coins sequence. But even here, one feels a savage analytical power at work: the anointing oil defining a familiar megalomania, the next line suggesting how, in the relationship, effort and suffering (sweat) have become first an intoxication and then, rather demeaningly, an acknowledged and exploited medium of exchange. (I must stress, though, how little I feel this moral reading exhausts the magical, medieval world these lines open.)

Grammatical ambiguities, too, contribute to the sense of cinematic montage, the indefinite boundary between metaphor and scene. The ambiguity in lines 10 to 12, where "each day" can be either modifier or subject, renders the subject of "unbandaging" in line 13 uncertain in turn: it can be "each day," or perhaps the "we" of line seven; or the clause may be taken as intentionally dangling. Consequently, one has the choice of taking the last two lines as part of the extended fire metaphor (as "blood-baked" suggests) or as an independent flash of real action. This in itself underlines the theme of the poem, the refusal of reality and the emotions to stand still, to submit to the frames of predictable interpretation within which they are tolerable, even when unpleasant, for us. (Indeed, the third person pronoun in the last lines ought to warn us that the action, in fact, is immediately being turned to fiction in its uses. A remarkable fact about the poem is its ingenious avoidance of "I," suggesting that identity becomes elusive when emotion is this tumultuous, and when one honestly recognizes the extent of the mind's mystifying stratagems.)

This new treatment of the flux of consciousness entails a new attitude toward the crucial theme of insanity. We have already noticed how Lowell's attitude changes from *Life Studies* to *Near the Ocean*. The *Life Studies* speaker's control and irony exactly mirror the psychoanalytic patient's desire for self-liberation through unmercifully objective self-scrutiny. In the succeeding books, Lowell's attention turns from the observably compulsive behavior pattern, the "hackneyed speech," to the inward experience of madness, including its secretly cherished joys. "What use is my sense of humor?" gives way to "O to break loose." Now, paradoxically (or perhaps not so paradoxically), at the very moment that the poet can hesitantly regard himself as *mens sana in corpore sano,* his capacity to record the irrational has taken an enormous leap forward, and his attitude has become much more complex. Where in *Life Studies* we essentially heard the poet's sane self telling us about his mad self, we now hear both (or perhaps many) selves, and are even allowed to share in an honest doubt as to which is which. A sense of humor (albeit a dark one) is in constant demand. "Long Summer 3" is a good example of this humor, and of the extremely complicated feelings—dread of self, dread of others, anarchic superiority, joy—that lie behind it.

> yet even on the steadiest day, dead noon,
> the sun stockstill like Joshua's in midfield,
> I have to brace my hand against a wall
> to keep myself from swaying—swaying wall,
> straightjacket, hypodermic, helmeted
> doctors, one crowd, white-smocked, in panic, hit,
> stop, bury the runner on the cleated field.

Religion, as well as psychosis, appears differently in the new medium. In *Near the Ocean*, as we saw, ecstasy and the "oceanic feeling" reentered Lowell's poetry, virtually for the first time since his Catholic period. But some pressure—perhaps simply the pressure of a strong ethical voice, bound to speak from belief— kept these elements outside of the poems, just before the beginning, just after the end, sensed rather than described. In *Notebook* this is no longer the case. The suspension of judgment permits a purely phenomenological approach; ecstasies, flashes, moments half out of time, even knowledge of God and the hereafter, "occur," in Wallace Stevens's phrase, "as they occur." Belief and analysis are, at best, secondary activities, even where the Deity is concerned; and this alone, perhaps, permits the Deity to be concerned. I shall return to the element of mysticism in detail later, for it seems to me to have subtle but important effects on Lowell's sense of himself, his personal morality, and his whole relation to the tragedy of history.

It would be easy to devote a long chapter, if not a book, to the aesthetic of *Notebook*. One might, then, consider the interaction of different kinds of language in the poem on a much more concrete level; one might follow a phrase, image, or anecdote from its initial context through all of its often disjointed recurrences, and observe its deepening, or accumulation, of meaning. Even more important would be a consideration of what concepts of total form are binding in the poem, how (or if) they influence what initially appear to be eccentric treatments of particular episodes. I am constrained by the limits of my project to forego this attempt, and to concentrate, rather, on the reappearance and development of the major public themes from Lowell's earlier poetry.

This approach will doubtless lead to some overemphasis on political poems; it will also, necessarily, emphasize isolable passages at the expense of interweavings. In a certain sense, to do so risks ignoring all that probably most interested the poet in writing this type of poem. On the other hand, I myself feel that the isolable poems are often the most central and moving ones—the non-isolable being, usually, not the more surrealistic or inward so much as the more jaggedly factual and allusive. It is my hope that this chapter, while remaining thematic, may be a partial guide to the centers of gravity of *Notebook*, and to poems worthy of being ranked with the masterpieces of Lowell's earlier career.

II

In spite of isolated passages more denunciatory than any in *Near the Ocean*, the general political tone of *Notebook* is gentler, sadder and more resigned, harder to categorize as "conservative" or "radical." Once again, this can be understood, at least partly, in terms of the temper of the times. 1968—with the assassinations, the police brutality, the steamroller operations by which machine politicians prevented any candidate opposed to the war from reaching the electorate—was a terrible year for the Left, a terrible lesson in the intransigence of Realpolitik, the "incestuous, complacent, inveterate evil" of Lowell's early work.[2] Unless a poet had the faith of Blake, or was willing to accept the remoter goals, the rationed sympathies and scruples of the realistic radical, the likely result was a return to a tragic sense—not, perhaps, the conservative tragic sense that says all revolt is negative, all violent will evil, but a deep recognition of fact, force, and human inertia.

Yet, for once at least, we must credit Lowell with prophesying rather than following history. For nearly half of *Notebook* was written before the tragic events of 1968, much even before the beginning of Senator McCarthy's campaign; yet the whole book belongs to our time, with its bitter sense of suppressed, unrelievable conflicts, and not to previous *élans* of reform or revolution. It takes no verbal or metrical pleasure in its own anger, and prefers to describe, not heroic or grotesque personalities, but massive buildings, impersonal procedures, moments of boredom, weakness, and realistic fear—even in the sonnets on the Pentagon March, for Norman Mailer and many others the climax of the white magic of the 1960s.

Yet, though the times are undoubtedly relevant, we must be careful of the tendency to assume ideological change in an author,

2. Jarrell, p. 192.

when we are in fact seeing something that has always been there suddenly brought into focus by a purely artistic transformation. Lowell's freer, more self-acceptant self-presentation in *Notebook* liberates him from the need to tailor each book into the expression of one consistent stance: the painful motive-searching, the almost paralytic liberalism of *For the Union Dead*; the angry, but not quite revolutionary, New Left position of *Near the Ocean*. Rather, Lowell allows his impulse or fantasy of the moment, whether radical or reactionary, to work itself out to its conclusion, not without internal irony, but without any externally imposed judgment. Lowell will acknowledge the strange distance and nonresponsibility toward one's own opinions that this method entails: "It's like 'going along for the ride'—you're not really driving, the ride itself is driving." [3] His justification would be the universality and irreducibility of the conflicts of value he finds within himself; as he says in the preface to *Prometheus Bound*, "These confusions . . . are irreconcilable with reason only if one wants to translate the old myth into marching orders." [4]

Aesthetically, this method has the same advantages and disadvantages as in the private poems. In following the poet's thought faithfully, it must often admit hackneyed opinions, expressed in editorial-speak ("arms given the people are always used against the people"), on the same terms as brilliantly original ones (a Leftist leader described as having a "Machiavellian Utopia of pure nerve"). The method's great advantage is that it enables Lowell to write about his politics as a partly irrational psychic event, set in its total context of generational and class experience, and of inner symbolic dramas. This, Lowell has always done to some extent—but the *Notebook* framework, and the suspension of the taboo against opinions he feels but may not consider "right," expand the possibilities enormously and produce some remarkable poems that could not be found in any of Lowell's earlier books.

It is probable that, if one approached this random mass of

3. The remark was made in conversation.
4. Robert Lowell, *Prometheus Bound*, p. vi.

political impulses statistically, one would find a numerical majority of conservative statements—nostalgia for the past, sympathy for the rich and the old, and for men of passive integrity, distrust of rebels—over radical ones. This does not necessarily mean that the book really does take a consistent position, or that it really is conservative, in comparison with the earlier books. Lowell has said, "Emotionally I am in sympathy with the 'Revolution,' intellectually I am doubtful that it would really make anything better." [5] One obvious deduction from this statement is that Lowell's radical side is likely to be found in the feelings animating the poems, while his conservative side would have the advantage when he is consciously being analytic, presenting an opinion. The fantasy previously quoted, from "Long Summer 3," of the mad poet as a football runner almost eluding the "helmeted doctors" provides a ready example. The clear desire for some act of total defiance, the vision of malice and panic behind society's most seemingly benevolent efforts to make the individual conform, betray an anarchism that remains a functioning part of Lowell's political self, whether or not it wins the approval of his theoretical intellect.

It is not my intention, however, to offer any inclusive tabulation of Lowell's individual statements on a Right-to-Left scale. It will be more interesting and useful, I think, to construct from the poems a portrait of Lowell's own radical and conservative selves, and then to turn to the poems—in particular, those dealing with the Columbia uprising—in which they come into direct conflict with each other.

An expression of Lowell's impulse to "break loose" in more direct connection with revolutionary politics is found in "Che Guevara." The poem is curiously divided between a detached, moralistic commentary on Che's career, and a sublicit identification of the poet with the revolutionary. The abstract judgment is, as one might expect, mixed. Lowell issues pacifist disclaimers of Che's sphere of action ("violence cracking on violence"), but grows more vehement in his revulsion at Che's murder: "then

5. In conversation.

gangstered down / for gold, for justice"—this, too, a pacifist disclaimer (of justice as a "higher" motive for killing), but also a suggestion that gold *is* justice for the Bolivian government and its CIA backers. Both societies, Bolivia and the U.S.A., are implicitly compared to the "oak [that] branch-lopped / to go on living, swells with goiters like a fruit-tree." The energy embodied in "the last armed prophet" is, Lowell recognizes, a necessary and life-giving one; the society that must destroy it in order to survive is already inwardly dying.

The identification of poet and revolutionary is made subliminally early in the poem: the phrase "held prisoner one lost day" has an incongruous "lost weekend" overtone which, in retrospect, seems to allude to the poet's "illicit" date in Central Park, another poignant moment briefly snatched back from the tyranny of society. Later in the poem, the poet's enemies and the revolutionary's are joined in a single symbol, the "sides" of the fashionable "high white stone buildings" that "overshadow" Central Park and its poor. These are Che's real killers, at least from a Marxist perspective; for the poet, they represent the world of surface respectability to which he will return, from which he perhaps fears detection and publicity.

The poem culminates in a kind of love/death moment, in which the poet seems completely identified with Che; in his own desires, the martyrdom, the transcendence-in-loss, and the "rest" of death find their counterparts.

> our clasped, illicit hands
> pulse, stop the bloodstream as if it hit rock . . .
> Rest for the outlaw . . . kings once hid in oaks,
> with prices on their heads, and watched for game.

The last line-and-a-half must be taken as an ironic qualification, since it refers to King Charles I.[6] Perhaps Lowell is actually

6. I considered an alternative reading: that Che Guevara is in fact being glorified, as the only figure of "king"-like stature in the world of the poem. The conferring of metaphorical royalty on a loser rather than a winner, to indicate his superior *virtu*, is a device that I have heard Lowell analyze, admiringly, in the

warning the reader that he is, after all, less Che Guevara than
Charles Stuart, less Marxist ascetic than blue-blooded libertine;
that his very sympathy for Che may be simply the pastoral game
of such a libertine—or simply a manic enthusiasm for both—and
all—dreams of power. These are devastating admissions; yet they
do not do away with our sense of the poet's real suffering in a
"branch-lopped" society, of his unlived potentiality for a "prophecy" as categorical and active as Che's, a potentiality which he
criticizes, but nonetheless regrets.

Given Lowell's perpetual concern with the intertwinings of
politics and sex, this direct emotional equation of sexual activity
with revolution demands more than a moralistic dismissal. It
comes up frequently in *Notebook*: in "Charles River 8," for
instance, the poet again treats his love affair as a direct defiance of
his too-regular surroundings, the cement freeways and cement-
block dormitories of Cambridge. If this impulse were carried to its
logical conclusions, we might see the emergence of a novel
Lowellian role: the Lawrencean sexual radical, calling for a
return to the body, its consciousness and its joy, with the faith that
this is the really necessary precondition for healthy social
relations.

In fact, Lowell does assume this role, for one joyous and
vehement moment, in "Wind," a poem about Paolo and Fran-
cesca. He assails "the folly of Christendom that loathed her flesh,"
and envisions instead a pagan utopia:

> seed winds, the youthful breath of the old world,
> when each progression of our carnal pleasure
> was a firm extension of the soul

Sexual mysticism is an important element in the world of *Notebook*,
to which we will return later; it can, perhaps, be considered an
important extension of Lowell's "radical" side. But the impulse
specifically under discussion here has a less healthy aspect, of

---

ballad of Sir Patrick Spens; and he employs it himself in "The Death of Count
Roland." But the fact that the king, here, is specifically Charles I, and that he is
mainly concerned with "game," led me to reject this interpretation.

which Lowell seems quite aware. In the "Charles River" poem, as in "Che Guevara," revolutionary feelings are only really satisfied in sexual intimacy when they alter the nature of that intimacy, infecting it with military fantasies:

> awake and naked, like a line of Greeks
> facing a second line of Greeks—like them,
> willing to enter the battle, and not come out . . .
> morning's useful traffic . . . the unbroken snore.

This is a kind of inversion of the usual idea of sublimation: sex is overburdened by being the sole expression of many social frustrations and angers. The tremendous amount of introjected violence, against the self and the beloved, which is present here if one takes the metaphor seriously, testifies to the unhealthiness of the situation; it suggests, again, that rebellion is a legitimate need of Lowell's creative individuality, and that the stillbirth of the Che Guevara in him was a source, as well as a prevention, of evils.[7]

However the balance may fall out intellectually, Lowell is certainly no more tender toward his emotionally conservative side than toward his emotionally radical side. At several points, he provides snapshots of himself satiric enough to please his worst detractors. There is Lowell the one-man literary Establishment:

> We say, "Everyone accepts our claim to greatness,
> our best photographers dare not retouch us.

7. From a Freudian point of view, the "Charles River" sequence is perhaps the central poem about the triple conjunction of sex, rebellion against authority, and insurmountable guilt in Lowell's mind. In the middle three sections, Lowell recounts how his father attempted to frustrate his first romance, on grounds of propriety, writing to the girl's father "that he knew / you'd been coming to my college rooms alone." Lowell confronted his father with the letter, then knocked him down in the living room of their home. That the act, for Lowell, amounted to parricide is made clear by the reference to his early poem "Rebellion," and by the concluding lines:

> I struck my father; later my apology
> hardly scratched the surface of his invisible
> coronary . . . never to be effaced.

If blood doesn't spurt from our eyelashes, when we meet
a work of art, it isn't art"

["Trunks"]

Lowell the poetic archaist, seen through the eyes of Allen
Ginsberg:

> Six skulls, the best minds of my generation,
> coiffure as out of style as what we write;
> six hands on the dusty bust of the microphone:
> "Read us your great collage, or something old,
> since nothing dead is alien to our tongue."

["Grave Guild"]

Lowell the paterfamilias and "male chauvinist":

> "But you and Harriet are perhaps like countries
> not yet ripe for self-determination."

["Outlivers"]

Finally, there is a Lowell gradually more deeply "reached" by
material good, more critical of the bad style of idealism:

> book-ladders on brass rods and rollers touch the sky—
> in middle age, the good costs less and less . . .
> Who can deduct these years? Become a student,
> graced with rebellion, hair and the caw of Shelley,
> his hectic hopes, his tremulous success,
> the ignominious and bitter death?

["The Golden Middle"]

"Here," Lowell concludes, a little defensively, Shelley himself
would have turned "with the tread of an ox to serve the rich."

Sometimes, it must be said, attitudes like the above emerge in
the poems without saving irony on the author's part. Particularly
often, Lowell is patronizing toward the young, and too ready to
see the least competitiveness or criticism directed toward their
elders as Oedipal murder—which is surely no truer than the
contrary belief that all adults are Kronos. Even in chivalrous

friendship, it is not fair to say that the young people who were bothered by Senator McCarthy's failure to be as passionate as themselves in his own cause were "coldly willing / to smash the ball past those who bought the park." (Isn't the park in question an old one? Aren't several distinguished American losers, and winners, wronged in this hasty disposition of the property rights?)

But in general Lowell does not (except in self-mockery) become complacent about such attitudes because they are appropriate to his age; still less does he consider them the wisdom of experience. Rather, there is often an intense and disquieted inquiry into the personal meaning of fame, position, and wealth; the latter subject is more prominent here than in any of Lowell's books since *Life Studies*.

Probably wealth has a constant appeal to the hypersensitive person for whom it is even a possibility. He feels that by "buying solitude," buying out of the pushiness, discomfort, and subjection to others' judgments that afflict him more painfully than most people, he will free his straitened internal economy for generosity, creativity, and inner ease—for the creation of an ideal self. Or perhaps the wealth itself seems sufficient compensation for inner inadequacies—even a kind of ontological confirmation. In practice, these hopes are seldom fulfilled. The difficulties are inner, and the individual must become more painfully aware of this fact when they persist in spite of increased comforts; he may come to feel social guilt as well.

In consequence, the comforts become narcotics that must be taken in higher and higher doses to provide the illusion of self-escape. Some such idea is summed up, for Lowell, in his refrain "the rich poor"; paradoxically, the rich are brought face to face with an essential human poverty which the poor are spared by the particularity of their struggles.

Fame, position, or even conventionality can serve some of the same psychological functions as wealth: a shield, a compensation for other sufferings, a hopeful condition of growth. Thus, Lowell understands Coleridge's lapse into conservatism as a result of his weakness and melancholia, his need to spend his forces as "passive courage" and endurance in a personal and metaphysical impasse which he was, in fact, not capable of growing beyond.

> For our passive courage, paralysis
> that held us upright like tenpins to face the strike—
> Coleridge's laudanum and brandy,
> his alderman's stroll to positive negation—
> his large plant with pith within, not heart of wood,
> power without strength, an involuntary impostor.

The result is that outer and inner selves become more and more distinct, and far from curing each other, drive each other to irreversible extremes: the hard alderman and the visionary, but now completely inarticulate, pessimist. "An involuntary impostor," Coleridge is less hypocrite than schizophrenic.

The same might be said of many of the conservative figures Lowell views sympathetically: his Thomas More, able to do evil actively but good only passively, "ready / to turn from executioner to martyr." One notes how easily Lowell slides to Coleridge from "us," that characteristic "us" that means everything from the editorial "we," to a specific milieu or clique in New York, to a kind of Platonic aristocracy of the baffled and the humane. In fact, Lowell applies much the same analysis to himself as to Coleridge, in one of the poems where his radical and conservative selves confront each other most directly. "Petit Bourgeois" describes an (apparently real) dream; but its title and its place in a section on the murder of Martin Luther King suggest a political interpretation, which can in fact be elaborated almost schematically, though with no illusion of exhausting the unconscious dimension of the symbols.

In the dream, the poet's apartment sanctum has been invaded, ambiguously, by toughs or by militant revolutionaries: "Our floor ganged, liberated." [8] But suddenly, the figure of youth metamor-

---

8. Professor Irvin Ehrenpreis objects to my political reading here, on the grounds that the boy is clearly a "jock," hence likely to be politically conservative and opposed to student uprisings. I would argue, in response, that the image of the young tyrannicide in Lowell's poetry is consistently athletic, blond, short-haired or

phoses from the attacker to a kind of savior:

> hand over hand on the one knotted rope, the boy,
> a cool crew haircut, tans above the ledge,
> smiling at me to mount his shoulders, swing
> down fifty tiers of windows, two city blocks,
> on that frail thread, that singed and swinging rope.

The description that follows is sardonically metaphorical:

> our building from here, a tapered, swaying rope,
> fat head and narrow base, Louis Philippe's
> face mirrored pear-shaped in a silver spoon.

The building clearly represents wealth and ruling-class privilege, the fat-headed, narcissistic other face conferred on the poet along with the "silver spoon." The poet would like to get down from this bad, and dangerous, eminence, down to the relative innocence of the afflicted masses; but the descent, too, is dangerous—indeed traumatic. The image of descent along a rope (which undergoes a nightmare multiplication when the building itself turns into a rope) is, at least arguably, a Freudian symbol of birth. Richard Tillinghast has suggested that the line "Crawling through fallen houses of his Troy" in "Between the Porch and the Altar" has this meaning; here, too, we have not only a burning house, but the image of an older man escaping on a young man's shoulder, which brings to mind Anchises and Aeneas.[9]

In the light of these associations, the command *"You must go down the rope to save your life"* has almost the force of the biblical injunction to be born again. But, Lowell says,

> long ago, this was answered by hallucination:
> if forced to walk to safety on a tightrope,
> if my life swung on my will and skill . . . better to die.

---

clean-shaven—from his mother's Siegfried, to Perseus and David in "Florence," to the "depilated stripling" in "Alcohol, 2." The substitution of an obviously archetypal figure for reality seems to me well within the logic of dreams; and the word *liberated* indisputably establishes a contemporary radical context.

9. Richard Tillinghast has argued (in conversation) that the fall of Troy is associated with a birth trauma throughout Lowell's work, and in Allen Tate's "Aeneas at Washington" as well.

It becomes, then, a question of the existential fear of freedom. To pass through such a transformation, one must depend on nothing but oneself, one's "will and skill"; one must, as Sartre would have it, create oneself gratuitously, ex nihilo, and this is the ultimate source of fear. (The fact that there is only one person in the hallucination-within-the-dream, where before there were two, suggests that the two, the man and the boy, are both really Lowell—the Old and New Man, the conservative and radical selves—in deadlock.)

The poem has a rather savage final twist:

> The crowds in the street were cheering, when we refused.

The line suggests Mussolini, or any tyrant, addressing crowds from a balcony; the psychological implication is that the great refusal, the passive martyrdom, can itself be merely an inverted form of the old desire for total power, for an intoxicating egocentricity. The passive conservative, like the tyrant, expresses the perfection of his own will in a closed, histrionic system rather than cast himself into the open territory of free choice, where right and wrong cannot be fully determined in advance.

In this poem, Lowell expresses a deep distrust of some of the motives for his conservatism—the fear of rebirth and of existential solitude, the attraction of the martyr's painful but guiltless power. The analysis applies not only to himself but to a generational mood of self-righteous defeatism, as we see when Lowell turns from the comfortable "we" voice to the castigation of old liberals, part of the "we" in its New York sense, who have turned into New Left-haters. In "The New York Intellectual," Lowell attacks such a writer for constructing a martyr image of himself while claiming to do nothing of the kind:

> 'without fantasies of martyrdom,'
> facing the graves of the New York Intellectuals,
> 'without joy, but neither with dismay' . . .

As seen through Lowell's satire, the writer has, like Coleridge, hardened into a set of gestures divorced from any authentic perception. Like his disclaimers of martyrdom, his moral "tact," tough-mindedness, and objectivity really exist only as intended effects of style; he himself is "the great brazen rhetorician serpent, / swimming the current" of national backlash. Lowell's exposure of this writer is unusually unkind, but it is perhaps as much a self-testing as a denunciation. After all, Lowell shares, and would not renounce, at least some of the doubts that have turned the writer against revolution and revolutionaries; but "Petit Bourgeois" shows clearly enough his fear that failure to advance beyond this passive stance, or at least to avoid becoming complacent about it, will turn him, too, into "an involuntary impostor." Only the most passionate self-criticism, if that, will countervail.

This conflict, and this mutual distrust of motives, between the two sides of Lowell's temperament, become dramatic when he is the direct observer of political upheaval, as he was during the uprising at Columbia University in May, 1968. The four poems dedicated to the event show, as one might expect, great vacillation, an almost mathematical pairing-off of attacks on Leftists with attacks on administrators, of revolutionary flashes of vision with conservative *sententiae*. The first poem, "The Pacification of Columbia," is the most important, and the most puzzling. Its first lines suggest Lowell's imaginative response to the kind of "revolution" the students envision.

> Patches of tan and blood-warm rooftile, azure:
> an old jigsawpuzzle Mosque of Omar flung
> to vaultless consummation and blue consumption,
> exhalation of the desert sand to fire.

The image of the jigsaw puzzle might represent both Lowell's mind, trying to understand an experience he views from the outside and with ambivalence, and the students' minds, trying to construct a revolutionary program out of their half-accidental gestures and confrontations. What half-emerges is the idea of visionary revolution at its most inclusive and serious, as preached by Blake and Shelley, by the Surrealists, and (perhaps) by the

Lowell of *Lord Weary's Castle*. This vision postulates a world formalized to the point of atomism and universal sterility ("desert sand"), suddenly transformed into a creative anarchy, taking on such flexible shapes as flow spontaneously from human warmth and imagination—an anarchy unvaryingly symbolized as "fire." The transformation is never held to proceed from institutional changes alone, but from a release of religious ("Mosque") and erotic ("Omar," "consummation") feelings. (Islam, it should be observed, fascinates Lowell throughout *Notebook*, because it is a non-ascetic religion whose vision of eternity is closely connected to unrestricted sexual fulfillment, at least for the male believer.) The Surrealists' slogan, "Prenez vos désirs pour la réalité," was explicitly revived in the French students' rebellion, and was latent in the mood of the American one, with its striking departures from traditional Marxist style and tactics. But Lowell's sympathetic understanding of this fact is mixed, even here, with the predictable doubts: this "consummation" may seem infinite only because it is incomplete ("vaultless"); such extreme longing for imaginary change may be a form of disease as well as of mysticism (the double sense of "consumption").

The real "message" of the scene, Lowell senses, is "one the puzzle never sent." It is the grim fact that "no destructive element" (a phrase coined by witch-hunting administrators to refer to students and "outside agitators" but probably applied ironically, here, to the police brutality as well) is likely to upset the institutional order of Columbia—or America—for very long. Nothing "emaciates" Columbia; the word is significant, for it looks back to "consummation" and "consumption," and forward to opposing images of inertial weight:

> the thickened buildings look like buildings out
> of Raphael, colossal classic, dungeon feudal

This is that same "kingdom of necessity," of "complacent, inveterate evil," that Jarrell saw in the earlier Lowell.[10] Its particular incarnation suggests the staging of Lowell's *Prometheus*

10. Jarrell, pp. 188, 192.

Bound at Yale, in which the rock was replaced by a fortress wall of mixed classical and medieval style, an atemporal Platonic form of oppression. Such order cannot change when put into question; it can only "thicken," become more harshly, unintelligently itself. The police horses ("higher artistic types than their grooms") and "Broadway's median trees" pathetically recall the cosmos of visionary revolution: "as if / nature were liberated . . .". If the police "meet and reason together," as the university was frequently accused of being unable to do, it is perhaps because such manipulative reason is satisfying only to pawns; what Lowell's symbols have revealed is an absolute and spiritual, or, as Blake would have put it, an Intellectual War.

One should not leave unmentioned the outstanding tonal characteristic of the poem—its constant, almost precious, allusiveness to art objects and artistic types. Perhaps this points, a little mockingly, to Lowell's remoteness as an observer, as, in literal fact, an artist seeking material; on the other hand, as the poem deepens with rereading, it seems to betray the Blakean belief that art is innately revolutionary, innately critical of the false solidities of the oppressor.

"The Pacification of Columbia" is, in the balance, unhopefully but sincerely sympathetic to the Left. The succeeding poems qualify this sympathy without wholly withdrawing it. "Can a Plucked Bird Live?" is a pacifist statement in response to a revolutionary glorification of action and "guns." Carefully balancing regal and revolutionary examples, and including Trotsky for good measure, Lowell argues that force always betrays those who trust it absolutely. His title refutes Tom Paine's criticism of Burke's pity for Marie Antoinette, in terms of the organic implications of Paine's own metaphor. These considerations lead Lowell toward a self-righteous quietism ("arms in the hands of the people are criminal"), but one which he partially retracts in the concluding lines:

> the only guns that will not kill the owner
> are forged by raised hands . . . fear made wise by anger.

This nice definition of wisdom leaves Lowell somewhere between the liberal, led by his fears to the lesser evil and a vote for Humphrey, and the pathologically fearless "Left adventurist," such a figure as the third poem portrays.

This revolutionary embodies all that Lowell fears in the new style of activism, whose artistic side he admired in the first poem. The man's whole character is summed up, for Lowell, in the phrase "Machiavellian Utopia of pure nerve." He is so caught up and existentially defined, for himself, in each moment of unflinching defiance, that he seems to need no further goal. He shows an obscenely open relish for martyrdom ("the predestined poignance of his murder"). A reference to Heidelberg duelling practices suggests that one of his motives is adolescent *machismo*. Words like *electric* and *plastic* serve to make him very much part of the age he condemns. There is something McLuhanish (for Lowell, obviously, repellently so) about his dependence on "nerve" rather than "sense" for his values, and on the "low current whir" in his voice for his rapport with his audience. Lowell reveals, here, the age-old conservative fear of communal ("mob") feelings.

But if the poem ends as violent satire, it begins in a much more ambiguous mode. It claims to be written from the point of view of "love" (whether Christian love, or a remaining personal affection is not said).

> Love will not bind it to his blind ambition,
>   or blinder courage (both sowed their dirty germs)
>   or some ostracizing glandular imbalance

In a line, Lowell has slid from love to the rhetoric of loathing, of depersonalization, as practiced by the self-proclaimedly normal Right—"dirty germs," "glandular imbalance"—a rhetoric, ironically, that he has sometimes had directed against himself. Does he mean to insist that ambition and courage may be pathological? Or is he being ironic, suggesting an element of crude hatred in himself—or else a bond with the satiric target that lessens his right to judge? The issue is not resolved, since Lowell quickly opts for a more "loving" and less reductive ground of judgment. The revolutionary, he feels, has surrendered his humanity and intelligence to his role—he has "closed his eyes." But, Lowell adds, he has done so because he has seen a "miracle"—presumably his experience, in "the [Civil Rights] demonstrations," of creating revolutionary hope by his own suffering in the face of realistically overwhelming power. This "miracle" has given him a "flesh of wood." Lowell quickly changes the metaphor from wood to plastic, but the two non-humanities are not the same—the first suggests medieval carvings of the saints, or of Christ. By these tortuous hesitations, Lowell sets off the destructive cogency of his satire; he makes us notice his own aggressiveness in dubious relation to his "love," his unresolved feelings about political sainthood in the abstract.

When "Leader of the Left" is followed by an equally personal satire on Columbia University's "old king," the balance is clearly intentional; the sequence becomes an ideological chiasmus. The poem springs from the celebrated remarks of the university president and the police sergeant on reentering the presidential chambers after the Bust:

> He halts at woman-things that can't be his,
> he says, "To think that human beings did this!"
> The sergeant picks up a defiled *White Goddess*, or is it
> *Secret Memoirs of the Courts of Europe*?
> "Would a human beings do this things to these book?"

The president's indignation is reduced to sexual prudery, the sergeant's, to a class hatred that, under other circumstances, might be overtly anti-intellectual. Beneath the slapstick, however, lies a more serious and abstract concern with the relation between order and "human" being. The president's blind and total identification of the two is fascist; while the students' disorder, though fraught with "malice," has much in common with the disorder in which the creative mind often thrives, finding, perhaps, an image of its own openness and dissatisfaction. The president's study under the students' regime is, Lowell says, "much like mine left in my hands a month." (The same point is made, more subtly, by the unrespectable titles of the books whose mutilation shocks the sergeant.) Even the "malice," as Lowell reconstructs it, strikingly resembles his own sense of humor, teasing and darkly just: "all the unopened letters have been answered." This destructiveness is symbol and theater, not violence; and we do not lose sight of the fact that real personal violence has been perpetrated by those who self-righteously blur this distinction.

In his own satire, Lowell comes back to his initial sympathetic identification with the artistic quality of the student rebellion. With this, the sequence has come full circle, and it gets no further resolution, though some of the following poems—"The New York Intellectual," a poem on De Gaulle, and one on the young Lowell's flamboyant commitment to a conservative aesthetic— provide additional perspective on Lowell's ambivalence. One would not really expect any absolute resolution, at this stage in Lowell's career; indeed, if the political poems in *Notebook* have one salient fault, it is the tone of weariness that creeps into them as Lowell again and again trots out the non-solutions that are his solutions. What is new is Lowell's willingness to enact his inner conflict within his poetry, to commit himself to defining the kind of revolution that he can still—at least in imagination—desire, and then the kind of scruples that would still hold him back. In the context of so many more automatic rhetorics, this becomes a moral as well as an aesthetic virtue; though it leads to no active commitment, it dramatizes inward qualities—"fear made wise by anger"—that, one feels, still hold out to Lowell the possibility of valid public response.

III

Apart from specific political stances, *Notebook* continues Lowell's examination of the effects of civilization, especially late-industrial civilization, on man's deepest psychic life. "Civilization" (from the "May" sequence) is the baldest statement yet in Lowell's work of the Freudian ground-theme: that an irreducible conflict exists between civilization and the instinctual life.[11] The immediate

11. In treating "Civilization" and "Sounds in the Night," contrary to my usual practice, I use the text of the first printing. The later versions are perhaps

occasion is sexual: a rather vulgarly dressed girl is, it appears, making up to the famous poet, who clearly enjoys both the temptation and the homage. But his impulse is in conflict with his standards—aesthetic, perhaps, even more than moral—and he lets us know this through a closely observed catalog of the girl's physical blemishes, in which, I think, one can detect a certain amount of sadism, of self-contempt turned outward. The conflicts —the imperfect compatibility of the aesthetic and the sensual, the feeling that a "lowering" sexual experience is especially exciting yet somehow to be atoned for—are classic enough, and fittingly lead to theoretical reflections:

> Civilization will always outrun life,
> its toleration means to bear and ache,
> hurt, hate oneself, as no one wants to twice.

Toleration is an odd word in this context, but it suggests that ambiguously polite ground of relationships in which the poet can neither "do it in the road" nor burn the girl as a witch to relieve his feelings. Such toleration has the effect of turning all impulses inward, to vent their energy destructively upon the self. Hence— again the old, inexorable insight—the neurotic desire to die: "no one wants to twice."

In other words, civilization first makes energy aggressive through frustration; then, by its "decent" overt morality, makes the only object available the self, which can conveniently be tormented in the very act of self-restraint. The "Liberal . . . sucks his own blood to bare his icy tooth." Hence there are no real "Liberals"—the situation is simply too sad and contradictory to be borne. (Lowell's own liberalism, constantly veering for emotional release to the wealthy-conservative and to the revolutionary, would probably bear witness.) In contrast to the liberal's life is some absolutely primordial experience: "if the god Eros arcs into the Virgin." This seems at once to be a perfect sexual experience and an epochal religious event. One thinks vaguely of

---

smoother, but, to my mind, the earliest ones capture psychological nuances missing in the others.

Yeats's *Vision*, Leda and the Great Year. Because this event can take place "once a moon," one also thinks of werewolves, the return to animality in its most frightening form (but which Yeats, as it happens, took as a symbol of transmogrification in the other direction, toward divinity).

This basic realm of archetypes, both animal and divine, frightens not only the liberal but "the worst bastard"; not even in evil can man escape, or wholly unite with, his archetypes. The maddening experience with the girl is in some ways analogous to this fright; it makes Lowell bear—also meaning, perhaps, give birth to—himself as a civilized man. (This scorn of the possibility of ever really getting back to the primordial ecstasy occurs elsewhere. In one poem, Lowell writes sardonically:

> It makes men larger to sleep with the sublime,
> the Magna Mater *had*, shivers under oak, moon, cloud.
> Such cures the bygone Reichian prophets swore to . . .

In another, he quotes Milton against the paradisiac claims of hippies: "Gardens, how far from Eden fallen, though / still fair!" But, as we shall see, he is not so ready to exclude the possibility from his own life.)

Notebook is Lowell's New York book par excellence, and nowhere in his work is the symbiotic relationship of the civilized psyche and the mechanized environment more insisted upon. A phrase from "Charles River," "the blood of the spirit lost in veins of brickdust," expresses the two crucial aspects of the relationship: the enervation, or loss of contact with the bodily self, involved in sublimation, and the sense of almost organic closeness to the non-human that arises from it. The two poems that frame "Civilization" in the original edition develop the theme. The ending of "Sounds in the Night" sets up a contrast between "man" and "the body of his work"—as if the "work" had almost taken the place of the half-forgotten "body," providing the erotic and ontological reassurances that originally came from physical well-being alone. Made cynical by the cross-purposes of civilized friendships, Lowell finds an outlet and perverse paradigm ("if any love is") of affection in the constancy and unvariance of machine sounds heard in the night. His absurd declaration of longing ("Each night, I drink their love") reverberates from his earlier dreams of an all-inclusive, oral paradise. But the real object of thirst is inward vitality itself: the "cat in heat," which, though "dungeoned" like the Columbia rebels by the monolithic thing-world, seems to say in its cry,

> 'Who cares if the running stream is sometimes stopped?
> Inexhaustible the springs from which I flow.'

The cat is "conservative" in the most ultimate sense: it does not change because its desires have never required projection beyond the limits of the body. Yet, in another meaning of the word, it knows perfectly well how to conserve itself, while man's accelerating history breeds a "prehistory."

In "The Diamond Cutters" the theme, civilized man's loss of his feelings to his objects, is carried over into a new sphere, money and value. Since "the Ur-kings' bank-account," the absurd yet unchanging choices, a certain metal, a certain stone, have swayed the largest of human issues: "loss of empire for a grain of dust." I think inevitably of Norman O. Brown, who devotes many pages of *Life Against Death* to explaining this and other economic arbitrarinesses psychoanalytically. What Lowell perceives is, if not exactly Brown's sublimated anality, some perverse human love for qualities as opposed as possible to finite flesh—an "essence, rare and hard and bright." "Herman Melville would have had the meaning" of this, presumably because of his fascination with ambiguous absolutisms. But he is a most ironic example, since the power of money ("dust") tore him from the sea he loved to the "grit" of New York—the "grit," or pure waste, civilization always creates side by side with "essence." But Lowell presses on to a further meaning, a violence implicit in the creation of value:

> no one can avoid the thoughts of man:
> mason's chisel on the throat of a stone . . .

The impulse to shape and perfect now appears murderous, an outlet for innate human aggressiveness. This is partly explained, no doubt, by the extreme denial of Melvillean "cousin"-ship involved in the assumption that man perfects nature (we are back, in a sense, to the terms of *Lord Weary's Castle*). Transformed nature becomes both man's victim and his object of self-abasing adoration—the sadomasochist paradigm extended to cosmic proportions. The poem ends on an extremely strange note:

> We were boulevarding out the time till lunch;
> the conversation was inaudible to You,
> eye brighter than the uncut sun at noon.

Who is the capitalized "You"? Various answers are possible: God; the diamond; or perhaps some loved "essence" quality in Lowell's friend, inaccessible to "conversation" yet supernally "bright" (a reading involving extrapolation, which is perhaps suggested to me by Lowell's tendency to admire a violent spiritedness in women). But all these meanings coalesce in the sense of a fearful adoration, one that bypasses, and seemingly transcends, the natural and earthly: the eye outshines the sun. The sun plays the same role in this poem as the cat does in "Sounds in the Night," though more emphatically, being the literal source of life. But the idea that it can be "cut" (by the edges of New York skyscrapers) like a diamond again suggests an apocalyptic issue of human alienation and destructiveness.

This analysis of urban consciousness extends ideas present in Lowell's work since "For the Union Dead." But the theme of the city, in *Notebook*, undergoes not only an intellectual elaboration, but a qualitative change in tone, in the manner of envisioning. Buildings are seen as characterless, as pure geometric forms (a strange development in a poet normally infatuated with the grotesquely particular). Or, if particularized, they seem excessive in some way, oversized, over-weighty, overdone to the point of caricature in style (like Columbia's "thickened" buildings "out of Raphael"). In "Che Guevara," the monosyllabic line "sides of the high white stone buildings" is really an anti-description, forcing the reader to see blocks and monoliths rather than individuated structures. In the immediately following poem, "Caracas I," the image recurs: "jerry skyscraper living-slabs." The mental simplification now goes to the point of turning a complex structure into a single stone, and carries a clear human message—that the inhabitants' lives must be a living death. Moving on to a description of the Venezuelan "White House," we encounter "petrified" guards, who are carefully not described as individuals, but whose weapons are described with technical exactness: arabic numerals leap up from the pages like buckshot. After a brief portrait of El Presidente, a minor Mussolini full of sexual braggadocio, the poem ends on yet another petrifaction image:

> This house, this pioneer democracy, built
> on foundations, not of rock, but blood as hard as rock.

The ideas here are familiar from earlier Lowell: that brutality is justified by being made to appear impersonally scientific; that power cements itself by making its misdeeds both enormous and habitual. But here there is a difference in degree, a banal perfection which suggests the process really is autonomous and irreversible. The underlying metaphor of the poem seems to be cancer; the idea of disorderly, rapid growth unites with that of deathly simplification of the units: "another of our cities without a center, as hideous / as Los Angeles."

In "The March," these symptoms are appropriately brought home to the seat of American power. Here the sense of excess, both in size and style, particularly predominates:

> Under the too white marmoreal Lincoln Memorial,
> the too tall marmoreal Washington Obelisk,
> gazing into the too long reflecting pool,
> the reddish trees, the withering autumn sky

The atmosphere is made even more unreal by the sense of duplication: Washington Monument paired off with Lincoln Memorial, both redoubled in the reflecting pool—the nearly endless replications another version of centerlessness. The effect is heightened, as a friend who heard the poem without having read it observed, by an auditory pun on *too* and *two*. Doubtless, this imagery is partly intended to suggest the narcissism of imperial America, screening out all reality that does not mirror its power and glory. But it also reflects darkly on the peace marchers, suggesting that they themselves are shadows or mirror-images; as they issue "remorseless, amplified harangues," the message of their medium seems stronger than that of their individual consciences. They are, in all too fundamental a sense, playing the Establishment's game. Like Norman Mailer, Lowell seems to place more faith in weapons of gaiety and improvisation, subliminal Civil War memories, but his final sense of the occasion seems to be of an (in its moral implications) appalling unreality. In the culminating scene of violence,

> An MP sergeant kept
> repeating, "March slowly through them. Don't even brush
> anyone sitting down." They tiptoed through us
> in single file, and then their second wave
> trampled us flat and back.

How innocent the scene of concealed intimidation in "The Opposite House" seems when one has read this! There is an almost schizophrenic de-realization of the action and its victims here, in the gratuitous parody of nonviolence, the ritual of not-touching; so that, mild as the actual violence is, we feel that, for a moment, we breathe the air in which Nazi-style atrocities become possible.

The new style of envisioning in these political poems cannot be reduced merely to an allegorical continuation of the attack on America's mystification-*cum*-mechanization of a brutal foreign policy—though that is certainly involved. What is really at issue is the whole direction of civilization and "progress" that nurtures such politics—a seemingly irreversible process of abstraction away from biological life, sufficiently pervasive to begin to generate massive feelings of unreality, and to incline frustrated energy toward a violence more psychopathic than tyrannous. The poems in *Notebook* make us feel nature retreating before our eyes like a mirage—as if the human/inhuman forms of civilization had an active desire to outrun, coat over, bury it, and so become themselves the all-inclusive reality. Two quotations from "Charles River" will illustrate what I mean:

> Roads on three levels parallel the river,
> roads pace the river in a losing struggle,

> forces of nature trying to breathe beneath
> the jacket of lava.
>
> No stars worth noticing; the lights of man
> lunge road and sky

But these forms, or tastes, are not only more destructive outwardly; they are the symptom, and the allegory, of an inward
deterioration. Our forms become less natural because our minds
become less natural, more bent on sublimation. But since nature
(including our own fleshly human nature) is the ultimate ground,
through metaphor, of all mental activity, any final flight from
nature can work only by a negative method, the denudation of
particular (recognizable) properties, an approach to pure mathematics. If this is in fact our collective neurotic project, it is small
wonder that it has so vastly accelerated the removal of natural
objects from the literal landscape. In "Long Summer 13" Lowell
relies on these connections to create a twentieth-century *Dies Irae*:

> stream of heady, terrified poured stone,
> suburban highway, rural superhighway,
> sprig of skunkweed, mast of scrub . . . the rich poor . . .

The building of a highway becomes the Dance of Death, in a
surrealistic montage of devastating suggestiveness. For, according
to Brown's extension of Freud's theories, we attempt to flee our
fate by thus making the universe more and more familiar; but in
doing so, we release a death and inertia as present within
ourselves as stone in flowing cement. Paradoxically, we think we
are trying to reimmerse ourselves in nature, in vitality; but we
decimate nature in the process, thus proving our inward altera-
tion, our inability to see farther into nature than a roadside.

The deathliness of modern "life-styles" provides another grim
parable in one of the finest of the *Notebook* poems, "Those Older,"
in which the replacement of a forest by a subdivision stands for
the change in an aging man's mind as his familar world becomes
more a part of death than of life:

> and even this dead timber is bulldozed rootless,
> and we face faceless lines of white frame houses,

> sanded, stranded, undarkened by shade or shutter—
> rich and poor . . . no trees in the sky—their stones
> so close they melt to a field of snow, if we pass,
> won from the least desire to have what is.

All these motifs and concerns seem to culminate in "Two Walls." This poem, written a few days after the assassination of Martin Luther King, is probably the emotional nadir of the book. Not even the Chicago convention seems to have produced in Lowell such feelings of exhaustion and dead end—and with them a "visionary dreariness," to quote Wordsworth, strong enough to arouse and disturb preconceived notions of the poetic in readers who would have thought they had none.

> Somewhere a white wall faces a white wall,
> one wakes the other, the other wakes the first,
> each burning in the other's borrowed splendor—
> the walls, once woken, are forced to go on talking,
> their color looks much alike, two shadings of white,
> each living in the shadow of the other.
> How fine these distinctions when we cannot choose!
> Don Giovanni must have drawn sword on such an avenger,
> two contracting, white stone walls—their pursuit
> of happiness and his, coincident . . .
> At this point of civilization, this point of the world,
> the only satisfactory companion we
> can imagine is death—this morning, skin lumping in my throat,
> I lie here, heavily breathing, the soul of New York.

The walls are the Platonic form of the buildings and objects I have discussed: characterless, mirroring, scarcely real; a human world that excludes nature totally, an artifact world that abandons human presence and use. Unlike its antecedents, this vision floats alarmingly free of locale or context; even symbolic meanings are elusive, though they are there. Nowhere has Lowell's New Critical training in the value of any slight suggestion, when controlled by a rigorous logic, served him to better purpose. We may suspect that this evasion is practiced to disquiet us, as the image itself does—offering another kind of solipsism, where we are trained to expect only fruitful relation.

Under this caveat, we proceed to symbolic readings. A political one suggests itself, because of the date and the conspicuous quotation from the Declaration of Independence, but is otherwise hard to prove specifically. Presumably, Lowell admired Dr. King, and fears that the assassination will harden all sides in America, and in particular will make the black and revolutionary side more merciless, more like their adversaries in morality and tactics. (This use of the mirroring image is familiar from all liberal critiques of revolution.) America is thus a Don Giovanni (how Hart Crane would have relished that comparison, in isolation!) who arrogantly sets in motion the machine of poetic justice that will destroy him. What follows then is easy to remember: the sword is drawn and proves totally useless; and, before Don Giovanni plummets to eternal damnation, there is the overwhelming image of his unbreakable handclasp with the man of stone, a union as cold and absolute as that of the walls themselves. (In this whole political context, it need hardly be pointed out that the connotations of *white*—skin color, ideological purity, deathliness—are staggering multipliers of irony.)

As one first enters into the poem, however, there is little hint of a political meaning. Rather, the first external context that suggests itself to the reader is probably marriage: the figure of the two walls "waking" each other. Later, there is much else to remind us of the view of marriage in "Near the Ocean" and "Long Summer": bored people "forced to go on talking" by *horror vacui;* a combat in which the roles of aggressor and victim, of autonomous individual and of parasite or suppressed "shadow," have become entangled beyond any hope of clarification. The paradox of "burning in . . . borrowed splendor" yet "living in the shadow" suggests another context, that of literary friendships and influences, of a writer's struggles and fame. This context, too, seems to be a constricting one, yet inescapable except through illusion; writing, like marriage, is a lesson in the nonexistence of pure identity or sincerity. (Lowell, in *Notebook*, quite characteristically mingles motives of literary politics with those that seem spiritual or sublime; see, for instance, *"The Literary Life, A Scrapbook."* Those who think this excessively worldly might recall that William Blake often wrote in the same spirit.) Beyond the strictly literary, these overtones are also surely intended to characterize New York intellectual milieus; the combination of battles over "fine distinctions" with helplessness is very fitting, especially where politics is concerned.

Yet important as these suggested contexts are, they are not encompassing; rather, they all seem to lead us toward metaphysical concerns—with the idea of "distinction" itself, with the Self and the Other, with the generally dualistic frameworks of Western thought. Put as philosophy, the argument might run thus: all definition, whether of the self or anything else, is relative (i.e. by relation). But if there are only the Two, and they never merge in the One, then all relation goes in a circle; real choice becomes impossible, and identities and values have no basis except in an infinite regression. In the poem, one notices, lines 2, 3, and 6 are all paradoxes that attack the notion of causality or priority. A dualism, or system of contraries, is thus not (as for Blake or Hegel or Marx) a condition of growth, but a nihilism. The Two do merge, in the revelation of their common emptiness that results from the increasing fineness of their "talking"—the same talking that gives them the illusion of separate existence. This, Lowell's implication of real contexts suggests, is the ultimate lesson to be gained from all existential encounters. It is also, presumably, the lesson of politics; since Lowell's political myth is of an unfructifying dialectic between authority and rebellion, in which he himself cannot choose sides, and, as he tries to prove by psychoanalytic ideas, nobody can with complete sincerity.

The conclusion of the thought seems to be, "the only satisfactory companion we / can imagine is death." Why should this be so? Perhaps it is because all other companionships reduce (using this word in both a logical and a moral sense) in the way shown above; perhaps because death alone remains a pure opposite, an unknown quantity. "Death / keeps our respect by keeping at a distance," as Lowell put it in the first version of "Long Summer 12." In facing death, one recovers the pure identity in pure

opposition that all life-relationships seem to take away. The
thought here reminds one of Heidegger more than of Freud or
Marcuse. But Lowell remains in touch with the latter by giving
his despair a historical setting: "this morning" he, or it, is "the
soul of New York." The reducing dialectic, however abstractly it
can be conceived, has happened in one way or another in history;
our civilization is the "talking" and thinking that have, "at this
point," restricted the soul to death as an object of love. And our
civilization's outward forms express this, in their simplification—
the weariness of particular relations, the desire for absolute ones
alone.

At one point in the poem Lowell seems to criticize, rather than
merely to describe, philosophical dualism itself. In lines 9–10, the
pronouns *their* and *his* make a distinction between "Don Giovanni" and the "two walls" of which we first thought he was,
symbolically, one. Thus there is a hint of a primary identity that
dooms itself by dividing into warring opposites—such opposites as
id and superego, will and fate (both of which might be suggested
by the plot of the opera), or even the self and the other. If Don
Giovanni is intended to represent America (or "civilization"), we
arrive at a more specific cultural criticism—of habits of mind that
tend to distinguish rather than unify, of a too purely active and
manipulative definition of the ego. But a larger, presumably
mystical, concept of selfhood does not enter into the poem, except
for the hint that it might exist.

In this poem, Lowell finds an ultimate image for the emptying,
the increasing formal purity and arbitrariness of modern life, its
perhaps final turning away from the animality that comforted, a
little, even in the "giant finned cars" of "For the Union Dead."
To convey these new sensations of alienness, Lowell ventures into
the categories of existentialist philosophy—but always, it seems to
me, by way of description, not of explanation. The existential self,
so constantly occupied in rarefied proofs of its own existence, is
perhaps too much a logical extension of old problems of the
Western ego to replace the psychoanalytic, or even the mystical,
self in Lowell's thought. In some ways, the familiar analogy of
civilization and mental illness is a more deeply useful tool.

In discussing the politics of "Florence," I invoked R. D. Laing's concept of "petrifaction" as a psychic weapon against outside forces. This concept has an obverse form, which corresponds very closely to Lowell's notion of an emptying world. According to Laing, the entry into a schizophrenic state often involves a willful self-deadening, an increasing rarefaction and internalization of all self-world relations, a withdrawal of affect from, and consequent formalization of, all external behavior. The initial purpose is the total protection of the inward self from all external dangers; the ultimate result is often that the sense of self disappears entirely, leaving only explosive fragments of fabricated selves and dis-owned impulses.[12] If for Laing's inward self one substitutes Lowell's "blood of the spirit," for his outward or false self "the veins of brickdust," one sees that the change in Lowell's view of civilization from "For the Union Dead" to *Notebook* resembles the change from a schizoid to a schizophrenic condition. A half-delib-erate numbing of the consciousness of man's biological-human nature gives way to monolithic eruptions of the purely not-human.

But as impulse, as well as the false self, breaks from the schizophrenic in dissociated forms, so the spiral of emptiness has its own mirror-image, its second wall: the spiral of energy into ever grander, more rapid, more destructive forms, with which Lowell was so concerned in "Waking Early Sunday Morning." This theme has a more minor place in *Notebook*: nuclear war is seldom mentioned, and is once, somewhat facetiously, put forward as the better alternative ("La Condition humaine"). For Lowell, as for the rest of us, the day is past when the Bomb seemed the one unthinkable possibility in an otherwise normal world. But the more general concept, or myth, recurs when Lowell treats of evolution: the beauty and terror of its acceleration and exfolia-tion; the fear that the process may be self-consuming by nature, the civilized perversity only a particular instance.

> the virus crawling on its belly like a blot,
> a hairbreadth an aeon, lives of love-in-death,

12. See R. D. Laing, *The Divided Self*, particularly chapter 9.

Venusberg in Venus fly-trap; to the tyrannosaur,
first carnivore to stand on its own feet,
to the Piltdown Man, first carnivore to laugh;
to the raised hand of Hitler, clenched fist of Stalin—
heaven descending from the hand of man.
But was there some shining, grasping hand to guide
me when I breathed through gills, and walked on fins
through Eden, plucking the law of retribution from the tree?
Did the Lord wish to enjoy the desolation?
Was the snake in the garden, an agent provocateur?

Lowell's adaptation of *Prometheus Bound*, written immediately
before *Notebook*, contains some of the clearest statements of his
myths as myths (I regret that my self-limitation to poetry prevents
a more lengthy illustration). At a climactic point in the action,
Prometheus foresees two apocalyptic possibilities, emerging without warning out of the normal cycles of power and rebellion, and
closely resembling the two spirals I have discussed.

I could settle for a succession of gods, each a little stronger
and more intelligent than the last. Small loss to us, and some
solace . . . All's shining, all stays in motion, the pace keeps
rising. Why rising though? Suppose the pace were to slow.
No one has ever seen bottom through this life-giving blank.
No one will step across the last line of space, or walk back
through the atoms and microbes to time's beginning. Think
of life cooling. No, I think of fire. Fire will be the first
absolute power, and the last to rule. Then the trivial order of
the gods, that scratch on space, will crackle. Zeus will then
be a small flame trickling and dying out among a million
dying flames, that were once alive, were life.[13]

One of Prometheus's fears is the autonomy of the accelerating,
organizing energy which, when limited, is the will-to-power
(Zeus), but is also life. His other fear, "life cooling," suggests
many now familiar forms of rigidification, simplification, and loss

13. Lowell, *Prometheus Bound*, pp. 55–56.

of feeling, including the existential man's illusion of "seeing bottom" through the "life-giving blank" of apparent meanings. (In a sense, these tendencies are embodied in the play's antagonists, the immobile Prometheus, soul of his world as Lowell is the "soul of New York," and the ceaselessly active Zeus.)

To conceive of these equal and opposite dangers is to imply that life is a balance and flow; and that the life of the spirit, or of society, might well obey an analogous law. This biological metaphor might thus provide a kind of ultimate rationale for Lowell's radical-conservative politics, as more simply derived ideas of balance have for similar thinkers. Lowell would never make a slogan of this metaphor—too many similar ones have been used in bad faith—yet one can see it operating all the more powerfully as an intuitive ground of judgment (for instance, in his conflicting reactions to the Columbia uprising). The judgments are seldom, as with the metaphor's misusers, wholly predictable: who else would consider Che Guevara too rocklike, or make a lady painter's chic conversation so convincing an embodiment of the dance? But the applications of the biological metaphor are more often tragic than affirmative. What concerns Lowell is the fact that the two elements go out of balance and pursue separate perfections in the face of more difficult conditions of life, far more readily than they grow in connection with each other to a new balance.

In this whole matter, one is again struck by the resemblance of Lowell's mind to the later Freud's; for when Freud set out to give his Thanatos and Eros metaphysical definitions, he arrived at exactly such terms as pattern and flow, the simplicity of separateness and the high-energy activity of connection.

But the reader may already have noticed how closely these categories, heat and cold, the rising or slowing pace, correspond to Lowell's description of manic and depressive states in himself. This fact is so implicated in the whole manner of envisioning, that to avoid mentioning it would be a wasteful tact. Further, we would be overlooking a crucial, enabling factor in the grand project of Lowell's later poetry, the broadening of subject from self and family to political life, to the "whole enterprise of civilization": the analogy between the disorders of the private psyche and those of societies.[14] (Again, as often in thinking about Lowell, I am reminded of Yeats who, at a similar point of crisis in his career, turned to a private and disreputable "given"—his spirit-messages—to provide the total organizing pattern his public self had been unable to forge.)

Life Studies gives us the basic paradigm, most explicitly at the end of "Memories of West Street and Lepke." Since madness is often a response to—indeed, as R. D. Laing has noted, a symbolic rebellion against—what is most unendurable in civilized life, madness may offer the metaphors to unlock the inward nature of civilization's contradictions and upheavals. In his succeeding studies of tyrants, Lowell draws the simplest, most easily comprehensible connection between madness and public life. Then, in "For the Union Dead" and *Near the Ocean*, Lowell turns to classes and communities, groupings of ordinary and clinically healthy people, and finds them also responding en masse to social restraint and unpleasure by various combinations of self-deadening and "breaking loose." Finally, in *Notebook*, the manic-depressive split is applied to civilization itself as an entity, to describe its tendencies to inertia and expansion, and the process by which these tendencies become autonomous and uncontrollable until extremes of dead order and violence are reached. "At this point of the world," Lowell finds our civilization on the verge of passing into pure schizophrenia, the total loss of the sense of a central self able to include conflicting tendencies, through the increasing impoverishment and falsification of that sense of self.

These theoretical terms must sound heavy as well as dark, so jammed together; I can only refer the reader back to the poems for the wealth of cultural observations, of individual portraits, of painful and profound insights, that is organized and clarified by them. Nor is the picture quite so dark as it appears: for to describe man's ills as illness rather than essential nature, is to open, at least obliquely, the question of cure.

14. Cf. Richard Tillinghast, *An Introduction to Robert Lowell's Recent Poetry*, chap. 3, p. 4.

IV

Where, then, shall hope and fear their objects find? What is to be feared is, perhaps, clear enough; but given all that tends to make of *Notebook* a Vanity of Human Wishes, it is harder to account for the seemingly joyful and expansive energy that pushes Lowell through his catalogs and digressions, as if sufficient vagary were bound to fall over the edge into revelation.

We must return, later, to the purely aesthetic character of this joy, but in the meantime it is worth dwelling on three more tangible sources of positive feeling in *Notebook*: the endurance of the ego, comedy, and transcendent experience. The first is the most familiar from Lowell's earlier poetry; but it will be useful, here, to pause and consider its psychological basis. Even if mankind cannot bear very much reality, the ability of the ego to stand up under a shattering revelation without resorting to some form of denial or defense is always a source of paradoxical pleasure: the ego enjoys its own strength, its ability to affirm life. This fact always makes literary judgments based on "optimism" and "pessimism" somewhat paradoxical and two-edged: they may reveal the critic's defensiveness, as well as the writer's melancholy or masochism.

In Lowell's case, this triumph of the ego is particularly evident. His essay on Sylvia Plath, his statements in interviews, all reveal an unquestioned assumption that work and discipline are forces of life—among the deepest things that keep one going. Since his own work so often moves toward dark revelations, one can only assume that to acknowledge darkness and articulate it to its full measure of threat is for him a strengthening process. Indeed, one cannot read aloud the jaw-gritting finality, the Miltonic stationing, of last lines in *Life Studies* and *Near the Ocean* without feeling this sense of triumph. Yet it is precisely because the tight-jawed element is less in evidence in *Notebook* that I choose to dwell on the ego's self-affirmation here; it has become almost a comic theme, and allies itself with other forms of comedy. Strangely, this happens most visibly in the most important section treating a theme that has always given Lowell deepest cause for depression—history and its tragic recurrences.

The style in which "The Powerful" is written is extreme even
for *Notebook*. Jazzy, dirty, irrepressible, it draws all of the past
without reverence or hesitation into the slang and knowingness of
the present:

> Like Henry VIII, Mohammed got religion
> in the dangerous years, and smashed the celibates . . .

> Orestes knew that Trojan chivalry was shit.[15]

Indeed, any age is absorbed into the terms of any other with equal
alacrity: Mohammed preaches *schrecklichkeit*; Roland dies in "the
Franco-Moorish War." What is implied in this mannerism, the
sameness of all history, is outrightly stated elsewhere: "his speech
is only the one all kings make"; "there are wars and wars."
Analytic passages have a similarly breezy, shorthand assurance.
Omnivorous of sources of metaphor, they seem almost to prefer
the most incongruous: sociological jargon, for instance, or the
literary in-jokes that Lowell loves to turn into parables. Lowell's
Clytemnestra "at sixty worked in bed like Balzac"; and was killed
because

> Orestes, the lord of murder and proportion,
> saw the tips of her nipples had touched her toes—
> a population problem and bad art.

Beneath the manner of "The Powerful," the matter is Lowell's
oldest and most serious political themes, especially the psychosexual ones. The passage just quoted amounts to an anthropological
interpretation of the *Oresteia*: a matriarchal society changes to a
patriarchal one; sexual morality, intellectual art, and social
planning arrive; the sanctity of human life loses ground a bit.
Elsewhere, Mohammed's vision becomes a classic sublimation;
the army of the Duc de Nemours, on the other hand, derives its
morale from open, ritualized bestiality, and the general inference
is that all war is "sexual delirium." The old theme of the

---

15. This degree of daring seems to have disquieted Lowell himself. In the 1970
Notebook, he substitutes the quotation, " 'I saw her knees to tremble, I enjoyed the
sight.' "

psychopathic appeal of power, the crossing of the dividing-line beyond which impulse is an absolute unto itself, is also very prominent: Hitler, Tamerlane, Richard III. Indeed, Lowell seems to acknowledge its attraction more frankly than elsewhere:

> What does he [Richard III] care for Thomas More
>   and Shakespeare
> pointing fingers at his polio'd body;
> for the moment, he is king; he is the king
> shouting: it's better to have lived, than live.

History does not lose its grandeur or terror in the breeziness of these poems. The simply recorded deaths of Anne Boleyn and the Japanese Admiral Onishi are as human and harrowing as similar actions in Lowell's more solemn works. "The Death of Count Roland," despite "the Franco-Moorish war," rises to the level of its passages of direct translation from the *Chanson de Roland*; its movingly heroic ending, in which the imagery subtly elevates the dead Roland over the conquering king, probably derives from another pre-literary work, the ballad of Sir Patrick Spens.

Yet, in Lowell's jazzy linguistic medium, all of these elements undergo a sea-change, and come out more black humor than tragedy, or even than satire. If traditional language remains noble when it describes individual heroism, it becomes its own parody and corrective when it tries to explain the deeper causes of disaster: "King Marsiliun in Saragossa / does not love God." The thorough application of the psychosexual theme, once a joking tone replaces the usual Freudian solemnity, tends to place all history on the level of an exhibition act in a brothel. By the sexual emphasis, by the disrespectful familiarity of tone, by many forms of incongruity, the powerful are reduced to absurd or farcical types: a scaling-down that establishes their common humanity, and even makes us love them, but at an obvious cost to ideology and charisma. The incongruity involving time and the use of uniquely modern perspectives has been discussed above. But the deepest form of incongruity is internal, and arises from the method of the character-portraits themselves, the concentration on idiosyncratic, obsessional, parochial characteristics, the links established between them and grand actions. We get a sense of solipsistic attitudes toward life, at once aesthetically perfect and completely absurd—a sense we are used to associating with Elizabethan "humor" characters, nineteenth-century dandies, or twentieth-century protagonists of absurd drama, but seldom, until now, with political portraiture, which tends, at worst, to assume evil but reality-oriented motives. The purest type of such a portrait is Lowell's Attila:

> Attila mounted on raw meat and greens
> galloped to massacre in his single fieldmouse suit,
> he never entered a house that wasn't burning,
> could only sleep on horseback, sinking deep
> in his rural dream.

When Attila is subsequently compared with Hitler, the effect is both to make twentieth-century reactionaries' rural dreams equally grotesque and solipsistic and to make Hitler curiously, almost lovably, quaint. The same double effect, deflating and humanizing, is intended and gained by the repeated comparisons between the idiosyncrasies of artists and the crimes of the powerful: Balzac and Clytemnestra; Berkeley and Attila; Titian, St. Francis, and Charles V; Yeats and the Duc de Nemours.

Black comedy and the celebration of the ego are deeply intertwined in the aesthetic effect of "The Powerful." To mock and tease the tyrants and tyrannicides, the figures of Lowell's nightmare—to restate their lives in his own daytime language, and get a laugh by doing so—is surely to enact a partial liberation from them, to "awaken," as Stephen Dedalus wished, from history. To scale the powerful down to purely human size, without hatred, is a kind of revolution, one that does not run the risk of reifying its victim. Even the constant references to art and artists, however casual-sounding, are an invocation of the artist's original magical power over the thing he can name—and over the consciousness that his terms can explain better than its own can.

The last poem of the sequence, "New Year's 1968," audaciously furthers this idea by comparing Lowell's own manuscript to the Rosetta stone, the revealer of a hitherto inaccessible language.

"The Powerful" thus goes beyond the affirmation of the ego's ability to survive the contemplation of the worst in history— though this, too, is stressed in "New Year's 1968"—to a celebration of its own mental energy, the deep import of its own playfulness. Like the Columbia poems (but more successfully, since the question of action cannot be raised), it testifies implicitly to human resources of insight which the power-cycle as yet neither draws on nor understands.

Moments of transcendent or religious experience are frequent in *Notebook*, and are handled without the kinds of authorial dissociation (very indirect symbolic presentation, irony) familiar to us from Lowell's other post-Catholic poetry. Richard Tillinghast has remarked that Lowell's "experience of infinitude . . . though it is often generated erotically . . . is still essentially a religious one." [16] And, in fact, the most explicit and powerful expression of mystical feeling in *Notebook* comes in a love poem, "Mexico."

There are a number of reasons, besides the intensity of the love affair, why "Mexico" should be a central sequence. The movement south ("South of New England, south of Washington, / south of the South") is for Lowell, as it was for Lawrence and Crane, a powerful symbol for an inward journey from death to life, from the constraints of the civilized self to an encounter with the fundamental life-force. This movement is doubled by the sense of a movement backward in time, through the Toltec remains, the tropical flora and fauna, as if toward some Eden or primordial event. The sequence is immediately, and presumably intentionally, preceded by a group of poems about prehistory, about a hypothetical moment when "I . . . walked on fins through Eden." On another level, the unorthodox Catholic setting (a monastery deconsecrated for its "heretical" innovations and now used, it appears, for writers' conferences or retreats), and the girl's own Catholic background, both conspire to reopen, at least to memory and contemplation, the dead issue of Lowell's own experience with the leap of faith.

16. Richard Tillinghast, *An Introduction to Robert Lowell's Recent Poetry*, p. 35.

And yet, despite all this, and despite the initial tone of tender irony ("The difficulties, the impossibilities, / stand out"), one's strongest impression from the first two poems is of violence: an enormous resurgence of Lowell's old tendency to equate eroticism and aggression. Within thirty lines, the love affair has been compared to the Aztecs' human sacrifices, the story of Cain and Abel, and (of all unlikely events!) the battle of Killicrankie. It is tempting to fall back on a pathological explanation for this obsessively recurrent equation; but it is at least puzzling that these ideas return so strongly in a situation in which, by the standards of reality, the poet's treatment of his lover is more than usually devoted and altruistic. For whatever reason, stronger feelings, fuller recognition of the lover as a person, intensify rather than allay the sense of violence. Without endeavoring to psychoanalyze the poet further, I would suggest that the violence here is at least partly metaphorical. Being an extreme and final human act, it can serve as an analogy for the most extreme: the exercise of Sartrian lonely freedom, the commitment made for its own sake against all the considerations—social approval, pragmatic reason, the future—which (Sartre would say) we value so much partly because they shelter us from the realization that we finally act alone. This feeling, the exaltation and terror of knowing one has only to choose, is clear in the two beautiful lines that precede the unlikely Killicrankie reference:

> Stand still, you'll feel the sureness, the delirium,
> rank and file certain of smashing the enemy . . .

In the beginning, this terrifying freedom rests more heavily on the girl ("you, God help you, must will each breath you take"); the poet knows how to act in such situations by "reflex and the ways of the world." But he, too, as he becomes wholly committed, realizes he cannot predict or control the consequences (internal, if not external) of the affair on his life, his compromises, his relationships. Violence is associated with the inclusiveness of the changes that can be wrought by love; Lowell says of the Toltecs,

> when they took a city, they too murdered everything:
> man, woman and child, down to the pigs and dogs.

But once the existential commitment is made, on both parts, violence seems purged from the experience and the poem; between sections 4 and 12, there is only a single violent reference.

Violence is associated in the first poem, not only with the idea of commitment, but with the idea of time, the poignant finiteness of the moments together if the relationship is to remain temporary:

> we two are clocks, and only count in time;
> the hand's knife-edge is pressed against the future.

Such a situation will make the present seem unusually, intensely, real; but it will also increase the sense that life is self-consuming, that all our actions are, in a way, human sacrifices, assaults on the sum of time and possibility left to us. This double consciousness of time is present throughout the sequence; yet, as the violence of commitment tends to purge itself in the exercise of freedom, the vision of devouring time is almost resolved in a mysticism of the present, such as Lowell approaches at the end of "Near the Ocean," but more fully reconciling here. We can see this in the farewell poem, section 6 (which perhaps receives its unlikely place at the very middle of the sequence because of this sense of transcendence).

Midwinter in Mexico, yet the tall red flowers
stand up on many trees, and all's in leaf;
twilight bakes the wall-brick large as a loaf of bread—
somewhere I must have met this feverish pink before,
and knew its message; or is it that I walk
you home twenty times, and then turn back on my tracks?
No moment comes back to hand, not twice, not once.
We've waited, I think, a lifetime for this walk,
and the white powder beneath our feet slides out
like the sterile white salt of purity; even
your puffed lace blouse is salt. The bricks glide; the commonest
minute is not divided, not twice, not once . . .
When you left, I thought of you each hour of the day,
each minute of the hour, each second of the minute.

This poem embodies the understanding that only a continuous present is real, not the abstract idea of time in which past, present, and future are coevals. When this is understood literally, each moment becomes not only an assault on the future, but an annihilation of the immediate past—and this annihilation is going on perpetually, not, as our calibrations suggest to us, at the comfortable distance of a second, a minute, an hour. (Lowell suggests this continuousness by his emphatic use of the verbs *slide* and *glide*). To live with this consciousness of time is a constant acceptance of death, in the small and in the large. But it is also, in a sense, a step out of time into eternity—for if the present alone is real, it is all-encompassing. Symbolically, there is much to suggest that this walk is an eternal present, an event outside of time. The first lines abolish the polarity of the seasons, summer and winter, and give instead a Keatsian plenitude where "all" is equally ripe. Paradoxically, this pure present seems to sum up all other time, to connect with it and yet to transcend it: the moment is at once the fulfillment of a déjà vu ("somewhere I must have met . . .") and the goal that "we've waited . . . a lifetime for." The simultaneous consciousness of time annihilating itself does not interfere with the sense of the absolute as much as might be supposed; if the numbers of clock-time can no longer make the past seem comfortingly available, neither can they "divide" the flow as long as consciousness—here the feelings of the lovers—remains unitary. Once time's strange and frightening immediacy is accepted, time may become, if not (as Lowell elsewhere quotes Heidegger as saying) "ecstasy," at least the possibility for ecstasy in consciousness.

Of course, the reality of loss in time remains. The "white powder" (suggesting an hourglass) stands for it in the poem, against the uncalibrated, undivided feelings the rest of the landscape conveys. Lowell even hints that his sense of eternal present, intense as it is, may be psychologically conditioned by a simple desire to hold off the future. Once the girl has left, he wholeheartedly desires to rebel against time on behalf of love, but can do so only through the negative unitary state of regret.

Nevertheless, the transcendent experience has happened, and

has included within itself far more than a changed awareness of time. As Norman O. Brown has argued, one cannot fully accept the present without also accepting the body and the physical space enveloping it. In "Mexico," Lowell shows both a new and moving sense of ease with the body in sexual experience, and a more general feeling of embodiment that presses toward philosophical expression:

> infirmity, a food the flesh must swallow,
> feeding our minds . . . the mind which is also flesh.

Concurrently, there is a philosophical devaluation of abstract mental activities: "What is history? What you cannot touch." In the poem quoted above, one notices how physical space seems to become fuller, closer, more real: the wall-brick that "bakes," enlarges, and intensifies in color in Lowell's vision, until it suggests a temporally (and epistemologically) primary scene, when one "knew its message." Elsewhere in the sequence, the entire landscape becomes sexualized, as though the lover's bodily consciousness became the measure of the more distant senses, and so gave a human proportion to all that can be perceived:

> the breath
> of the world risen like the ripe smoke of chestnuts,
> a cleavage dropping miles to the valley's body

> I ask only coolness, stillness, intercourse—
> sleep wastes the day lifelong behind your eyes,
> night shivers at noonday in the boughs of the fir.

Thus, Lowell seems to arrive at a kind of total reality or central being, within the unique yet encompassing present and the actual yet humanized place. In this sense of reality, the love affair which is the subject of the poem and the primitive religious history which is its persistent backdrop come together—though I do not know how far Lowell is aware of the intellectual bases of the connection. Mircea Eliade, in *Cosmos and History: The Myth of the Eternal Return*, holds that primitive or traditional man, in all the crucial (that is, archetypal) events of life, feels that he steps out of "profane time" into "mythical time"—literally, into the time of the creation of the world and the prototypical acts of the gods. There is an

> abolition of time through the imitation of archetypes and the repetition of paradigmatic gestures. A sacrifice, for example, not only exactly reproduces the initial sacrifice revealed by a god *ab origine*, at the beginning of time; it also takes place at that same primordial mythical moment; in other words, every sacrifice repeats the initial sacrifice and coincides with it. All sacrifices are performed at the same mythical instant of the beginning; through the paradox of rite, profane time and duration are suspended. And the same holds true for all repetitions, i.e., all imitations of archetypes. . . .
> The abolition of profane time and the individual's projection into mythical time do not occur, of course, except at essential periods—those, that is, when the individual is truly himself. . . . [One such is] ceremonial sexual union; the individual ceases to live in profane and meaningless time, since he is imitating a divine archetype ("I am Heaven, thou art Earth," etc.). . . . [Likewise] profane space is abolished by the symbolism of the Center, which projects any temple, palace, or building into the same central point of mythical space.[17]

According to Eliade, this return to mythic time (which, to the primitive mind, is always desirable, as "history" and duration are always distasteful) is ceremonialized in all New Year festivals. At the New Year, time literally ends; there is a descent into chaos, followed by a new cosmogony, all symbolically enacted in the rituals of the occasion. Hence, symbolically at least, the world is never more than a year old. The Aztec human sacrifice was a New Year's rite, and clearly conformed to the pattern. The ritual king died to replenish the sun for the coming year, and was

17. Mircea Eliade, *Cosmos and History: The Myth of the Eternal Return* (New York: Harper & Row, 1959), pp. 35–36. I am grateful to my student, Neal Snidow, for introducing me to Eliade's work, and for suggesting its relevance to "Mexico."

himself identified with the sun-god. Lowell's affair, of course, also takes place at a New Year. And in his attitude toward it there is something like the primitive feeling of the New Year, in both its aspects: it is at once a pure present, a new and unconditional beginning; and a return to archetypes, an identification with earlier and more absolute forms of life—the "Toltec Eden," the Christian Eden, the personal déjà vu of section 6, the Battle of Killicrankie, the lizard, the "saurian sunset."

Perhaps it is for this reason that Lowell can modulate (in section 5) from almost Petrarchan rhetoric to terms of "bull and cow," without sounding vulgar or cynical. In this poem, "the dark downward and vegetating kingdom / of the fish and reptile" is paradise regained; but because of the myth of eternal return (return, in the deepest sense, to unity with one's own life), it is a human and ethical paradise after all.

In fact, there is a good deal of ethical meditation in the poem. Interestingly, it takes the form of a debate between two kinds of consciousness, one of which treats the relationship as a part of the sequential time of Lowell's usual life, the other as essentially outside it. The second consciousness insists that the relationship can be judged only by its own terms, and must be allowed to develop its own ethic in its own time—

> love demanding we be calm, not lawful,
> for laws imprison as much as they protect

—or, as Lowell puts it, speaking with evident admiration of the girl's values, "unballasted by honor or deception."

The other consciousness relies on abstract (and temporally diffused) criteria, whether it be to condemn adultery, or to condemn the moral cowardice involved in not perpetuating the illicit relationship, or to rely cynically on "the ways of the world." The second attitude tends to be associated, throughout, with a rather negative set of images: "the sterile white salt of purity," or, in a quarrel situation,

> As if we chewed dry twigs and salt grasses,
> filling our mouths with dust and bits of adobe,
> lizards, rats and worms . . .

or

> We're burnt, black chips knocked from the blackest
>   stock . . .

All of these images of ash and salt relate, at least distantly, to the passage in section 8 where Cuernavaca is called a "city of the plain." The biblical allusion can be read in two ways. Mention of Sodom suggests that the lovers' pleasure is sterile or perverse, and that an inevitable punishment attends on it; but the story of Lot's wife suggests an opposite moral—that one is turned to salt (the sterile salt of purity) by turning back from the present to the past, and doubting the angelic command to set out for a new and autonomous life.

In the last poem, the in-time, abstractly moral perspective seems to win a partial victory. We are back to Lowell's familiar, violent terms: self-consuming energy, Lucifer and Lilith, the guilty Puritans who "turned / the wilderness to wood, then looked for trees." In the question with which the poem ends,

> how can I love you more,
> short of turning into a criminal?

there is no longer an alternative to "law," except for "criminal"— and this in itself prejudges the question, since for Lowell negative definitions of oneself are always bad definitions, private closed systems that exclude the fullness of experience. Yet the question is put as a question, and leaves open more than it at first appears to: for instance, the very fact that up to the time of writing this final line Lowell has not considered his love criminal, even though it fails to fit into any of the abstract moral schemata invoked. And in the penultimate lines, the relationship seems to continue its organic growth up to (almost past) the end—to be capable, in potential, of extending its mythic time indefinitely:

> Now our hesitant
> conversation moves from lust to love;
> friendship, without dissension, multiplying
> days, days, days, days . . .

One species of eternal return in "Mexico," that enriches the poem and calls for particular notice, is Lowell's implicit reassessment of previous experiences of transcendence and new beginning: his Catholic conversion, and the psychoanalytic reinterpretation of himself which necessitated his major change of style. There is a pointed allegory of Lowell's spiritual progress in the very history of the setting: a monastery dedicated to art ("avant-garde crucifixes"), which is eventually disbanded by a papal commission for making psychoanalysis compulsory and tolerating irregular sexuality. Implicitly, Lowell views the love affair, and the existential-mystical sense of time and physical being it has brought him, as a third conversion or centering experience. Judging from his comments on the monks, Lowell now refuses to view any of these conversions as either uniquely valid or categorically invalid: he wryly equates the monks' "depth-transference" with Paul's conversion, and sums up the whole situation as "one revelation healing the ravage of the other." All revelation is thus both a "healing" and a "ravage"; like present time and illicit love, it is double-edged. It is both a return to a central self, and an embracing of the incalculable and destructive, an opening to new forms of existential jeopardy. One might say, thus, that Lowell's Catholic vision led to forms of power-identification and bad faith that *Life Studies* healed, but that book in its turn created a dryness, a dissociation of part of the self, which must be healed in the new sensuous explosiveness. A paradox remains; nevertheless, in the passionate but wholly terrestrial terms of "Mexico," Lowell seems closer to marrying his rationalistic and religious selves than at any previous point in his poetry.

Moments of transcendence—of an escape from, or more often a centering in, time and space—occur in many other contexts in *Notebook*. They are glanced at in dozens of short passages and single images:

> if we leaned forward, and should dip a finger
> into this river's momentary black flow,
> the infinite small stars would break like fish.

> Spring the echo of heaven's single day

In "Randall Jarrell: 1914–1965," the intense sharing of experience between the two young friends creates its own kind of mythic
time, to which Lowell can still return after Jarrell's death:

> Grizzling on the embers of our onetime life,
> our first intoxicating disappointments,
> dipping our hands once, twice, in the same river,
> entrained for college on the Ohio local

Out of the memory grows a vision—primitive, Oriental, and very
suggestive of Eliade's ideas—of a before-time, a perspective from
which all events are relative and equidistant, like the circumfer-
ence of a circle, rather than linear.

> the scene shifts, middle distance, back and foreground,
> things changing position like chessmen on a wheel,
> drawn by a water buffalo, perhaps
> blue with true space before the dawn of days

After these lines, however, the facts of Jarrell's death bring Lowell
back to a tragic vision of living in time as a narrowing, entrapping
process.

In "The Pacification of Columbia," as in *Lord Weary's Castle*,
Lowell associates a more intense, apocalyptic vision—of a sexual
and imaginative "consummation" of the "desert sands" of the
universe—with political change or revolution, but his moral and
realistic scruples prevent an extended development of the theme.

One arena of transcendence that deserves lengthier discussion is
marriage. It is true that the descriptions of married life in *Notebook*
are almost unremittingly painful. Yet, as I noted in discussing
"Two Walls," there is a kind of back-handed, existential praise of
marriage, not as bourgeois stability but as its opposite: the one
encounter so unremitting that it breaks down all our normal and
solipsistic ways of conceiving our relationships—as fulfilled fantasy, as power and manipulation, as identification, as a social
arrangement—and forces us to acknowledge the person as beyond
all our frames of reference, *an* other and *the* Other. If this sense of
absolute connection can be called love, the praise is no longer
entirely back-handed:

> And neither of us the wiser or kinder—torn
> darlings, professional sparring partners; and
> but for the impossible love, a loyalty
> beyond abasement, outside anywhere:
> all icy pandemonium.
>
> ["Half a Century Gone"]

Such a marriage could indeed be "outside anywhere," in terms of the respectable and ethical limits imposed on more stable—or more distant—relationships; but it is also "outside anywhere" in the sense of being "beyond abasement" by these or any other categories. It is the fully experienced un-wisdom, and even unkindness, that, in true Socratic fashion, become their opposites. Elsewhere, "Half a Century Gone," like "Two Walls," stresses the wearing nature of the process, the unending tension that may well prepare one to view death's blanker otherness as a release ("With us, no husband could sit out the marriage"). But if this is true, it is conversely true that marriage makes one live with (and so, perhaps, accept or expiate) one's own desire to murder, an insurmountable source of guilt in so many other areas of Lowell's life, especially the political.

In "Ulysses and Nausicaa," one of the best new poems in the revised (1970) *Notebook*, the same point is made even more emphatically. Here, adultery is "landhugging," while marriage may be "a cover for the underworld, / dark harbor of suctions and the second chance." Marriage expresses longings that are more ultimate, more dangerous (perhaps because, in Freudian terms, they are more directly and openly related to the original longings of childhood), hence may be the true journey into the unconscious, the true opportunity for the death and rebirth of the self. In this poem, "husband and wife" are once again united by shared disillusionment, by the loss of all projects for escape ("because their ships are burned and all friends lost"). Their identities at last coalesce into "one Greek smile"—that enigmatic feature in which the modern eye seems to detect at once resignation, impersonality, and coyness—a configuration more ancient, and, therefore, Lowell suggests, more basically human, nearer "Eden," than the clearer smiles of romantic love or pansexual tolerance. In deepest paradox, a state of union, with each other and with the great human archetypes, is achieved.

Structurally, the placing of "Half a Century Gone" and other marital poems at or near the end of *Notebook* adds to the sense of an inclusive experience, much as, in *Ulysses*, Molly Bloom's erotic memories seem at once to dissolve and to find an archetype in the final memory of her courtship with Bloom. This seems the more true because the three principal extramarital episodes are selected with more than "a puritan's too literal pornographic honesty" in view.[18] They form a kind of three ages of love: adolescence (or the attempt, later, to return to adolescence) in Cambridge; romantic maturity, in "Mexico"; and the fullness of experience, with its combined resources of cynicism and compassion, in New York. The same kinds of relationship seem to coexist within the marriage, not only as phases of its past but as simultaneous levels of its present. (To prove this would require much quotation and comparison, but I believe that in "Half a Century Gone" the three ages are betokened by the "serfs with the pageboy bob of Shakespeare's kings," the "loyalty beyond abasement," and the "professional sparring partners.") Yet Lowell is ultimately too honest to allow the experience of "Mexico" (or that of the other extramarital episodes) to be diminished from without by a mere architectural arrangement, and the last poem in the book, "Obit," leaves the final choice somewhat ambiguous.

The poem begins, it is true, with Lowell's strongest philosophi-

18. In "Mexico," the poet asks his beloved, "those other *yous* . . . are they meaningless *in toto?*" Sometimes one feels like readdressing the question to him, so ubiquitous (and blankly apostrophic) are his uses of the second person. This is doubtless done to forestall gossip, but poetically speaking, it succeeds all too well in blurring the women's personalities, and the poet's special feelings for each of them. But, on rereading, a plot does emerge. "Through the Night," "Charles River," and "Harvard" seem to belong to the same episode, one whose dominant tone is the quest to recover and improve lost youth. "Mexico" is the second story. "April" seems to tell a third, the only one in which the woman approaches the poet's own age and sophistication. "April" seems a kind of defense of older love, since it begins in apparent cynicism yet leads up to the beautiful Lawrencean celebration, "Wind."

cal statement of the value of the experience of aging-in-marriage.
In terms derived from Marcuse, Lowell describes a sense of union
with his own destiny, his own natural time, involving a realization
that the flow of life cannot be transcended or submitted to a single
pattern, and that one never escapes from existential jeopardy.

> Before the final coming to rest, comes the rest
> of all transcendence in a mode of being, stopping
> all becoming. I'm for and with myself in my otherness,
> in the eternal return of earth's fairer children,
> the lily, the rose, the sun on dusk and brick,
> the loved, the lover, and their fear of life,
> their unconquered flux, insensate oneness, their
> 　　　painful "it was . . ."

Like the ecstasy of "Mexico," this darker unity succeeds in
abolishing the sense of self-division into an "I" and an "other."
Yet also like "Mexico," the poem ends on a question:

> After loving you so much, can I forget
> you for eternity, and have no other choice?

The rest of the ultimate encounter is not quite ultimate; it does
not quite abolish the fear of death, the desire for more time or,
perhaps, for other encounters (I take the words "no other choice"
ambiguously).

The parallel to the final question in "Mexico" seems quite
deliberate (both the grammar and the rhythm echo); and it
establishes the opposition between "Mexico" and the concluding
marriage poems as the axis of the personal *Notebook*. On one level,
the opposition is simply (like so much else in the book), a dialectic
of conservative and apocalyptic impulses, consciously unresolved.
But the questions themselves are more parallel than opposite:
they express a commitment felt as absolute in itself, but in terms
that reveal it as contradicted, indeed betrayed at the very
moment, by the "unconquered flux" of life. Also, both questions
are expressions of last-ditch or absurd hope. Within Lowell's
attitude toward his opposite commitments—to lover and wife, to
immediate transcendence and cumulative "being"—lies the same

sense of the double-edged nature of all profound encounters, revealing and confusing, regenerating and destroying.

Finally, there is a kind of transcendent aspiration in the whole project of *Notebook*—the characteristics treated at the beginning of the chapter, surrealism, banality, the jarring levels of moments, the stretched definitions of "plot" ("monster yawning for its mess of pottage") to which one must resort to get through the book, or often, through a single poem. To use such arbitrariness or exhaustiveness is, for Lowell, a form of existential freedom, the liberating of a "monster" (cf. "For John Berryman": "we used the language as if we made it"). But to use it, as Lowell evidently does, with conviction of purpose is to raise Wallace Stevens's "a great disorder is an order" almost to an article of faith. I think that, for Lowell, the act of following one word with another has, even in ordinary conversation, an element of real quest which it lacks for most of us (this is probably our loss: we know too well how our words are bound to single frames of reference). In "Myopia: A Night," Lowell spoke biblically of "thought stitched to thought, / as through a needle's eye," as if every consecutive thought were at once a near impossibility and a conceivable entry into paradise. In a scene from *Prometheus Bound*, Prometheus describes his own unclassically random style of talking in these terms:

> I was trying to feel my way toward truth. One word led to another. Each one might have hit on something that would have helped Io. I myself might have been helped. . . .
> I think I should have been more loyal to the idiocy of things, or bolder, or more careless. . . . Even here, something stirs in my heart. . . . Around some bend, under some moving stone, behind some thought, if it were ever the right thought, I will find my key. No, not just another of Nature's million petty clues, but a key, *my key*, *the* key, the one that must be there, because it can't be there—a face still friendly to chaos.[19]

Already, the idea that wilder, as it were more multimedia, forms

19. Robert Lowell, *Prometheus Bound*, pp. 49, 52–53.

of talking ("loyal to the idiocy of things") are more likely to hit on truth has emerged as a natural corollary of the basic assumption. Much of this passage is incorporated into the opening poem of *Notebook*, though the application to language is there unstated:

> I slice through fog, and round
> the village with my headlights on the ground,
> as if I were the first philosopher,
> as if I were trying to pick up a car
> key . . . It can't be here, and so it must be there
> behind the next crook in the road or growth
> of fog—there blinded by our feeble beams,
> a face, clock-white, still friendly to the earth.

In "These Winds," one of the *Notebook* poems most explicitly about creativity, Lowell creates a metaphor for his own method:

> I see these winds, these are the tops of trees,
> these are no heavier than green alder bushes;
> touched by a light wind, they begin to mingle
> and race for instability—too high placed
> to last a day in the brush, these are the winds . . .

The more things one sees moved by the wind, and the slighter, the more delicate they are, the more one seems to "see" the wind. Later in the poem, wind is equated with "inspiration"; while the small, unstable branches that respond even to a "light wind" might be the slight, indefinite materials on which Lowell leans his poems, in contrast to the "brush" of heavier themes. Lowell's method, he suggests, allows him to see the shape of his inspiration (and perhaps an intrinsic shape in his experience), as he could not by more traditional and forceful means. But "wind" becomes more than inspiration in the last line: "in these, too, the unreliable touch of the all." The line seems to say that the "touch of the all" is most surely felt in the "unreliable"—perhaps because what has no adequate contingent cause must fall back on the fundamental Cause, the whole interweaving of the cosmos. If there is room for a God in Lowell's current thought, God would have to be this design of the undesigned, this "face still friendly to

chaos." We remember that Lowell (in his "Afterthought") classes
his daughter's definitions of God after "a seaslug" as "declining";
and that elsewhere ("No Hearing") "belief in God is an
inclination to listen." In this light, Lowell's own randomness
becomes a kind of prayer—or at least an effort to attune himself
with, to discover in himself, the "touch of the all." In a sense,
Lowell has arrived at one of the commoner solutions to religious
embivalence in modern poets. Such poets do not (as their
Christian detractors have said) worship art; but they find in the
artistic act the type, or the gesture, of a self-transcending religious
attitude toward the cosmos, abstracted from any specifically
supernatural content, or reward.[20]

But Lowell's method has a naturalistic implication as important as the religious one. By bringing in so much of the

20. All the same, the concept "God" has been making a surreptitious comeback
in Lowell's poetry—couched in satiric terms in "Fourth of July in Maine," more
openly and seriously presented in *Notebook*. Lowell, it appears, instinctively believes
in an Old Testament God, very personally interested in the doings of His servant
Robert Lowell:

> Our God; he walks with us, he talks with us,
> in sleep, in thunder, and in wind and weather;
> he strips the wind and gravel from our words,
> and speeds us naked on the single way.
>
> ["Helltime"]

> God is design, this ugliness confides
> the goodness of His will, and gives me warning—
> the scrape of the Thunderer's fingernail . . . .
>
> ["The Flaw"]

At some point in his "sickness," the need to have such a God merged into the wish
to *be* such a God ("High Blood"). (This confession, it seems to me, adds weight to
my interpretation of the ambiguities of "The Quaker Graveyard in Nantucket,"
and suggests that guilt may have been a motive for the disappearance of the
religious dimension from Lowell's poetry.) In this light, the pantheistic or Eastern
conception of a nonpersonal God who *is* everything ("the air I breathe," "the
unreliable touch of the all") seems a healthy corrective—and deeply akin to the
morality of *For the Union Dead*, and the mysticism of the present of "Near the
Ocean" and "Mexico."

surrounding world without the semblance of prior ordering, it creates a continuum, even a marriage, between inner and outer, between writing and living. The real winds "have crossed the wind of inspiration." A poetry that brings back moments with their physicality, their endless and inseparable strands of being, unimpaired, creates its own kind of central time and space; just as a poetry that shows the shape of its own inspiration creates a central self. Thus, writing, too, becomes a kind of eternal return, though this is accomplished, paradoxically, by the inclusion of raw historical disorder.

All of Lowell's work since *Life Studies* might be seen as an attempt to find a center for his enormously complex and self-divided personality in the act of finding a totally adequate language. Such a language would have to be at once deep and spontaneous enough to reach the innermost recesses of feeling, and versatile enough to catch all responses to the outside. The sense that, if one could find this central point, one could move the world, is not unique to Lowell; it is there in every poet who undertakes such a quest for the absolute language, even if he merely wishes to move the world into his poems. But in Lowell's case, the claim is more serious, more philosophical, than in most, due to the movement of his work toward microcosmic-macrocosmic orderings, his psychoanalytic view of history.

In *Notebook*—despite its unevenness, and despite its many moments of roughness, crudeness, banality—Lowell seems to me to come closer than ever before to achieving this central language. The unmediated, surrealistic flow of consciousness, the comic vision, the ecstatic vision, the less restrictive view of the self, the mystique of randomness and "the unreliable touch of the all"—all of these changes seem to belong together and to move the book in the same direction, which is at once into the center and onto the existential edge. For this reason, despite its objectively somber view of human destiny, *Notebook* seems to me Robert Lowell's happiest book, in a sense akin to Rilke's "praise": a happiness that arrives of itself when no moment of experience, however trivial or painful, is regarded as wholly negative or wasted—that is, for an artist, as unusable.

Index